SLAVERY TIMES IN KENTUCKY

SLAVERY TIMES

in Kentucky

By

J. WINSTON COLEMAN, JR.
Author of
Stage-Coach Days in the Bluegrass, etc.

Chapel Hill

THE UNIVERSITY OF NORTH CAROLINA PRESS

1940

TYPOGRAPHY, PRINTING, AND BINDING IN THE U. S. A. BY
KINGSPORT PRESS, INC., KINGSPORT, TENNESSEE

TO

WILLIAM H. TOWNSEND

PREFACE

IN KENTUCKY, there were few, if any, large plantations, and great gangs of slaves to till them were not common, for the system of African bondage was never profitable here as it was in the Lower South. From an agricultural standpoint, it was more of a domestic than a commercial institution, as the master-directed farm, of medium size with five or six slaves, was the rule rather than the exception.

Situated directly below the free states of Ohio, Indiana and Illinois, Kentucky was not far enough south to be one of the cotton or sugar-cane states, where slavery was proverbially harder and the absentee system of ownership prevailed. Numerous accounts have been left in the journals and diaries of travelers who visited this commonwealth with an open and unbiased view, that they saw slavery in Kentucky in its mildest form, better than in any other slave state, with the possible exception of Maryland or Virginia.

With the increased demand for "cotton hands" in Mississippi and Louisiana after 1820, actuated somewhat by the increase of Negroes and the unprofitableness of slavery in this state, there grew up a large slave trade between Kentucky and the Cotton Kingdom, despite the public's unfavorable views toward the trader and his business.

As the capital of the rich Bluegrass region, Lexington was "the very seat and center" of the slave trade in Kentucky. At an early date many of the leading traders made it their headquarters. In their private slave pens and "Negro depots" were assembled slaves gathered from all over the state, who were kept there until a sufficiently large cargo, or coffle, could be made up for shipment to the Southern markets, Natchez or New Orleans.

Much of the material for this book, hitherto unpublished, has been found in the yellowing court records which played an important role in directing life and labor in ante-bellum Kentucky. It is largely from these records, which took cognizance of the lowly as well as the well-to-do, that I have drawn to present an account of the life, manners and customs of the "peculiar institution" as it existed in the Bluegrass State. It is not my purpose to write an economic or political history of slavery, nor to attack or defend the institution, but, rather, to present the records and let them speak for themselves.

Kentucky as a border slave state came in for its share of anti-slavery agitation and, being close to free territory, it afforded the agents and "conductors" on the Underground Railroad ample opportunities to ply their trade and spirit hundreds of slaves northward in their frantic quest for freedom. More than thirty years was necessary to convince the Kentucky Colonization Society of the futility of its social experiment plan of transporting and colonizing freed Negroes in its African colony in Liberia.

In order to put the reader more in the spirit of the period under consideration, generous use has been made of the phraseology of the times. A great many sources have been examined, including those in the appended bibliography. Much firsthand information was gained on the old slave days by personal interviews with many of the oldest and best informed persons of the state, as well as with a number of old slaves.

To those who have aided me with valuable court records, personal recollections, family papers, pictures or letters, I make grateful acknowledgments, my thanks being especially due John E. Richardson, of Glasgow; Otto A. Rothert, of Louisville; Judge Gordon Sulser, of Maysville; Evelyn Phillips, of Henderson; Mrs. Mary T. Moore, of Bowling Green; E. E. Hughes, of Smithland; Mrs. Lutie Poage Martin, of Brooksville; Lovel H. Liles, of Greenup; D. D. Dowell, of Hardinsburg; Judge George B. Kinkead, Charles R. Staples, Robert G. Lunde, J. C. Meadors, Dr. J. S. Chambers, of Lexington; Wilbur H. Siebert, of Columbus, Ohio; Rogers G. Davis, of Natchez, Mississippi; Louis A. Warren, of Ft. Wayne, Indiana; John T. Vance and Frederic Bancroft, of Washington, D. C.

To William H. Townsend and Thomas D. Clark, of Lexington, I am especially grateful for assistance and encouragement in the preparation of the manuscript, for furnishing much valuable source material and photographs, and for enjoyable companionship on numerous excursions in search of data. Judge Samuel M. Wilson, an outstanding authority on Kentucky history, has read the manuscript and generously given me the benefit of his wide knowledge and sound judgment. Fletcher Hodges, Jr., of Pittsburgh, and Hambleton Tapp, of Louisville, have also read the manuscript, or parts of it, and furnished many valuable suggestions and criticisms which have materially improved each chapter.

It is my wish that the reader may find something within these pages to awaken his interest in those colorful days of ante-bellum Kentucky when one man was considered good enough to rule another.

J. Winston Coleman, Jr.

April 15, 1940
Winburn Farm
Lexington, Kentucky

CONTENTS

ILLUSTRATIONS

SLAVERY TIMES IN KENTUCKY

CHAPTER I

BONDAGE IN THE BACKWOODS

SMOKE CURLED lazily from clay-chinked, wooden chimneys of Harrod's Fort, the first permanent settlement in "Caintucky." On this particular spring morning in the eventful year of 1777, Captain John Cowan was making history within the rude stockade walls, though, strangely enough, his implements were pen and ink instead of hunting knife and rifle. The captain, one of the original settlers of the fort, had just finished the first census ever taken in the Western Country —a complete list of all human inhabitants of this frontier outpost—and was busily recording it in his journal:

"Men in service	81
Do, not in service	4
Women	24
Children above ten years old	12
Children under ten years	58
Slaves over ten years old	12
Negro children under ten years	7
Total,	198" [1]

It will be observed that at this time, when Harrod's Fort constituted the principal organized settlement in

1. McAfee Papers, Draper MSS No. 4CC30, May 1, 1777, Wisconsin Historical Society, Madison.

Kentucky, there were nineteen slaves in a total population of nearly two hundred people. The exact date when the first slave came over the Wilderness Road cannot now be ascertained, but it is known that, on March 25, 1775, at or near the site of "Twetty's Fort," in what is now Madison County, a Negro man in Boone's party, together with Captain Twetty, was fired upon by Indians and killed,[2] and that two years before Cowan's census, Benjamin Logan had brought his "slaves & cattle out to Caintucky," where even the haunting fear of Indian raids could not prevent the "peculiar institution" from taking root in frontier soil.

Thus it was that slavery, established in Virginia in 1619,[3] spread to Kentucky as naturally as it spread to other sections of the Old Dominion. Those who had slaves brought them to their new homes in the wilderness. Few families, however, had more than two or three slaves,[4] since the plantation system was not yet developed, and, at this early period, they were used more in the manner of free laborers.

The struggle for independence prevented any large immigration from the "old settlements," but the Yorktown campaign closed the five dreary years of the Revolution and released many from service, who, ruined by economic disruption of the war, now sought to restore

2. Thomas Speed, *The Wilderness Road,* pp. 31–32.

3. In the month of August, 1619, a Dutch man-of-war sailed up the James River until it reached the small Virginia colony at Jamestown. There the Dutch trader sold twenty Negroes to the tobacco planters, and Negro slavery was thus introduced into the English-American colonies.

4. Daniel Boone owned, at various times, at least three slaves. In 1784 he secured from his relative, John Grant, a Negro girl named Easter, worth about seventy-five pounds, and on March 4, 1786, he bought "one Negroe gurle named Loos" for ninety pounds.—John Bakeless, *Daniel Boone, Master of the Wilderness,* p. 329.

their fortunes by hunting and exploring trips beyond the hazy Alleghenies.

Many of those who had received land warrants for services during the French and Indian War either located their claims on desirable tracts in the Bluegrass or sold their warrants to speculators who hurried westward to "take up" the available lands. Moses Austin noted in his journal the eagerness of settlers to penetrate the wilderness and acquire land in Kentucky. "Have you got any [land]?" he asked one of the emigrants. "No," he replied, "but I expect I can git it." "Have you got anything to pay for land?" "No." "Did you ever see the Country?" "No, but Every Body says its good land. . . ."

Austin was astounded at both the determination and the utter lack of good sense, as he thought, in the crowds starting westward. ". . . can anything be more absurd than the conduct of men," observed the disgusted Austin, "travelling hundreds of miles, they know not for what, nor whither, except it's—Kentucky!" [5] Undoubtedly the unfaltering purpose, as William Calk wrote in his journal, was to "start early and git down to Caintuck." [6]

Unheeding the counsels of the cautious, or the imminent dangers and hardships, these intrepid emigrants pushed eagerly forward to reach the much-talked-of land of promise and certain fortune. There were no roads for wheeled vehicles and thousands of men, women and children, braving incredible privations and perils, moved in successive caravans over narrow trails

5. Eugene C. Barker, *Life of Stephen F. Austin,* p. 8.

6. Entry of April 20, 1775, manuscript in possession of Mrs. William Calk, of Mt. Sterling, Kentucky.

blazed by the tomahawk—men with trusty flintlock rifles on their shoulders driving stock and leading pack horses; women walking beside them or riding horseback with children in their laps, or in paniers slung over the saddle, and the older children trudging along on foot. Along with his cattle, horses and household goods the settler also brought his human chattels. But, in the solitudes of the wilderness and the isolations of the scattered settlements, slaves were more than property—the irrepressible longing for the society of humankind made the companionship of master and slave an essential condition to the contentment and happiness of the backwoods home.

If "Uncle Ben" or "Black Sam" felled the trees for fencing and fuel, plowed the corn ground, or hoed the garden, "Marse Tom" often bore a hand with him; and when he did not, they knew he was scouting Indians, supplying the wants of the household with the prowess of his hunt, or sharing in some other manner the arduous toil and exposures incident to the precarious existence which constantly confronted master and slave alike. If "Aunt Jenny" plied the loom, spun the yarn, or cooked the meals, "Mistis Ann" was always present to direct and aid, or was diligently occupied in the performance of other duties.

Master and slave often fought side by side in the defense of their homes and loved ones against their common enemy, the red man. A few instances will suffice to illustrate the fidelity of the slave in this respect.

On March 19, 1782, deserted rafts drifting down the Kentucky River created suspicion at Boonesborough that Indians were lurking in that vicinity. On receipt of this information, Captain James Estill left his station, which was fifteen miles from the Boonesborough fort, organized a scouting party of twenty-five men and started at once in search of the invaders.

On the following day a band of Wyandots crept through the early morning mist, surrounded Estill's Station, caught and tomahawked the daughter of a prominent settler as she milked a cow just outside the stockade walls, and captured Monk, a shrewd, stocky, powerfully-built "young negro, five feet five inches in height, weighing 200 pounds, who belonged to Captain Estill."

Since the searching party had taken every able-bodied man from the station, the remaining inhabitants, women, children and four invalid men, faced immediate massacre. Monk, however, was equal to this fearful emergency, and his captors were so impressed with his story of the forty sharp-eyed, grim-visaged men then in the station moulding bullets that they beat a hasty retreat, taking their crafty informant with them.

Two days later, Captain Estill, having received news of the occurrence, overtook the Wyandots at Little Mountain, on the outskirts of what is now the town of Mt. Sterling, and both sides, equal in number, quickly maneuvered for battle. A veteran in backwoods warfare, Captain Estill detailed Lieutenant Miller, with six men, to guard the horses and protect his flank. As the Indians were attempting the very movement which Estill sought to forestall, Monk's voice rose above the crack of rifles, shouting: "Don't give way, Massa Jim, there's only about twenty-five of the red-skins, and you can whip 'em!" The bravery and optimism of this faithful slave greatly encouraged his master and the main body of Estill's command, and the tide of battle seemed definitely in their favor, when Lieutenant Miller and the six men of his detachment suddenly beat a retreat, allowing the horses to stampede wildly through the woods.

Greatly weakened, but undismayed by this desertion, the remainder of Estill's men, within a range of fifty yards and for three hours, fought a bloody, stubborn but losing battle until thirteen pioneers lay dead or gravely wounded on the brown, withered leaves of this forest battleground, and Estill himself had succumbed in a hand-to-hand encounter, with a hunting knife buried in his breast. In the midst of the struggle, Monk managed to escape and carried one of the survivors, whose thigh had been broken by a rifle ball, on his broad back almost the entire distance of twenty-five miles to Estill's Station.[7]

Undoubtedly Monk was one of the finest specimens of his race in the new country. From some source he had learned the art of manufacturing powder and on many critical occasions he supplied Boonesborough and his own station with ammunition—the first ever manufactured in Kentucky—which he had made from saltpeter found in a cave in Madison County.[8]

As the husband successively of three wives and the father of thirty children, Monk was no laggard in the propagation of his own race in Kentucky. One of his sons, the first colored child born at Boone's fort, became a Baptist preacher and lived at Shelbyville. Shortly after the engagement at Little Mountain, which has come to be known in history as "Estill's Defeat," Monk's new master, young Wallace Estill, freed him, and his old master's family as evidence of their affection provided

7. Zachariah F. Smith, *History of Kentucky,* pp. 193–95; Robert S. Cotterill, *History of Pioneer Kentucky,* p. 180.

8. Smith, *op. cit.,* p. 193.

liberally for his comfort and support as long as he lived.[9]

Edmund Cabell was a pioneer who, at an early age, brought his family across the mountains and settled them in the wilderness. Shortly afterward he returned to Virginia for a brief visit, leaving his wife and children in the care of Mrs. Cabell's uncle and "Black Sam," a trusted slave.

One hot, sultry night, Black Sam, who slept on a pile of new-mown hay at the edge of the clearing, was awakened by savage shouts and the blaze of his master's burning cabin. Crouched behind the hay, the unarmed Negro helplessly watched the massacre of the Cabell household and for a time believed that all had perished. However, as the Indians emerged from the cabin, carrying furniture, dishes and other plunder, one warrior held in his arms Cabell's little daughter, Augusta, apparently only half conscious, and laid her down about halfway between the cabin and the spot where the slave was concealed, and then rushed back for more loot. The burning logs by this time cast a glaring light for many yards around, while Black Sam, in imminent danger of detection, wriggled and squirmed through the tall grass and weeds until he was able to seize the dazed and bewildered child and escape into the woods.

Heading for the nearest fort, carrying little Augusta upon his back, Sam traveled all night but by noon next day he found that he had completely lost his direction. Exhausted from lack of food, his exertions and the fear of being overtaken by the Indians, the slave and little child wandered through the trackless woods until they came to a spring and a patch of bushes bearing ripe berries. Refreshed, they continued their journey, but it

9. *Ibid.*, p. 194.

was slow and tedious. Now and then cautious Sam, with eyes and ears alert for danger, concealed Augusta among the thick boughs of fallen trees and hid himself until every suspicious sign or sound had disappeared. After three nights the fort was reached, and weary, faithful Black Sam, leaving his little charge in safe hands, hurriedly set out again to the scene of disaster so that he might meet his master on his return and tell him that one member of his family still survived.[10]

"Miss Gussie's saved, Mas' Edmund. Little Miss is alive," shouted Black Sam as he found Mr. Cabell bowed in anguish over the ruins of his home. And then the master had an opportunity to show the kindly and thoughtful relations which in many instances existed between master and slave. Speechless with emotion, Cabell pointed toward his travel-stained wagon, which contained Sam's mother and father and his wife, Maria, whom Cabell had brought with him from Virginia.[11]

One Sunday morning, in the spring of 1782, Settler Woods, who lived near Crab Orchard, rode over to a near-by station, leaving his wife, his daughter Hannah and a lame Negro man in the cabin. Not long afterwards, Mrs. Woods, who had ventured a short distance from the house, discovered the presence of a band of Indians and she ran screaming toward the cabin, hotly pursued. As she stumbled through the front door, the foremost Indian, wearing the hunting shirt of Absalom Mount, a trapper recently killed and scalped at Station Camp Waters, forced his way into the cabin, where the crippled slave met him in a death grapple.

After a short, fierce struggle, the slave and his savage

10. Norman B. Wood, *The White Side of a Black Subject,* pp. 287–89.
11. Emma M. Connelly, *The Story of Kentucky,* pp. 111–12.

adversary fell heavily to the floor, but the Negro, though underneath, held his assailant tightly in his sinewy arms, calling loudly to "Miss Hannah" to get the broadaxe from under the bed. Miss Hannah hastily seized this combined weapon and tool of the backwoods and promptly went into action. Her first stroke nearly severed the Indian's arm from his shoulder. The next blow killed him and, according to the journal account of a contemporary, "Whilst young Miss Woods dispatched his life, the Old Lady Barrd the Door & Kept it shut." [12]

When the besiegers began splintering the clapboard door with their tomahawks, the slave suggested to his mistress that the Indians be admitted one at a time to be given individual attention by the Negro, who had now procured a gun, and by Miss Hannah, who had wielded the broadaxe with such deadly precision. However, before this strategy could be put into effect, as the pioneer journal recited, "A neighbor hearing the savage screams fired his gun & relevd the house." [13]

The records contain accounts of many other slaves or family servants who rendered valuable service other than in matters of defense in those days when life was hard and uncertain. Near the end of December, 1778, settlers and their families, who had lived on Corn Island at the Falls of the Ohio, while General Clark conquered the Illinois Territory, moved into the fort they had built on the present site of Louisville, at the foot of what is now Seventh Street.

According to the custom of the times, the celebration of this first Christmas in their new quarters was to be a

12. Whitley Papers, Draper MSS, IX, 37, Wisconsin Historical Society, Madison.

13. *Ibid.*, p. 38.

feast and dance. With the river teeming with fish and the woods full of game, it was easy enough to have the feast, but the matter of music for the dance presented a more difficult problem.

Cato, a slave, had furnished the music at all festive occasions during the summer and fall, but age and hard usage had left only one string on his dilapidated fiddle. All efforts of the usually resourceful Cato to find a satisfactory substitute for "cat gut" had resulted in utter failure. Hair from a horse's tail had emitted the most unearthly screeches when Cato's black hand wielded the bow. Deer sinews gave out only hoarse moans "like the melancholy hoots of a night owl," sad as the hearts of old and young as they anxiously witnessed the results of Cato's patient but futile experiment.

On Christmas Eve, just when things looked darkest for the terpsichorean part of the celebration, a boat loaded with traders on their way to Kaskaskia tied up at the new landing for repairs. The next day, with true Kentucky hospitality, the voyagers were invited to the feast and after dinner the news quickly spread around that one of their number, a Frenchman, was a skilled violinist.

Almost within the twinkling of an eye, a large place was cleared on a smooth dirt floor and tall backwoodsmen in fringed buckskin hunting shirts and moccasins and the stockade girls in linsey dresses and stout brogan shoes stood eagerly awaiting the first strains of music.

But the Frenchman knew nothing but the fashionable music and intricate figure-dances of his native land, with which these sons and daughters of the frontier were wholly unfamiliar. Obligingly he tried to teach them the branle, but his pupils, willing though they were, got out of time and figure. Then he showed them the stately minuet and played the music for it, but the participants hopped rather than glided, and, instead of bowing gracefully, "bobbed their heads up and down in quick succession like geese dodging a shower of stones."

In a last despairing effort to improvise a dance suitable to the music in his repertoire, the Frenchman suggested and attempted to illustrate certain other movements, but all in vain. By this time the dancers were thoroughly confused, disorganized and discouraged, while the baffled Frenchman stood against the wall, his fiddle under his arm, a picture of complete frustration, rage and despair.

At this critical moment, "a charcoal face with ivory teeth between thick lips, grinning from ear to ear," bounded into the room, flourishing a battered bow, his trusty fiddle clutched tightly in the other hand. Secretly Cato had traded the Frenchman four raccoon skins for fiddle strings, and now he walked up to the foreigner, and with the finest tact and politeness asked if he might play while Monsieur rested. Gladly the Frenchman assented, and Cato, tucking his rehabilitated instrument under a black pudgy chin, swung into the familiar strains of the old Virginia Reel. Instantly the atmosphere and spirit of the rude, improvised ballroom changed as if by magic. Discouragement, uncertainty and awkwardness vanished. Quickly and naturally the dancers fell into position, selected their partners, and, without prompting, wheeled and turned, bowed and circled with assurance and ease. Then, in quick succession, the faithful and tireless fiddler played other pieces of varied tempo, which had tickled the toes of backwoodsmen since childhood—jigs, hoedowns, shuffles and pigeonwings—until past midnight, when need of sleep broke up the party, and the weary revelers showered thanks upon old Cato who had given their holiday such a happy ending.[14]

By 1783 the population of all the settlements of Kentucky was considered to be about twelve thousand.[15] The suspension of Indian hostilities and the return of peace tempted home-seekers from the Atlantic states. Many of these settlers, particularly from Pennsylvania and New England, during this formative period of Kentucky's history, came down the Ohio River by flatboat to Limestone, now Maysville, then overland to Lexington and central Kentucky. Over the Wilderness Road through Cumberland Gap and along trails worn bare by the feet of many predecessors came swarms of settlers —all eager to carve out a home in the wilderness. And, like the earlier settlers, they brought their household goods, their slaves, their domestic animals and, later, their books and even printing presses.

In the spring of 1784 it was estimated that the population had increased to more than twenty thousand.[16] Few movements of population in America can compare in momentum and magnitude with this influx of immigration during the next decade and a half. However, unlike similar movements in the older states, the new inhabitants of Kentucky exhibited much less class distinction. The patrician element visible for a moment on the surface of the tide became quickly submerged in the overwhelming flood of so-called plebeians—artisans,

14. Smith, *op. cit.*, pp. 122–24.

15. John W. Monette, *History of the . . . Valley of the Mississippi*, II, 143.

16. Cotterill, *op. cit.*, p. 244.

hunters, surveyors and speculators. Cheap land and equal opportunity for the accumulation of wealth further served to level any artificial social distinctions among the population. So that Kentucky, instead of duplicating or imitating the definite caste system of the Lower South, developed a social structure of its own, where wealth and power reposed in the hands of the middle class, with the upper and lower classes conspicuously absent.

By 1790, out of a total population of nearly seventy-five thousand, Kentucky had twelve thousand slaves.[17] Yet slavery here came to be and remained, for the most part, quite different from what it was in Mississippi, South Carolina and other so-called "cotton states" or, for that matter, different even from what it was in Virginia. Master and slave, in the earlier days, worked together in the fields, marched together against the Indians, and slept side by side in family cemeteries. Here, in this picturesque country, so largely endowed by nature, the patriarchal type of slavery prevailed, and it does not seem too much to say that this system of bondage was the mildest that existed anywhere in the world.

It will not do, however, to give the so-called middle class entire credit for the development of Kentucky or to blame them wholly for the introduction of slavery. Many well-to-do gentlemen or members of the landed gentry of Maryland and Virginia, learning of the rich and verdant meadows beyond the mountains, were quite anxious to augment their fortunes there. Treasury warrants, purchased at the Virginia land office in Richmond, gave them inchoate title to numerous acres in the wilderness, and some representatives of this class,

17. Ulrich B. Phillips, *Life and Labor in the Old South,* p. 76.

unwilling to undergo the hardships and rigors of pioneer life, sent forward their overseers with slaves to clear the land, plant crops, build cabins and make other necessary improvements. Then, in a year or two, when conditions became more livable, the master and his household migrated to the newly-established home in Kentucky.[18] This practice, of course, greatly increased the slave population, which kept steady pace with the prosperity and development of the country.

Writing back to the "old settlements" in Virginia in September, 1789, a resident of Lexington thus described the town's rapid growth: "It is astonishing how fast this town improves . . . it is by far the largest in the district and it is expected the emigration this fall will be greater than ever . . . report says there are seventy families now on their way to Kentucky." [19]

During the same year, Polly Davis, of Spotsylvania County, Virginia, wrote her brother in the Bluegrass region: "A great many people here are talking of settling in that country [Kentucky], for their land is getting poore & money is hard to get hold of." [20] And three years later: "God must be prospering you if you can have a Silver Teapott & Shugar Dish. I did not think Lexington was big enough to have a silversmith . . . we made a pore crop [of] Tobacco this year, the crop of

18. An excellent example of this procedure is that of Colonel Samuel Meredith, of Amherst County, Virginia, who in 1789 sent his overseer, Dr. Philip Roots, and a number of slaves to Fayette County, Kentucky, to locate and settle his two-thousand-acre grant. His plantation later became known as "Winton," located seven miles north of Lexington, a portion of which is still in the possession of the descendants of Colonel Meredith.

19. Letter of Mrs. James Wilkinson, *The Pennsylvania Magazine of History and Biography*, LVI (January, 1932), 52.

20. *Virginia Magazine of History and Biography*, XII, 435–36.

corn is pretty good. Money seems harder to get hold of than during the war. . . ."[21]

As the turn of the century approached, it was apparent that the institution of slavery, deeply entrenched in the social and economic life of Kentucky, found few voices to dispute its steady insidious growth. Indeed, the old mother state, reposing with the dignity of age beyond the Blue Ridge, in consenting to the admission of her young vigorous daughter to statehood, had expressly stipulated that slavery should not be molested.[22]

By 1800 there were fully two hundred and twenty thousand inhabitants of Kentucky, of whom forty thousand were "persons held to service" for life. Probably few of these sturdy pioneers realized, as they accepted slavery to provide the additional labor required to clear their lands, to build cabins and to aid them in wresting a livelihood from the backwoods, that they were introducing an economic and social factor that would later go far to shape and mould Kentucky's system of agriculture and to determine the texture and tendencies of her society. Even at this early date, as the pioneer period was passing, the number of slaves which a family possessed was rapidly assuming a pronounced social significance.

21. Phillips, *op. cit.*, p. 84.

22. Kentucky adopted the statutes of Virginia for the treatment of her slaves and slavery problems, but after six years of statehood the legislature, on February 9, 1798, passed "An Act to reduce into one, the Several Acts respecting Slaves, Free Negroes, Mulattoes and Indians," which contained forty-three articles and remained the basis of all legal action throughout the entire period of slavery.—William Littell, *The Statute Law of Kentucky,* II, 113–23.

CHAPTER II

FOLKS IN THE BIG HOUSE

During the first quarter of the nineteenth century, the social and economic life of Kentucky changed greatly. Land was rapidly cleared; log cabins gave way to stately brick mansions; coonskin caps and buckskin hunting-shirts were replaced with fashionable attire from the East; business expanded rapidly, and the fine arts were cultivated. All attested an era of growing prosperity.

"From dirty stations, or forts, and smoky huts," remarked an early adventurer, "Kentucky has expanded into fertile fields, blushing orchards, rising villages and trading towns. Ten years have produced a difference in the population and comforts of the country, which to be portrayed in just colours, would appear marvelous." [1] Many wealth-seeking families poured into Kentucky until it appeared "as if these immense and fertile regions were to be the asylum common to all the inhabitants of the globe. . . ." [2]

Game was growing scarce, but plenty of cattle had

1. Gilbert Imlay, *A Topographical Description of the Western Territory,* p. 168.

2. François A. Michaux, *Travels to the West of the Alleghany Mountains,* p. 161.

FOLKS IN THE BIG HOUSE

The Grange, Bourbon County
Scotland, Franklin County

Lynnwood, Mercer County
Grassland, Fayette County

HOMES OF WELL-TO-DO PLANTERS

been brought into the state; large flocks of sheep and herds of cattle grazed on the cleared land. Apple orchards and vineyards had been planted. Mechanics and tradesmen had come from the East and were plying their trades in the young towns and villages over the state. Wagon trains coming into Kentucky, especially the central portion, brought china and queensware, mahogany tables, tall clocks, lace berthas and books—all signs of the inevitable rise of an aristocracy in this remote frontier region.[3]

For the decade and a half following the turn of the century, the tide of emigration toward Kentucky was still very strong. Those who had passed the barrier of the Allegheny Mountains and established frontier homes in Kentucky carried back to the "old settlements" glowing accounts of the fertility of the soil, the magnificence of the timber and the general wealth of the new state.

Many younger sons of the best families of Virginia, unable to realize their ambitions to become great planters, packed up their goods and chattels, collected their horses and slaves and set out for Kentucky, the land of promise.[4] A vivid picture of such a trip from the Old Dominion is related by Francis Fedric, a Virginia-born slave who emigrated with his master to Kentucky, escaping years later to England where he wrote his memoirs.

3. *Ibid.,* p. 212. This early traveler through Kentucky visited the Revolutionary general, John Adair, whose plantation was "situated near Harrodsburgh, in the county of Mercer." Here this Frenchman, in 1802, found "a spacious and commodious house, a number of black servants, equipages, every-thing announced the opulence of the General."

4. Robert Carter Harrison is a good example. In 1805 he purchased some two thousand acres of land in Fayette County, Kentucky, and moved there from Virginia with his family, cattle and fully one hundred slaves. Shortly afterwards he built a substantial residence known as "Elk Hill," in the northeastern part of the county, seven miles from Lexington.

"My master determined to give up his plantation in Virginia," recounted Fedric, "and go to Kentucky. We set out [from Fauquier County] with several waggons and a sorryful cavalcade [it was] on our way to Kentucky. After several days journey, we saw at a distance the lofty ranges of the Allegheny Mountains . . . our journey was, I must say, almost interrupted every now and then, by immense droves of hogs, which were bred in Kentucky, and were proceeding from thence to Baltimore and places in Virginia. These droves contained very often from seven to eight hundred hogs."

Fedric's caravan slowly made its way to Kentucky, traveling by day, halting at improvised camps at night. Indian corn baked on griddles and salt herring constituted their only food. "Two or three times during the night," wrote this ex-slave, "one of the overseers would call our names over, every one being obliged to wake up and answer. My master was afraid of some of us escaping, so uncertain are the owners of possession of their slaves.

"The howling of the wolves and other wild animals, broke the stillness which reigned widely around us. Now and then my master would fire his gun to frighten them away from us, but we were never in any way molested. Perhaps the fires kept them at a safe distance from us.

"My master had bought a plantation in Mason County, about twenty miles back from Maysville. When we arrived there we found a great deal of uncultivated land belonging to this purchase. The first thing the negroes did was to clear the land of brush and then sow blue grass seed for the cattle to feed on. Then they fenced in the woods for what is called woodland pasture. Some of the neighboring planters came and showed my master how to manage his new estate."[5] In a few years additional slaves were added to Fedric's group; the lands were cleared and a suitable residence was erected for the master and his family.

Similar groups of landed gentry from Virginia, Maryland[6] and Pennsylvania, such as Fedric described, had settled in the rich farming sections of Kentucky, and especially in the Bluegrass region. The pioneer log houses were fast being abandoned for the more commodious and stately brick mansions indicative of the rank of Kentucky slaveholders and well-to-do planters. In many instances, the early log cabins, which had afforded shelter for the master and his family, were now consigned to the use of the slaves, and when these were not sufficient to house the groups of black people which went to make up some of the larger plantations, additional cabins or groups of cabins were constructed just back of the "big house" of the master.

Thus, in Kentucky, as in Virginia and England, the term "gentleman" came to be associated with landed estates and manor houses. Success at the bar or in trade was signalized by the purchase of a country seat. John Speed, owner of seventy slaves, built "Farmington" on Beargrass Creek, near Louisville;[7] William C. Bullitt had his slaves and one thousand acres at "Oxmoor" in

5. Francis Fedric, *Slave Life in Virginia and Kentucky,* pp. 15–17.

6. Josiah Henson, a Maryland-born slave, sometimes incorrectly referred to as the original Uncle Tom of *Uncle Tom's Cabin,* came to Daviess County, Kentucky, with his master in April, 1825. He found "the situation was in many respects more comfortable" than he had left it in Maryland. His master's new farm in Kentucky "was larger and more fertile, and there was a greater abundance of food, which is, of course, one of the principal sources of comfort of a slave."—*Father Henson's Story of His Own Life,* p. 56.

7. James Speed, *James Speed, A Personality,* p. 4.

the same county, while Charles A. Wickliffe, in 1813, built the magnificent "Wickland" in Nelson County, and not far distant another slaveholding planter and barrister, Judge John Rowan, had some years before erected "Federal Hill," both of the latter homes being near Bardstown. "Grass Hills" in Carroll County was the handsome show-place of Lewis Sanders.

John Breckinridge had early removed from Lexington to his country estate, "Cabell's Dale," some five or six miles from the city. In 1806 he was the possessor of one hundred and twenty head of horses, seventy head of cattle and slaves so numerous that many were hired out to Peter January, John Nancarrow and other merchant-manufacturers of Lexington. General William Russell occupied stately "Mt. Brilliant"; Colonel David Meade his pretentious "Chaumière du Prairie," and Henry Clay, the well-known "Ashland," while General Levi Todd had his "Ellerslie"—to mention a few of the estates which made the beautiful country around Lexington a region "of finely cultivated fields, rich gardens and elegant mansions."

Henry Clay, like Jefferson and others who favored gradual emancipation, farmed his estate with slave labor, and "the slaves of Kentucky," said a visiting British Whig, were "better fed, better lodged, and better clothed than many of the peasantry in Britain." [8] Clay's slaves increased from six in 1805, to fourteen in 1808, to eighteen in 1811. Many immigrants to Kentucky were no more favorable to slavery than was Henry Clay, but, after a while, they quietly took on the color of their environment, finding life exciting, diverting and, on the whole, agreeable.

8. John Melish, *Travels through the United States, 1806–1811,* II, 206.

During the twenties, thirties and forties, many imposing homes were being built throughout the state. Some of the more pretentious ones were "Xalapa," "The Grange," "The Larches" and "Runnymeade" in Bourbon County; "Buck Pond" and "Woodburn" in Woodford County; "Ridgeway" and "Montrose" in Jefferson County; "Stockdale" in Shelby County; "Scotland" in Franklin County; "Castlewood," "White Hall" and "Woodlawn" in Madison County; "Cleaverhouse" in Boyle County; "Arcadia" in Lincoln County; "The Oaks" in Logan County; "Grassland," "Winton," "Mansfield," "Richland," "Greentree" and "Hedgewood" in Fayette County.

While Kentuckians were reaping a bountiful harvest from fertile virgin soils and planning and building elegant mansions, they were not unmindful of suitable furnishings for their homes. In these fine homes of the landed gentry were to be found oil portraits of their families done by such masters as Stuart, West, Harding and Earle, and the best local artists of the day—Matthew Jouett, Oliver Frazer, Joseph Bush and others.

The art of dining and entertaining was a source of much pride for these early settlers. Good food, beautifully served, was a cultural art for the ante-bellum Kentucky hostess. Well-to-do planters of that period had their own silverware, services and mint julep cups made to order, hammered out by local artisans, Asa Blanchard,[9] Robert Frazer, B. B. Marsh, Edward West and others of central Kentucky, while S. D. Choate, W.

9. Asa Blanchard, of Lexington, was master of all the early Kentucky silversmiths, and even today his name on a piece of silver has as much significance in Kentucky as that of Paul Revere in New England. Blanchard specialized in spoons, soup ladles and mint julep cups, all hammered from pure coin silver.

Kendrick and S. W. Warringer, of Louisville, supplied hand-wrought tableware to discriminating patrons of that section.

While this exquisite silverware graced their tables, their furniture and draperies were often the best that New Orleans, Philadelphia or Baltimore merchants could supply.[10] Even as early as 1818, one Kentuckian living near Versailles wrote: "The steam-boats have brought New Orleans to our doors, and West India fruits are as common here now as in your [Virginia] Sea Port towns. . . ."[11]

Timothy Flint, a New England preacher and traveler, while touring Kentucky in 1826, observed that the better class of Kentuckians were "a high-minded people and possess the stamina of a noble character. It cannot be truthfully said, as is said in journals and geographies, that they are too recent and too various in their descent and manners, to have a distinct character as a people. They generally are of one descent, and are the scions from a noble stock—the descendants from affluent and respectable planters from Virginia and North Carolina."

Further noting the planter class, this traveling divine wrote in his journal: "There is a distinct and striking moral physiognomy to this people; an enthusiasm, a vivacity, and ardor of character, courage, frankness, generosity, that have been developed with the peculiar circumstances under which they have been placed. . . .

10. "The majority of the inhabitants of Kentucky trade with the Lexington merchants; they receive their merchandise from Philadelphia and Baltimore in 35 to 40 days, including the journey of 2 and ½ days from Limestone where they land all goods destined for Kentucky."—Michaux, *op. cit.*, p. 202.

11. Nathaniel Hart to James McDowell, MS in McCormick Agricultural Library, Chicago.

They seem to feel that they have an hereditary claim to command, place and observance. This perfect repose of self confidence is in fact their good star. . . ." [12]

"In points of comforts, of luxuries and even elegances," wrote a visitor in 1845, "the Kentucky farmer compares well with the English, Irish or Scotch gentleman-farmer *in every respect.* Their houses generally speaking have been built within the last 30 years; are of brick; well and tastefully planned; large and roomy; and if any fault is to be found at all they are too magnificently furnished for a 'farmer's' residence. They all stand some distance from the road and are approached by a wide avenue, shaded on either side with large forest trees, and the ground immediately surrounding the dwelling is invariably tastefully laid out in shrubbery, ever-greens and flowers.

"Every farmer or planter, has his elegant family carriage,[13] and his one-horse buggy for himself, with horses and saddles innumerable for the younger branches [of his family] to use when their inclination leads them to gallop uncontrolled from one neighbor's house to the other. . . ." [14]

"A Kentucky planter," observed another traveler, "has the manners of a gentleman; he is more or less refined according to his education, but there is generally a grave, severe dignity of deportment in the men of middle age, which prepossesses and commands respect." [15]

12. Timothy Flint, *Recollections of the Last Ten Years,* p. 70.

13. "The farms in the neighborhood [of Lexington] are well cultivated, and the farmers are generally rich and opulent, and many of them have coaches and carriages, made at Lexington, that cost one thousand dollars. . . ." *Niles' Weekly Register,* VII (January 28, 1815), 339–40.

14. *The Cultivator* (Albany, New York), N.S., II, 373.

15. Elias P. Fordham, *Personal Narrative,* p. 216.

These visitors were speaking of that well-to-do and aristocratic class of slaveholders, whom the slaves, when fortunate enough to be owned by them, were proud to call "quality folks." In these homes were many contented servants, born and reared for several generations in the families of their present masters, who served them with unswerving loyalty and devotion, and who, in turn, were held in genuine affection. Many of these family servants of the "big house" were privileged characters, and under no circumstances would they have accepted their freedom from their beloved "white folks."

During the ante-bellum days the population of Kentucky was divided, generally, into slaveholders, non-slaveholders on principle, wage earners, poor whites, slaves, and free Negroes. Of the slaveholder class there were various grades, ranging all the way from the modest master of only one slave to the quality folks, who were known far and wide for their wealth and position, as well as for the number of their slaves.

It was a mark of considerable pride and distinction among slaves to belong to the quality folks class. "I'se a quality folks nigger," was the proud boast of many servants who went around feeling the importance of their masters. This is well illustrated in the incident related by Thomas W. Bullitt of a wealthy and aristocratic planter who ordered his carriage to drive into the county seat. He and "Ole Mistis" were driven by the aged coachman, who felt to the fullest the importance of his white folks family. It was the first trip to town since a local railroad had gone into operation.

As the carriage approached the track, the train was coming on at a moderate rate of speed, but the old driver paid not the slightest attention to it and drove on over the track. The locomotive just grazed the rear wheel, turning the carriage over and pitching the old driver into a near-by clover patch. Nobody was seriously hurt. When he had gotten out, the old gentleman turned to the driver and said: "Henry, didn't you see that locomotive coming?" "Yes, Marster," replied the discomfited Henry. "Why the hell did you go up on the track?" demanded the master. "Why, you know, Marster," said the old Negro, "I thought when dey seed it was we-alls kerridge, dey would stop!" [16]

On a well-established Kentucky plantation, or farm, of the quality folks class, was to be found the mansion, or big house, of the master,[17] usually located some distance from the road in a grove of beautiful trees. In a detached group at the rear of the manor house were the slave cabins, usually constructed of logs, but often of stone or brick. These were familiarly known as the "quarters." Not far distant were to be found the coach-house, the stables or barns for the carriage or riding horses, the hemp-house, the ice-house, weaving and spinning room, smoke-house, wash room, dairy, stone spring-house, blacksmith and carpenter shops.

Sometimes, the meat-house, or smoke-house, usually constructed of brick and barred with heavy doors, served a dual purpose. In addition to its regular use for storing and curing the meat supply, it was used as a lockup for refractory or recaptured slaves.

Situated directly behind the mansion of many of the

16. Thomas W. Bullitt, *My Life at Oxmoor,* p. 67.

17. "The houses of the Kentucky planters are built of brick and stone, and generally a verandah runs right around them; the kitchens are situated at a short distance from the houses, so that the cooking may not be smelt. . . ."—Fedric, *Slave Life in Virginia and Kentucky,* p. 94.

wealthy planters was the kitchen, detached from the house so that the cooking could not be "smelt" by the occupants of the big house. Plain, rough, uninviting as it would appear to modern eyes, this archaic cooking arrangement offered facilities far beyond the capacity of the modern range. Usually the kitchen was a simple room of brick construction; the wash room being under the same roof. Both the floor and hearth were of brick. There was no well or cistern near-by, but water was "toted" by the "young uns" from a spring.

In front of the large open fireplace, fully six feet wide, swung several huge iron cranes, with a nondescript assortment of kettles and cooking utensils. The live coals and hot ashes in the fireplace or on the hearth provided ample means for frying, baking, stewing and other forms of cooking.

Then, on some plantations, there was a "tin kitchen," a contrivance for roasting a turkey or other fowls or meat. The "kitchen" was a half cylinder of tin, mounted on legs and open on the side next to the fire and at the bottom, arranged so that a whole turkey could be placed in it, exposed to the heat of the ardent blaze and turned from time to time, so as to be cooked through, the grease drippings being caught in a pan on the hearth. Many of these detached kitchens had a Dutch oven. Over this quaint culinary department, with her varied equipment of pots and pans, ruled the old black cook who was undisputed mistress of her own domain.

Such was the compact and practically self-sustaining unit of a Kentucky plantation, with its self-perpetuating labor supply, with its hamlet of carpenters, blacksmiths, farm hands, cobblers, weavers and other manufacturing artisans, with its own supply of cereals, meats, fruits and dairy products. Ice that had been gathered from near-by ponds and stored in the ice-houses, packed with sawdust or straw, cooled the drinks of the planter and his family. Here, a little community within itself, were produced various kinds of rough clothes for the everyday use of the slaves. From impulse of humanity, as well as from motives of prudence, the black people were well fed, well clothed, well housed and, when ill, were cared for by the neighborhood doctor, usually the same, indeed, who attended the planter's own family.

Many of the leading physicians of the day, clothed in the garb of their profession, long-tailed coats and stovepipe hats, made yearly contracts with planters and slave owners to furnish them medical attention at prices ranging from two to three dollars per person.[18] As one examines the ante-bellum doctors' account books, there are found many entries for services rendered both the planter and his slaves. Usually the master was designated as "Self" and his wife as "Lady" in these old record books.

Dr. James M. Bush, a prominent Lexington physician and member of the Transylvania medical faculty, rendered his account for services to Caleb Wallace, a Fayette County slaveholder:

"June 17, 1833	To curing case of Cholera, Self	$6.00
June 26, "	To visit Daughter, 8 doses, eye water & ointment . .	2.50
July 10, "	To dose pills, negro woman	.25

18. From his office in Jordan's Row, Lexington, Dr. Robert C. Holland sent the following statements for his annual services: "David Laudaman, March 10, 1836. To Engagement by the year for fifteen persons—$30.00." To Lewis Barbee, on March 15, was rendered a similar account, which read: "To medical contract by year—$24.00."

July	12,	"	To pres[cription] & Med [icine] negro woman . .	.25
July	23,	"	To dose Tarlton (little son)	.25
July	24,	"	To call visit, Lady & pres [cription]	1.00
Aug	10,	"	To setting & dressing fracture bone (Daughter) .	5.00
Sept	13,	"	To (night) visit negro boy & dressing head . .	2.00
Oct	17,	"	To 3 visits, negro Jane, pres[cription] & Med[icine] and large blister . .	2.00" [19]

Another well-known Lexington "family physician & surgeon" was Dr. Robert C. Holland, who visited the family and slaves of Smith Laudaman, in 1834, and for his services presented the following account:

"July	1,	To visit Self & Lady & 2 children	$3.00
July	6,	To visit Lady & Consultation .	5.00
July	14,	To visit negro child & 3 doses Med[icine]	2.00
Aug	3,	To extract tooth, negro girl . .	.50
Aug	17,	To vaccinating 7 persons till they took virus	5.00
Sept	4,	To services negro woman (Charlotte) during spell of sickness, about 2 weeks & med[icine]	7.00
Oct	10,	To obstetrical services for Amy (black)	8.00
Oct	19,	To visit negro child, pres[cription], 2 cathartics & worm oil .	1.75
Oct	23,	To 2 visits Self & two negroes & pres[cription]	2.50" [20]

19. Manuscript account book of Dr. James M. Bush, in possession of Dr. J. S. Chambers, Lexington.

20. Dr. Robert C. Holland's account book, in possession of Dr. J. S. Chambers, of Lexington.

Likewise, during 1835, Dr. Holland's horse and buggy was often seen hitched in front of the imposing Lexington residence of General Leslie Combs, where he treated both master and slave with equal skill and attention:

"To sundry visits, Self, day & night, medicine & attendance	$4.00
To three visits, negroes	3.00
To 14 visits, two negroes & med[icine] .	14.00
To visit Lady & medicine	2.00
To 2 visits negro (Sarah) & pres[cription]	2.00
To visit negro woman (America) burn .	1.00
To visit negro woman, Bleeding & med[icine]	2.50
To visit Self & pres[cription]	1.50
To visit (night) negro, fractured skull & bruises	3.00
To visit negro girl & consultation [with] Dr. Hopson	5.00
To visit Lady, med[icine] & pres[cription]	1.50
To setting & dressing arm negro (Ben) .	4.00
To Emetic pills, blisters & six powders for girl (black)	.75
To 3 visits negro girl (Mary) & sundry med[icine]	4.00
To extract tooth for old negro man (Joe)	.75
To visit and pres[cription] for Self . . .	1.50" [21]

Every manager of a Kentucky estate, whether planter or overseer, had to possess some knowledge of the many arts and crafts. Not the least of these was that of medicine. Physicians were often unprocurable, especially by

21. These entries from Dr. Holland's account book run from August 10, 1835, until late in the fall of the same year. There are several other manuscript account books in the University of Kentucky Library which very clearly prove that it was the rule, rather than the exception, for Kentucky slaves to receive the same medical attention as their masters and other members of his family.

those living some distance in the country, and the care of the sick had to be attended to by those on the place. Most of the slave owners realized that a day's sickness meant a day's work left undone, so they prescribed in many cases where home remedies would suffice, and the ailments were not too chronic.

In a well-stocked medicine chest in the planters' homes were likely to be found many family remedies: Dr. Hahn's "anti-bilious pills" and "genuine eye water," Dr. Hamilton's "worm destroying lozenges," Dr. James' "fever powders," Dr. Gardener's "fever and ague pills," Dr. Sherman's "all-healing balsam," Dr. Hooper's "female pills" and powders, "tooth-ache drops," "rheumatic bitters," various tinctures "for the asthma" and "phthisic," and some that were good "for the fits," "nerve ointment," "healing salves" of various kinds, Dr. Crumbacker's "anti-dyspeptic pills," emetic drops and powders, syrups of all kinds, and a picturesque, if not always palatable, lot of home-concocted remedies. There was also Dr. Pedro's "sootherine" for "cranky children" and his "cherry pectoral" for ailing adults.

Most of the Kentucky planters felt that their slaves were a trust and that it was their business to hold and use them as humanely and fairly as possible. Robert Wickliffe, familiarly known as the "Old Duke" and the largest slaveholder in Kentucky, with fully two hundred Negroes, provided in his will that all of his "black people" be permitted to attend his funeral, "and that they be not required to labor on the day previous, nor on that day, nor for two days thereafter." Gravely concerned over the future welfare of his servants, Wickliffe further charged his executors, if it became necessary to divide the slaves, that they regard in such sale, "the relation of husband, wife, parent and child, and see that they *be not sold and divided separately . . . and sold to good and humane masters.*" Moreover, he enjoined his children "to treat such of them [slaves] as may pass to them with humanity and kindness. . . ." [22]

Humanitarian feelings and personal attachment of masters for their slaves are reflected in numerous wills, many of which make provisions for the comforts, freedom and happiness of the blacks. Polly Ficklin, of Fayette County, emancipated all her slaves by her will and gave them the village of "Kirkville," where they lived, to be held in common for the benefit of all, "particularly those who from age, infirmity or infancy are unable to support themselves." [23]

Richard Higgins, another prominent slaveholder of Fayette County, set his six slaves free at his death, and his executors were further directed "to prevent any of those slaves from suffering after they are set free, to which they are hereby directed to retain in their hands $600 out of my estate to be used as they think best." [24]

In many instances, where freedom was not granted at the death of old "Marster," the slaves were given the privilege of selecting the person whom they wished to

22. Fayette County Court, Will Book X, p. 95, February 18, 1853. Wickliffe was also concerned about his own funeral and directed that he "be buried in a plain and decent manner, without show or parade . . . it is my wish that they [his family] do not wear the usual habiliments of mourning or sorrow for my departure from this to a better world I hope."—*Ibid.*

23. *Ibid.*, Will Book S, p. 272. Many present-day settlements of colored people in the rural districts of Kentucky are the results of kindly masters' leaving plots of ground for their old and faithful servants, whose descendants now occupy them. Examples of these settlements are: "Little Georgetown" and "Slickaway" in Fayette County, "Bibbtown" in Logan County, "Firmantown" in Woodford County, and "Salsbury" in Muhlenberg County.

24. Fayette County Court, Will Book P, p. 482, April 28, 1840.

serve. Amelia Stanhope, of Fayette County, mentioned in her will "three old and faithful servants" and provided that, "they shall have the liberty to choose the place they shall live, and wherever they should be placed, to receive special care and consideration." [25] Likewise, Horace Coleman willed that his faithful slave, John, was "to have some indulgence for his kindness, and that he shall have the right to choose his master and be not sold publicly." [26]

By the will of James LaRue, of Hardin County, all of his slaves were to have their freedom when they reached the age of thirty, "unless they be guilty of stealing or trading off property from their masters or mistresses or any other person. In that case they shall serve five years longer, and if any one of them shall be found guilty of such practice more than once, the one so found shall serve for life . . . or if the blacks should attempt to raise to force their freedom, they shall be slaves for life. . . ." [27]

There were many Kentuckians who had no desire to hold their slaves in bondage, but believed that in doing so they did whatever was best for the slaves themselves. Many of the slaves were so old they could not provide for themselves, others were women and children whom no one was willing to feed and clothe for their labor. Then too, there rested on the master the responsibility of liberating his slave, for in doing so he had to post a bond, usually from four to five hundred dollars, guaranteeing to the county that his manumitted black would not become a public charge.

25. *Ibid.*, Will Book S, p. 252, August 13, 1849.
26. *Ibid.*, Will Book R, p. 202, 1846.
27. Otis M. Mather, *Six Generations of LaRues and Allied Families*, p. 146.

FAYETTE COUNTY HEMP FIELD

OLD SLAVE WITH HAND HEMP-BRAKE

Henry Clay, the owner of some fifty-odd slaves at "Ashland," long known as an advocate of gradual emancipation, could not bring himself around to turning his blacks loose upon society without some means of support. He was once taken to task over this matter, when he was addressing a large assemblage of Whigs at Richmond, Indiana, in the fall of 1846. He was approached by a member of the crowd, a Quaker named Mendenhall, with a petition signed by a considerable number of names urging him to emancipate all of his slaves.

As Clay well knew, some of his slaves would not accept freedom if it were given to them, others were his helpless charges, dependent upon him.[28] All were well cared for. What would be their condition if he turned them loose upon the world? Would it not be an act of cruelty to turn them out without any means of subsistence or support? Clay waxed vigorous toward the close of his remarks at Richmond, telling Mendenhall to "Go home and mind your own business, and leave other people to take care of theirs," and he added, as an afterthought, that he was willing to liberate his slaves provided the Quaker abolitionist and his associates would raise fifteen thousand dollars for their benefit and support.[29]

Nor were the Kentucky planters indifferent to the comfort of their grey-haired old slaves whose days of usefulness had passed. Many exhibitions of the master's kindly feelings toward them are known. They were

28. Clay, in enumerating his slaves, related that some eight or ten of them "from age, decrepitude, or infirmity, are wholly unable to gain a livelihood for themselves, and are a heavy charge upon me. Another class is composed of helpless infants, with or without improvident mothers. Do you believe as a Christian that I should perform my duty toward them by abandoning them to their fate?"

29. Glyndon Van Deusen, *The Life of Henry Clay,* p. 361.

usually addressed in a mild and pleasant manner, as "Uncle" or "Aunty." These faithful old slaves were allowed to spend their last days in ease in their little cabins, those not too infirm cultivating small truck patches, some of the products of which they sold for pin money.

In Kentucky, "Marster" or "Massa" was usually pronounced with the broad Virginia *a,* as in ah. "Mistress" was never pronounced "Missus," but "Mistus" or "Mistis"—generally the latter, and applied to the head of the house as "Marster" did to the whole plantation. It was not unusual to hear a slave speak of "Ole Marster," "Ole Mistis," or simply "Old Marse" or "Ole Miss"; likewise of "Young Marster," "Young Mistis." The younger members of a planter's family, however, were usually addressed and spoken of as "Mahs Tom" and "Miss Car'line."

Over the affairs of thc big house ruled the wife of the planter. Mother of a romping brood of her own, and supervisor of the pickaninny throng, she was the chatelaine of the whole establishment. Working with a never-flagging constancy, she carried all the keys, directed the household routine and all the various domestic industries, served as head nurse, and taught morals and religion by precept and example. Her hours were long, her diversions few, her voice quiet, her influence firm and inflexible.

The master's concern was chiefly with his crops and his livestock. He laid the plans, guessed the weather, ordered the work and saw to its performance. He went out early and returned late; he directed, taught, encouraged and, on occasion, punished. Yet he found time for visits to the county seat on court days, visits to the "watering-places" during the hot summer months, took time for politics and enjoyed sports and social affairs.

The one big item in the lives of the ante-bellum Kentucky planters was their inherent and abiding love of hospitality upon a large scale. There was a constant interchange of visits between the homesteads. No invitations were necessary and hospitality was unbounded. Guests drove up unannounced, sent their horses to the stables, had their portmanteaus and trunks carried into the big house, and lingered for weeks. Such frequent visits are indicative of the easy, pleasure-loving life of the planters and their families, which gave life a gracious informality.

On the larger estates in Kentucky the house servants and field hands were the major groups only; within each of these there was much division of labor. In the domestic establishment of a well-organized plantation there were gardeners, coachmen, hostlers, nurses, chambermaids, housemaids, waiting-maids, butlers, washerwomen, ironers, seamstresses and a cook, with one or two assistants. Some of the wealthier and more fashionable families had a head butler, usually an aged Negro major-domo with a "biled" shirt and correct dress-coat, who, in his bearing toward guests, was the paragon of civility and politeness. To him was intrusted that all-important duty of mixing and serving the frosted mint juleps in finely-wrought cups of coin silver.

As was customary in the household of a gentleman of the Bluegrass, Robert S. Todd's cellar was always well stocked with the finest Kentucky whiskies and rare brandies, and it was freely conceded among those whose opinions were respected in such matters, that not even Henry Clay's Charles "could mix a mint julep like Robert Todd's Nelson." [30]

Nowhere did the yoke of bondage rest more lightly than on the servants in the household of Robert Todd, the father-in-law of Abraham Lincoln, who was a large slaveholder. Like other "gentlemen" of the period, Todd had a summer home, "Buena Vista," in Franklin County. Here, as in his town house on West Main Street, Lexington, faithful Chaney was in undisputed control of the kitchen; pompous old Nelson ruled the other servants with a high hand, "while black Mammy Sally, despot of the nursery, gave orders to the little Todds, which even their mother did not dare revoke." [31]

Life among the planters, with their fine homes, large families, fertile lands and numerous servants, was a life of ease and elegance, of grace and distinction. Slave labor afforded leisure to the planter who enjoyed thc diversions traditional to Virginia, Maryland and the Carolinas.

"Were we obliged to labor personally," reasoned one pro-slavery advocate, "to apply our hands to all the menial offices of the kitchen and stable, when our friends or strangers visit us, their approach would not be as welcome as it is now and their continuance would hardly be solicited with as much warmth and sincerity.

"When the master," further contended this Kentuckian, "is called perpetually to the details of manual occupation and the mistress must leave the parlour and dining-room for the drudgery of preparation, required by the table and by the apartments where her guests

30. William H. Townsend, *Lincoln and His Wife's Home Town,* p. 63.
31. *Ibid.,* p. 81.

are to be lodged, the pleasure of their society and conversation must be so interrupted, so diminished, so cut up into paltry parts, that the spirit of hospitality would be greatly withered. . . ." [32] And, certainly, above all other things, there was to be no lack of lavishness when the friends and relatives of a Kentucky planter did him the honor of an extended visit.

A multitude of family servants, as some claimed, was a serious detriment to the wives of the planters—made them idle, weak and undeveloped. Cassius M. Clay admonished the valetudinarian ladies of the plantations thus: "Make up your own beds, sweep your own rooms, and wash your own clothes—throw away your corsets and nature will form your bustles." And continuing, he held out high hopes, "you will have full chests, glossy hair, rosy complexions, velvet skins, rounded limbs, graceful tournures, eyes of alternate fire, sweet tempers, good husbands, long lives of honeymoons, and—*no divorces*." [33]

Clay's enticing appeals, however, had little weight with the planters, who had no thought of giving up their family servants and, as one traveler very well observed, "Kentuckians have servants, and whatever may be the future consequences of slavery, the present effects are in those respects most agreeable and beneficial. . . ." [34]

Aside from the well-established custom of long and lavish entertainment in the rich homes of the planters and well-to-do slaveholders, there was another kind of entertainment and social diversion equally popular with "Marster" and "Mistis." This was the frequent

32. *Western Review,* Lexington, Vol. 1, No. 5, William G. Hunt, editor.
33. *The True American,* Lexington, June 17, 1845.
34. Fordham, *op. cit.,* p. 216.

and sometimes long-extended visits to the well-known springs or watering-places for which Kentucky was famous. During the three middle decades, the thirties, forties and fifties, when the pioneer had passed, when the stage-coach was the acme of travel, and when labor-saving inventions had not standardized life, there were in Kentucky more than a half dozen watering-places of national importance and reputation, and numerous others locally popular.

Among the best known resorts were Graham Springs, or Old Greenville, at Harrodsburg; Crab Orchard Springs in Lincoln County, which rivaled Graham as the Saratoga of the South; Paroquet Springs in Bullitt County with accommodations for eight hundred guests; Grayson Springs in Grayson County; Cerulean Springs in Trigg County; Drennon Springs in Henry County; Estill Springs, with its "superior band of music"; the ever popular Blue Licks Springs in Nicholas County, where the accommodations were "all that the most fastidious could desire"; and the well-known and historic resort, Olympian Springs, in Bath County, which was known as Mud Lick in the earlier days.

Large numbers of prosperous Kentuckians, accompanied by their wives, children and family servants, flocked to these springs or watering-places during the summer and early autumn months "to take the waters" and enjoy the gay whirl of the social season. These famed Kentucky resorts were "the grand summer rallying ground for Southern belles and beaux, and the realm of romance and flirtation." At these celebrated springs everything conspired "to restore the invalid and amuse those who seek relaxation." Music, dancing, swinging, riding, hunting and other exercises were the order of the day.

These watering-places of Kentucky were, indeed, gay places—more given to "cards, billiards, horse-jockeying, &c, than to the use of the waters for medicinal purposes." [35] There was much flirting, sometimes by "married charmers, thirsting for universal dominion." And, at times, the duelling pistols of sensitive gentlemen shattered the tranquility of "the romantic and picturesque scenery."

To escape the "sickly climate" of the South, many wealthy cotton and sugar-cane planters came with their families and servants [36] to spend the watering season, as well as many Northern visitors equally anxious to partake of the gay life of the springs.[37] Upon the arrival of a well-to-do family at one of these Kentucky resorts, the family servants who came with them pitched in and worked side by side with those attached to the establishment, and, in this manner, large crowds of guests, sometimes from four to six hundred, were handled with comparative ease.

The Kentucky planter was a kind of feudal lord over his house, his family, his plantation and his black people. Money invested in the purchase of a man or woman brought the solution of the owner's labor problem; it obviated re-hire, as possession extended over the

35. Fortescue Cuming, *Sketches of a Tour to the Western Country,* pp. 211–12.

36. Isaac C. Snedicor, of Green County, Alabama, offered a reward of $100 for the return of his slave, or "body-servant," named Claiborne, who "ran away from the subscriber on the 8th inst., while returning from Olympian Springs in this state to his residence in Alabama."—*Lexington Observer & Reporter,* August 29, 1838.

37. J. Winston Coleman, Jr., *Stage-Coach Days in the Bluegrass,* p. 183.

life of the slave, and it brought natural increment as it vested the owner with title to all the slave's offspring. Once a man had a force of slaves equal to the needs of his plantation, his labor problem seemed not only to be solved temporarily, it seemed solved for all time, for the supply, which involved only a moderate investment, was self-perpetuating.

Many farmers and planters from the tobacco-growing districts of Virginia and Maryland came to Kentucky with their slaves, where they resumed the culture of this plant upon a large scale. But they soon found that, on account of tobacco being "low in the market"—two or three cents a pound—and with the dangers and difficulties of getting it to market, it did not pay them to plow up their rich Bluegrass woodlands, which were worth considerably more for the raising of livestock.

When the culture of tobacco was introduced into Kentucky, the only available market was New Orleans, and the only means of transportation was by water. This arrangement resulted in long waits for returns for tobacco and restricted production to river and near-by river counties. From the old papers of James Crutcher, of Meade County, there is a record of a flatboat trip from Curd's Warehouse, at the confluence of the Kentucky and Dick's rivers, to New Orleans. This faded old document relates that a cargo of corn, tobacco and lard was started down the Kentucky River, March 19, 1819, and reached its final destination June 1: "36,648 pounds of tobacco shipped by William Akin, Danville, Ky., on board the good flatboat *Eliza,* whereof James Crutcher is master for the present voyage, now lying in the Kentucky River and bound for the port of New

Orleans. To be paid [for freightage] at the rate of 1 cent a pound, ½ at New Orleans, ½ at Danville." [38]

Probably this cargo of planter Akin's tobacco, upon arrival at New Orleans, sold for about three or four cents a pound. With one cent off for carriage, and the risks of a safe overland journey back to Kentucky, such undertakings were indeed hazardous enterprises and certainly not very profitable. Even at Henderson, Kentucky, on the Ohio River, in 1830, tobacco was selling for only two and three-quarter cents per pound.[39]

Hence, the rich slaveholding counties of the Bluegrass—Fayette, Bourbon, Woodford, Scott, Clark and Jessamine—paid little attention to tobacco culture.[40] While some of the less fertile river counties grew it in larger quantities, the small profits derived were in keeping with the difference in the soil. In 1840 the largest tobacco-producing counties in Kentucky were, in order, Daviess, Christian, Todd, Henderson, Caldwell and Barren—any one of which produced more than all of the five rich Bluegrass counties surrounding Lexington, the county seat of Fayette.[41]

With the cleared forest lands in rolling pastures and woodlands, livestock soon became the one big industry for the Bluegrass planter, and for many years led the

38. George L. Ridenour, *Early Times in Meade County, Kentucky*, p. 55.

39. Richard H. Collins, *History of Kentucky*, II, 335. Although a hogshead market was established in Louisville in 1825, all tobacco had to be prized into hogsheads for shipment and the difficulty of transportation had its drawbacks.

40. In 1840 the tobacco poundage of these counties was: Fayette, 52,900; Bourbon, 4,361; Woodford, 13,860; Scott, no report; Clark, 82,410; Jessamine, 73,793.—*Compendium, Sixth U. S. Census*, p. 264.

41. Daviess County led Kentucky in pounds of tobacco produced in 1840, with a total of 8,589,900 pounds, and Christian County second, with 3,409,502 pounds.—*Ibid.*

state in the list of farm products.[42] Hemp likewise soon became a very profitable crop for Kentucky and was grown principally in the heart of the slaveholding counties—Fayette, Mason, Scott, Clark, Bourbon, Woodford, Jessamine, Shelby and Franklin. By 1840 these counties were producing more than two thirds of the total crop grown in Kentucky, which ranked first, with Missouri second, as a hemp-growing state.

Of all of Kentucky's crops in the ante-bellum days, hemp was believed to afford the greatest remuneration to the planter for his slave labor and lands.[43] It was estimated that three slaves could cultivate fifty-one acres, produce 35,700 pounds of fibre at an average of 700 pounds per acre.[44] Hemp, when manufactured into a coarse cloth or bagging, was well suited for holding the bales of cotton together, and this product came to be known as "cotton bagging." Rope made from hemp found an extensive use for tying the cotton bales for shipment. These products—"cotton bagging" and "bale rope"—were grown and manufactured in Kentucky and shipped by boat to the rich cotton markets of the South. Kentucky planters, faced by a growing demand for these products, were basking in the light of prosperity and enjoyed a good revenue from their hemp crops,[45] which were grown with a comparatively small amount of slave labor.

42. The value of livestock in Kentucky in 1850 was $29,661,436, and in 1860 it had grown to $61,868,237.

43. In the early eighteen-fifties there were 3,520 hemp plantations in existence in Kentucky, on which the acreage yield was estimated to be 650 pounds.—*Report of the Superintendent of Census, 1852,* p. 178.

44. *Kentucky Farmer,* Frankfort, March, 1859.

45. For several years in the late eighteen-twenties, Kentucky hemp brought an average price of one hundred dollars per ton. Hemp and livestock were the chief exports of the Bluegrass; hemp being second to livestock.—*Niles' Weekly Register,* XXXIII (February 28, 1828), 432.

Corn, food crops and pasturage for livestock permitted the handling of large acreage by small personnel; and in tobacco and hemp production there was little advantage of largeness of scale. Kentucky, therefore, did not develop great plantations nor import hordes of slaves to till them. In fact, the word "plantation" had by 1835 become almost obsolete in Kentucky, the term "farm" having taken its place. Likewise, "planter" and "farmer" soon became interchangeable.[46]

From an economic point of view, Kentucky was not suited to the development of slavery. By far the larger number of slave owners held less than five slaves each. Out of 38,456 slaveholders in Kentucky in 1850, only fifty-three owned from fifty to one hundred slaves, and only five owned more than one hundred. Holders of more than one and less than five slaves constituted the greatest number of Kentucky slaveholders, fully thirteen thousand coming within this class.

Agricultural pursuits were not so favorable in the eastern or mountainous sections of Kentucky, and the farmers were proportionately poor—many not able to own a single slave.[47] What little work there was to be done, the mountaineers did themselves, or swapped work with their neighbors. Slavery among this class of mountain whites was almost unknown, and many of them rarely, if ever, saw a Negro, or had any contact with the slaveholders of the "flat country" or cities, and were, therefore, little influenced by the institution. They were, however, more prejudiced against the slaveholders than against the Negroes themselves. Except for

46. Phillips, *Life and Labor in the Old South,* p. 80.

47. In 1860 the smallest slaveholding counties of Kentucky and their total number of slaves were: Jackson, 7; Johnson, 27; Magoffin, 71; Perry, 73; and Pike, 97.—Kennedy, *Preliminary Report of 8th U. S. Census,* p. 176.

this class of mountain whites, pro-slavery sentiment heavily prevailed in Kentucky.

While the evils of the absentee landlord system of the Lower South, with its cruel overseer and large hoe and plow gangs, were never prevalent in Kentucky, there were, nevertheless, many farms or plantations [48] which employed an overseer or general manager. With fifteen to twenty slaves, or more, to look after, many Kentucky planters found it necessary to employ an overseer.[49] William P. Hart, a prominent slaveholder of Fayette County, advertised in the fall of 1844:

> "AN OVERSEER WANTED!
>
> "Fair wages will be given for a man experienced in the culture of hemp and the management of slaves, provided he can also come well recommended for sobriety, industry and morality. None other need apply." [50]

Sometimes a widow who had a good sized farm and a number of slaves needed someone to manage her estate. Mrs. E. B. Coleman, of the northeastern part of Fayette County, applied through the local newspaper for a capable farm overseer: "I wish to employ a man well suited to superintend my farm and negroes; a sober, steady and industrious man, with a capacity for farming business and a small family." [51]

48. Primogeniture and entail never gained a foothold in Kentucky, the land being equally divided among the heirs. This and the high price of land in Kentucky account for the lack of large plantations as were common in the Far South.

49. "Overseer Wants a Position!—A man long accustomed to farming and the management of negroes wishes a situation as overseer the next year on a farm in this or any adjoining county."—*Kentucky Reporter,* September 29, 1829. Many such notices of overseers seeking employment are found in the ante-bellum Kentucky newspapers.

50. *Lexington Observer & Reporter,* October 30, 1844.

51. *Ibid.,* November 14, 1860.

Fortunate, indeed, was the Kentucky planter who had an overseer, or farm boss, whom he could thoroughly trust, who understood the lands and managed the slaves in a satisfactory manner. With such an arrangement he could visit the springs or watering-places with his family in the summer and fall, or in the city in the winter, without anxiety. He thus had much leisure for hunting, horse-racing, politics and other diversions, as his varied tastes might lead him.

Slavery in the Bluegrass State, as has been pointed out, was much more a domestic than a commercial institution. And it was in this environment of lavish nature, prodigal outlay, ample hospitality and benevolent bondage that the folks in the big house lived and enjoyed life in those colorful and romantic days of antebellum Kentucky.

CHAPTER III

MASSA'S PEOPLE

THERE WAS always much excitement and speculation down in the quarters when word came that a "play boy" was to be selected for young "marster." William, a slave born on the plantation of Dr. John Young, of Fayette County, described how such a selection was made in his boyhood days, which was substantially the same as in many other cases.

"When the planter's son became old enough to need a playmate to watch over him," wrote William, "mistress called all the young slaves together, to select one for that purpose. We were all ordered to run, jump, wrestle, turn somersets, walk on our hands, and go through the various gymnastic exercises that the imagination of our brain could invent, or the strength and activity of our limbs could endure.

"The selection was to be an important one, both to the mistress and to the slave. Whoever should gain the place was in the future to become a house servant; the ash-cake thrown aside, that unmentionable garment that buttons around the neck, which we all wore, and nothing else, was to give way to the whole suit of tow linen. Every one of us joined heartily in the contest, while old mistress sat on the piazza, watching our every movement—some fifteen of us, each dressed in his one garment, sometimes standing on our heads with feet in the air—still the lady looked on.

"With me it seemed a matter of life and death; for, being blood kin to master, I felt that I had more at stake than my companions. At last the choice was made, and I was told to step aside as the 'lucky boy,' which order I obeyed with an alacrity seldom surpassed. That night I was put to soak, after which I was scraped, scrubbed, washed and dried.

"The next day, a new suit came down to the quarters; I slipped into it; the young slaves gathered around me, and I was the star of the plantation." With his mother's blessing, William bade farewell to the log cabin and dirt floor of the quarters and started for the big house, where his mistress received him and sharply "laid down the law" which was to govern his future actions.

"I give your young master over to you," cautioned his mistress, "and if you let him hurt himself, I'll pull your ears; if you let him cry, I'll pull your ears, and if he wants anything and you don't let him have it, I'll pull your ears." And, according to William, "right well did she keep her promise." [1]

To be young master's play boy was a coveted honor, as William well knew, which would later enable him to become a house servant,[2] one of the most desirable

1. William W. Brown, *The Black Man,* pp. 11–12.

2. Francis Fedric, a Kentucky slave who was promoted from field hand to house servant, wrote: "I was now made a house slave. My duties were to wait on the table and help in the kitchen. I was extremely glad of this promotion as it afforded me a better chance of obtaining good food. At this period I had a good time of it, waiting on the table and listening to the conversation going on. I learned many things of which field hands were entirely ignorant."—Fedric, *Slave Life in Virginia and Kentucky,* p. 26.

positions on the whole plantation. The house servants formed a class quite distinct from, and socially above, the field hands; in fact, the social lines among the slaves [3] were often more rigid than among the whites. The slaves of a rich or well-to-do planter, or a socially and politically prominent master, were absurdly proud of their connections with greatness and power, and would have little to do with their fellow bondsmen who were held by poorer or inconspicuous slave owners.

On the whole, the life of the house or family servant was far more pleasant than that of the farm slaves. His food was likely to be the same as was served at his master's table. Clothing was frequently identical, being worn or castoff garments of masters and mistresses, or their children. Quite a few of the house servants could read and write "tolerably well." Generally they copied the manners and habits of their masters and the dignity of the big house was safe in their keeping.

Family servants of this class assumed an air of superiority over the field hands and sometimes refused to recognize them. This is indicated in a brief conversation between a smartly dressed coachman and a footman:

"You know dat field nigger dey gwine to sell, George?"

"No, he field nigger; I nebber has no 'quaintance wid dat class."

"Well, nor no oder gentlemens would." [4]

Also, slaves often rated their social standing by their

3. Malinda, a light-skinned mulatto slave of Oldham County, Kentucky, "moved in the highest circle of slaves and free people of color." She later became the wife of Henry Bibb, the runaway slave who set up and edited the anti-slavery paper, *The Voice of the Fugitive,* in Sandwich, Ontario. —Henry Bibb, *Narrative of the Life and Adventures of Henry Bibb,* p. 33.

4. Joseph H. Ingraham, *The Southwest,* II, 30, 56.

OLD SLAVE CABINS AS THEY LOOK TODAY

OLD SLAVE COUPLE, MERCER COUNTY

value in the market. "I'se a fifteen hundred dollar nigger," proudly boasted one Fayette County slave to another who had recently brought only eight hundred and fifty dollars, thereby putting himself on a much higher social level according to the slave method of reckoning one's rank.

In Kentucky, as in other slave states, the field hands were regarded as the lowest and "last link in the chain of human bondage"—confined to the seclusion of an extensive plantation, which was their only world, beyond whose horizon they knew nothing (their walks were limited to the area between the quarters and the fields), their knowledge and information gained from the rude and unreliable gossip of their fellow slaves, straggling runaways, or house servants, and most of the time without seeing any white person, except their master or overseer. To their owners they were variously known as "hands," "force," "field hands," "black people" and "niggers," but rarely ever called or spoken of as slaves.

As the group of cabins, familiarly known as the quarters, was the center of all slave life and activity, it was deemed expedient to place them some distance from the big house. One authority on recommending their layout advised that they should "be placed a convenient distance from the master's house on a dry, airy ridge—raised two feet from the ground—so they can be thoroughly ventilated underneath, and placed at distances apart of at least fifty yards to ensure health. In this construction, they should be sufficiently spacious so as not to crowd the family intended to occupy them —with brick chimneys and large fire-places to impart warmth to every part of the room."

Further stressing the need of well-designed quarters, this writer called attention to the fact that "more diseases and loss of time on plantations are engendered from crowded negro cabins than from almost any other cause. The successful planter should, therefore, have an especial eye to the comfort of his negroes, in not permitting them to be overcrowded in their sleeping quarters." [5]

From the description of the quarters visited in Kentucky by a New England traveler, it is quite evident that most Kentucky planters were cognizant of these conditions and paid especial attention to their Negroes' houses. "On the evening of the second day of my arrival," wrote Franklin Wilmot, "we took a stroll through the 'quarters.' We passed to the front and entered the yard of the 'quarters.' Groups of negroes were scattered around in different attitudes. There were seated on a bench under the trees, some two or three older ones, whose patriarchal appearance and gray locks attracted my immediate notice. Around them was a group of younger ones, who listened to the conversation of their seniors.

"There was another set stretched at full length on the green grass—happy and contented. There was a troop of noisy children, who stopped their gambols on the velvety sward to crowd around their master, who spoke kindly to all. Bursts of laughter, as pleasant as the tinkling of a silver bell, went forth from them when they replied to his questions. They came around us—a merry, grinning group; they examined my dress, and handled my watch without fear or hesitation.

"At the doors of some of the houses were seen sitting

5. *The Practical Farmer & Mechanic,* October 6, 1857.

the inmates quietly smoking their pipes, while ever and anon a snatch of a hymn, would issue from the tenements of the pious. All were free from care, and happy in the possession of enough.

"We now entered several of the houses. They were furnished very plainly, but were clean. A bed in the corner, and perhaps two; clothes hanging on pegs around the room; a pine table, and a few chairs or stools, together with a rude chest, and a plentiful supply of cooking utensils, completed the list. . . ." [6] What Wilmot saw of slave life in Kentucky was indeed a true cross section of the system. Generally speaking, the slaves were a happy, contented and carefree race; well fed, as their looks testified, well-lodged and not overworked.

"How do you feed them?" inquired Wilmot. "On Sunday morning," replied the master, "the overseer goes to the meat house, and there assemble the negroes; four pounds of pork are weighed out to each one, and they get a peck of meal, and a half gallon of molasses; beans, sweet potatoes, and other vegetables they raise in moderate quantities. They are allowed to raise chickens and always have a supply of eggs."

"What time do they go to work?" further asked this traveler.

"At daylight, and stop at sundown; rest two or three hours during the middle or heat of the day; but have every Saturday afternoon to wash and mend and cultivate their little truck patches." [7]

It is true there are to be found some disparaging accounts of Kentucky bondage as it was, but these were

6. *Disclosures and Confessions of Franklin A. Wilmot, the Slave Thief and Negro Runner,* pp. 20–22.

7. *Ibid.,* p. 25.

written for the most part by Northern abolitionists who were eager to believe the worst about slavery and who used, as if they were typical, stories which had to do with highly exceptional conditions and occurrences. Anti-slavery societies in the North likewise seized, rewrote and highly colored several of the fugitive slaves' stories and circulated them for propaganda purposes; yet, these overdrawn and often distorted views can hardly be considered as affording a fair picture of the "peculiar institution" as it existed in this state.

Many travelers of the ante-bellum period, who traveled in the slave states, noted in diaries and journals that they saw slavery in Kentucky in its mildest forms. Even Harriet Beecher Stowe, whose world-famous book, *Uncle Tom's Cabin,* gave a lurid picture of the horrors of slavery in the United States—an account that was not free from gross exaggeration—was fair enough to admit that, "perhaps, the mildest form of the system of slavery is to be seen in the State of Kentucky." [8]

That Kentucky slaves, under ordinary circumstances, were well fed, well clothed, happy and contented, is further substantiated by the number of newspaper accounts of runaway slaves, who, after experiencing "a spell of freedom" in Northern territory, often in Canada, were glad to return to their old homes and masters.

A typical case occurred in the fall of 1858, when William R. Crean, a planter of Bourbon County, received a letter from his two runaway slaves in Canada stating that they were tired of freedom and earnestly requesting their master to bring them back to the only home they knew. Arriving in Toronto, Crean had no

8. *Uncle Tom's Cabin,* p. 9.

difficulty in locating his fugitive blacks, who had been "barely eking out a very precarious existence" since reaching free territory.

"They stuck to their determination to accompany their old master home," said the *Cincinnati Commercial,* "and yesterday he arrived with them in this city, en route to 'old Kentucky' and servitude, and they seemed much pleased at the prospects of again being among friends and familiar places. . . ." [9]

Another case of this kind, and one which brings out more fully the benevolent side of Kentucky bondage, occurred several years later. A young Bracken County slave, in the early part of May, 1861, escaped from the Negro jail of Bolton, Dickens & Company, in Lexington. Nothing more was heard from this runaway until nearly a year later, when his former owner received a letter from Halifax, England, addressed, "Mr. George Humlong, County of Bracken, Kentucky, America," in which this erstwhile Kentucky slave implored his old master to take him back:

> "Dear Massa. Halifax, March 18, 1862.
>
> I am going to deliver myself up to you. I hope you won't flog me when I come to you. I shall leave England on the 9th of April, and arrive at New York about the 23rd. I run away May last and would rather be your slave than free. If you will write to the New York Post office to be called for, and state where I am to meet you, I will meet you anywhere you like, but I would rather meet you in New York. You can do what you like with me; sell me where you think proper. I am quite tired of being knocked about in England. I would fifty times rather be a slave than free.

9. September 5, 1858.

I hope you will meet me. I am 22 years old and can work [in] iron first rate. I was a slave in Lexington and escaped from Bolton & Dickens depot . . . I will give myself up and you can do what you like with me.

Your faithful slave,
John Brown." [10]

It is from observant European travelers who visited Kentucky with an open-minded attitude that we obtain some of the truest pictures of the actual condition of Negro bondage in the Bluegrass State. James Silk Buckingham, an Englishman, who visited here in 1842, saw many instances of black and white laborers —slave and free—working together in the same fields between Frankfort and Louisville. "As large gangs [of slaves] are not employed in the cultivation here," he observed, "as they are in the cotton, rice and sugar-cane lands of the South, the discipline is much more relaxed, and the condition of the negroes, as to food, clothing and light labour, struck me as being better in Kentucky than in any other [slave] state that I had yet visited. . . ." [11]

Among the black people the slave preacher was a person of great consequence. Strange, yet how true, that the more ignorant he was, the more power of influence for good or ill he carried among his fellow beings. "Uncle" Peter Cotton, an old slave preacher residing in Fayette County, filled two important vocations in his community, exhorter and wood chopper. One moment Uncle Peter might be seen chopping away at his woodpile; the next, kneeling down beside it praying. His

10. Original letter in the possession of Mr. Graham Humlong, Germantown, Kentucky.

11. *Eastern and Western States,* III, 8.

mistress fashioned a long jeans coat for him and, at his request, embroidered various texts of scripture on the coat tails. Thus, literally clothed with righteousness, Uncle Peter went from plantation to plantation, cabin to cabin, faithfully administering to the sick, baptizing, preaching the word and marrying members of his own race, according to the slave fashion, in a kind of common-law wedlock.[12]

Legally, there were no binding marriages among the slaves. They were not citizens, but mere property. The men were urged to take their wives, or mates, from among the women on the home estate, provided a suitable companion could be found. But if not, they eventually secured one in the neighborhood, and the master usually allowed his slave a pass to visit his reputed spouse once or twice a week, or, in some cases, only on Sundays or at weekends.

In many parts of Kentucky, and especially in the rural districts, slave weddings were important social events among the black people. It was not unusual for the master or mistress to provide an elaborate supper in the kitchen or yard of the big house, invite in all the bride's and groom's friends of the neighborhood and make a gala occasion of the affair. Many of these marriages were celebrated in true slave fashion, by the quaint ceremony of "jumping over the broomstick." [13]

12. James Lane Allen, *The Blue-Grass Region of Kentucky,* p. 79. "Almost every neighborhood had its negro preacher, whose credentials, if his own assertion was to be taken, came directly from the Lord."—Lucius P. Little, *Ben Hardin: His Times and Contemporaries,* p. 544.

Rev. Elisha Green, the property of John P. Dobbyns, of Maysville, was a well-known slave preacher of that section. In Lexington another familiar preacher was the Virginia-born slave, familiarly known as "Old Captain," founder and for many years pastor of the First African Baptist Church.—Robert H. Bishop, *Outline of the History of the Church in the State of Kentucky,* pp. 230–34.

13. "Aunt" Addie Murphy, an old ex-slave of Lexington stated: "To

This old practice was derived from some ancient marriage ceremony in Europe, which had been handed down with many variations by the "white folks" over a long period of years.

When no colored preacher was available, the master simply read a few passages of scripture, had the couple go through the ceremony of "jumping over the broomstick," and then pronounced them man and wife.[14]

In performing the marriage ceremony, the Reverend London Ferrill, a Virginia-born slave preacher residing in Lexington,[15] united several hundred couples in wedlock "until death or *distance* do you part," [16] and many were the partings *by distance,*[17] when families were broken up or when the best pecuniary interests of the "nigger traders" were jeopardized. It was generally understood that when married slaves were sold to different masters and the distance between the respective places of residence of man and wife prevented their liv-

---

get married in those days, they got a new broom and would jump over it and they were married, but they had to have a preacher."—J. C. Meadors, interview, August 13, 1938.

14. Rev. John R. Cox, ex-slave of Boyd County, Kentucky, remembered that his mother was married "by the ceremony of laying a broom on the floor and having the young Negroes step over the broomstick."—C. F. Hall, interview with Cox, at Catlettsburg, December 23, 1936.

When asked if his old aunt and uncle were married while they were in bondage, Henry Smith testified: "They said they were married in slave days and jumped over the broom stick as they called it."—Mike Cayson, *et al. vs.* Unknown Heirs of Henry Cayson, Barren Circuit Court, File 10,878, May 6, 1919.

15. *The Liberator,* Boston, October 17, 1854, carried a notice of Rev. Ferrill's death on October 12, 1854, and stated that "he had built up one of the largest churches in the United States, his communicants numbering 1828." He was credited with having baptized "upwards of five thousand persons."—*Kentucky Statesman,* October 13, 1854.

16. Sometimes the ceremony varied: *"or as long as circumstances will permit."*

17. "The custom was that if one moved off or was sold at a distance, he took up another, or if they got separated they took another mate. Distances in those days were the same as divorces."—Deposition of Lud Brooks, colored, Cayson *vs.* Unknown Heirs, *supra.*

ing together, they were then considered as divorced.

While slave marriages were without legal sanction, they were often held as sacred and binding as the legalized unions of the white class. Dick, a Lexington slave, escaped and fled South, as his master believed, "for he had often been heard to say that he was determined to go to New Orleans" to see "his wife living in that city." [18]

One of the most peculiar cases of slave marriages, and one that well illustrates the insecurity of the black marital ties, occurred in Garrard County during the summer of 1856. Steve Kyler, a "free man of colour," had belonged to Joseph Kyler, a prosperous, kind-hearted farmer, who had allowed him to hire himself out, and with his earnings Steve had purchased his freedom. When the owner of Cynthia, Steve's wife, moved away from the neighborhood, the good master purchased Cynthia and assigned the bill of sale to Steve. It was a sad day for these faithful servants when they buried "Old Marster" beneath the honeysuckle in the garden.

Steve was somewhat "pestered in his mind," for with freedom came responsibility. Debts had gradually piled up. Two creditors, refusing to wait longer, had already obtained judgments against him at the last "law day" in Lancaster. It was a relief, however, to reflect that, having no property, he would not be harassed by court officials, and could thus pay his debts as it became possible for him to do so.

But the next day Constable Arnold came to his cabin and seized Cynthia under two executions which had been issued on the judgments rendered against her husband. Steve, dazed and panic-stricken, rushed to the

18. *Lexington Intelligencer,* July 7, 1838.

county seat to consult Lawyer Allen Burton, later Lincoln's minister to Columbia, who hurriedly filed a petition in the Garrard Circuit Court and obtained a temporary injunction preventing Cynthia from being sold until the case could be fully heard upon its merits.

For Steve and Cynthia, Burton argued that "it being the understanding and agreement between all parties" that Steve "should take her as a wife only, he acquired no property in her aside from his right as a husband to her comfort and society."

For the creditors, the Honorable George R. McKee argued that Cynthia, being the slave of Joseph Kyler, her master, "did no act by which she would, at any future time, be entitled to freedom. He sold her as a slave; in the hands of a purchaser she is liable to sale for his debts . . . it is a fraud on the creditors for him to claim her but as a wife." This, as Burton claimed, was a "barbarous and piratical doctrine" which no "enlightened and humane public sovereignty" would tolerate.

Losing their case in the circuit court,[19] Burton appealed to the highest court of the state at Frankfort. In the winter of 1857 Chief Justice Wheat delivered the opinion for the Kentucky Court of Appeals, in which he held that the deed passed the title in Cynthia to Stephen and, by the laws of Kentucky, slaves were subject to execution for debts of their owners the same as other real and personal property. "Marriages between slaves have no legal effect," said Justice Wheat, "and marriages between free negroes and slaves are not recognized but to a very limited extent."

"Upon an attentive examination of the record," concluded the learned jurist, "we have not been able to

19. Dunlap *vs.* Kyler & Wife, Garrard Circuit Court, Fall Term, 1856.

perceive any error to the prejudice of the appellants. Wherefore, the judgment of the Circuit Court is affirmed." Thus ended one of the strangest and most tragic cases in all the history of Kentucky's "peculiar institution," a case where a home was broken up, the devoted wife seized and sold on the auction block by "merciless creditors" and "remanded back to slavery." [20]

There was one feature of slave life which gravely and at all times concerned the master. This was the act of his bondsman's running away. So long as a black family remained together upon one plantation, the love of its members for one another operated as the strongest bond to prevent their unceremoniously leaving. But, upon the breaking up or separation of families, with no prospect of reunion, the firmest and often the sole tie which held them together was severed. There was then little left to hold them back. In some cases, harsh treatment and severe punishment were the motives for runaways. And lastly, the fear of being sold "down the river" into the rice and cotton fields of the Far South caused many slaves to desert their Kentucky homes.

Very little attempt was made to find a runaway slave through his friends; for the Negroes almost universally aided and shielded imperiled people of their own race. If advertising failed, the next step was to hunt with dogs, and professional slave catchers advertised bloodhounds [21] that "can take the trail twelve hours after the

20. Kyler & Wife *vs.* Dunlap, *Kentucky Reports,* 18 B. Monroe 447, Winter Term, 1857.

21. Harry Smith, a Spencer County slave, wrote that Jim Lewis, who lived on the Bardstown turnpike, ten miles from Louisville, was regularly engaged in raising and selling thoroughbred bloodhounds, or "nigger dogs," for catching runaway slaves, and that he "would often collect $50 for catching one."—Harry Smith, *Fifty Years of Slavery in the United States,* p. 114.

nigger has passed" and "catch him with ease." The use of these "nigger dogs" was distasteful in Kentucky, but was not in itself an inhuman method of locating the fugitive, although many slaveholders looked upon it as a barbarous practice. It was often the fury of the pursuers and the desperation of the quarry that led to resistance and even to shooting.

Runaway Negroes were a source of great worry to their owners and somewhat of terror to the community. In some instances, when the master did not feel disposed to go after his slave, he "sold his nigger running" —that is, transferred the title to a purchaser who took the risk of finding the slave. Sometimes, such a "chancing bargain" was made with a professional slave catcher who had never seen the Negro, and had no other interest than to get him back and sell him for a profit.[22]

On October 13, 1834, John Reed, of Mason County, purchased a twenty-two-year-old slave, Elizabeth, and her two-year-old child, Rachel, for four hundred and fifty dollars from John D. Morford, of Bracken County. Curiously enough, this slave had run away at the time of the transaction, and there was written on the reverse side of the bill of sale: "The said negro has run away and the said Reed runs the risk of finding her. John Reed. October 13, 1834." [23]

Ordinarily the runaway took nothing with him in his hazardous excursion into the broad world except the clothes on his back. Slaves' clothing was of a large

22. William Ellis, of Fayette County, in 1829 paid $100 for the title to Tom, a runaway slave. Ellis pursued this slave to the "Indian Nation, on the Northwest territory," where he captured him, and, after bringing him back to Lexington, sold him for $750.—Wm. Gosney's Heirs *vs.* Wm. Ellis, Fayette Circuit Court, File 757, April 15, 1829.

23. Original in the possession of John Reed's grandson, Mr. Justice Stanley F. Reed, of Washington, D. C.

variety, from the young lady's waiting-maid who wore the still fresh dress that had been her mistress's own, down to the little pickaninnies of three or four years who went "as nature made them." Young Negroes usually wore a shirt that reached to their knees, while the grown-ups received clothes which varied according to the taste or whim of their master.[24]

Fairly accurate descriptions of slave clothing can be found in the advertisements of fugitive slaves that jailers and sheriffs prepared and published in the Kentucky newspapers. Among the materials frequently listed were: blue and brown Attakapas, plaid and striped osnaburgs, plantation twills, Kentucky jeans, cassimere, plain linsey, "gay calicoe," duffels, kerseys, cassinette, blue linen, check linen, "hard time" cotton, tow linen, linsey-woolsey, cottonade, fustian, duck, bombazette, French drilling and Lowell cotton. Numerous arrays of colors were added to this assortment. There were surtouts, roundabouts, round-coats, frock-coats, waistcoats and several other kinds, differing in color, weave and fabric almost as much as the trousers or pantaloons.

Campeachy hats, fur hats and woolen caps, coarse socks and russet brogans,[25] together with mixed jeans, cotton flannels and linseys seem to have been the stock in trade for many Kentucky merchants who catered to the slaveholding planters and farmers.[26] In practically

24. "Our clothes were made of jeans and linsey in winter, and in the summer we wore cotton clothes."—Statement of "Uncle" George Henderson, ex-slave of Garrard County, to the author, summer, 1934.

25. The term "brogan" was widely used in Kentucky and indicated a heavy and stout-made work shoe, very hard and clumsy, and sold to planters at prices ranging from $15.00 to $17.50 per dozen pairs.

26. *Georgetown Gazette,* March 25, 1858; *Kentucky Tribune,* Danville, October 6, 1843; *Western Citizen,* Paris, February 1, 1839.

all advertisements, a distinction was made between clothing for Negroes and clothing for white people. The former, when advertised for sale, was usually designated as "negro goods" and, if the merchant's stock of goods warranted it, there was a separate description of "fashionable clothing for ladies and gentlemen."

Homespun was largely worn on many plantations or farms, especially those in the more remote parts of the state. When bad weather interrupted work in the fields, the hands, both men and women, were required to spin or weave and, in the winter months, many of the slave garments were thus made. Many slaves who were old or unfit for field work regularly labored in the loom-house carding wool, spinning cotton and wool, weaving, dyeing and making clothes.[27] Homespun was often dyed with sassafras bark or the juice of berries, although indigo was sometimes used, when available to the slave owner.

It is evident, from the runaway advertisements, that Kentucky slaves, whether domestic, town or agricultural laborers, performed many different kinds of work. These notices reveal that slaves were employed as laborers in the iron works of Bath County, at the salt works of Clay County, worked in the iron and lead mines of Caldwell and Crittenden counties, served as guides in Mammoth Cave, in Edmonson County, and were employed in building many of the limestone fences throughout central Kentucky.

27. Josiah Henson, a slave of Daviess County, said of their clothing: "Our dress for the children was tow-cloth with nothing but a shirt; for the older ones a suit of clothes, consisting of hard-time cotton, this was for the men's breeches and shirts; and then cheap calico dresses and a hard-time shirt for the women. Besides these, in the winter we had a round jacket or overcoat, a wool hat once in two or three years, for the males, and a pair of coarse shoes once a year."—*Father Henson's Story of His Own Life,* p. 17.

Among the more specialized occupations listed were: a man "with considerable mechanical genius," "a superior blacksmith and engineer," "a first rate boot and shoe maker," "an excellent waggoner," "a good post & railer," "a first rate blacksmith," "an experienced weaver and chair spinner," "a skilled rope spinner," "a good hand for a rope-walk," "an excellent carpenter," "a very valuable Ostler," "a good race-horse rubber," and a "good groom for a stallion." Besides these specialties, there were the common notices for "first-rate field hands," experienced carriage drivers, house servants, seamstresses, dairy-maids, nurses, gardeners, stable boys and the like.

While slave labor executed in a fairly satisfactory manner most all of the menial tasks, both in the field, factory and the home, chattel slavery, on the whole, did not pay in Kentucky. Agricultural conditions and the climate of Kentucky were not suited to the profitable all-the-year-round employment of slave labor. Then, too, the slave owner had to look after every interest and need of his slave—his food, clothing, shelter, health, habits and discipline, and not for the working slave alone, but also for those who were incapacitated for work by sickness, old age or infancy. And this watch-care and upkeep had to be maintained by the master in hard times as well as in "flush," for the worthy as well as the unworthy slave.

Warner L. Underwood, a prominent slaveholder of Warren County, after giving agricultural labor in Kentucky a fair trial, was thoroughly convinced, as were hundreds of others, that it did not pay. "I may as well, here as elsewhere, record the fact," wrote Underwood, "that never have my slaves been a source of profit to me. That it has taken all that the profitable ones could produce to support the old, the young, and the unproductive, so that *I have supported my negroes and not they me.*"[28]

In view of these adverse conditions, many Kentuckians maintained that it was cheaper to rent or hire slaves than to own them.[29] To further substantiate this contention, one Louisville newspaper presented figures for the annual use and upkeep of a "likely field hand," valued at six hundred dollars:

"Interest on the cost of the slave	$ 36.00
Average insurance	21.00
Diet	36.00
Lodging	5.00
Clothing	20.00
Expenses in sickness	5.00
Loss of time	5.00
Pilfering	10.00
Neglect of business	10.00
Taxes	1.90
Waste and destruction	20.00
Grand total	$169.90"[30]

From the slaves' standpoint, they were far better off than many of the white workingmen in the Northern states. They had no rent to pay, no doctor's bills to settle, naught to do with either grocer or butcher, and nothing to worry about from physical infirmities or old

28. Manuscript diary of Warner Lewis Underwood, in the Western Kentucky State Teachers College, entry of April 17, 1833. Ben Hardin, a prominent lawyer and slaveholder of Mercer County, wrote of the unprofitable side of Kentucky slavery. "If it were not," said he, "for supporting my slaves, I would never go near a court-house."—Little, *Ben Hardin,* p. 544.

29. "There are more men able to own slaves in Kentucky who do not own them, than there are slaveholders."—*Frankfort Commonwealth,* March 10, 1857.

30. *The Examiner,* Louisville, August 14, 1849.

ICE HOUSE, FAYETTE COUNTY

DETACHED KITCHEN, WOODFORD COUNTY

100 DOLLARS REWARD!

Ranaway from the subscriber on the 27th of July, my Black Woman, named

EMILY,

Seventeen years of age, well grown, black color, has a whining voice. She took with her one dark calico and one blue and white dress, a red corded gingham bonnet; a white striped shawl and slippers. I will pay the above reward if taken near the Ohio river on the Kentucky side, or THREE HUNDRED DOLLARS, if taken in the State of Ohio, and delivered to me near Lewisburg, Mason County, Ky. THO'S. H. WILLIAMS.

August 4, 1853.

EMILY RUNS AWAY

age. Kentucky slaveholders were legally and morally bound to look after and provide for their black bondsmen.

These people, dwarfed by the ignorance of ancestral provenance and environment, were the subjects of many superstitions. The slave's vivid imagination conjured up a host of strange myths and fears. They fully believed in the distorted creations of the mysterious and preternatural and held firmly to belief in the sway of witches. At night, they were often overmastered by their abject fear of "hants" and ghosts—"sperits"—which were the chief objects of their superstitious fear and awe.

There were many kinds and forms of witches. One was a sort of wood-sprite, which perpetrated strange and mischievous pranks. Horses running in pastures, partly marshy and containing briar patches, frequently appeared in the morning splashed with mud and with curious tangles in their manes. To the white folks this simply meant that the horses had been wallowing in the mud or wandering among the briars. But the more-knowing and better-informed darkey quickly discerned that the horse had been ridden by a witch, and knew that the knots and tangles in his mane were "witches' stirrups."

The slaves' belief in ghosts was universal and absolute. Every deserted house, secluded or weird-looking nook or corner of the plantation or farm, was supposed to be haunted by some sheeted ghost or disembodied spirit, which jealously guarded its inviolable premises and resented nocturnal intrusion. "Doan you nuvver let a sperit see you," they would caution one another. "Ef he once sees you, he gwine to allus ha'nt you."

There was one thing that the slaves could not bear, the thought that their dead should be put away without a suitable funeral. Very few masters ever denied them this privilege. Such a funeral, with mournful manners and sorrowful outcries, had all the earmarks of an elaborate social function with festive accompaniments. It was characterized by the gathering of the kindred and friends from far and near. Usually an all-day meeting, often in a grove, it drew white and black alike, sometimes in equal numbers. There was much staked on the fame of the officiating brother, who was always one of their color and a man of celebrity. They needed just such a man "to plow up their emotional depths," with plenty of freedom to indulge in the extravagances of their sorrow. These demonstrations were their invariable tribute to the dead and were expected to be fully adequate to do honor to the surviving family of the deceased. Often the slaves' burial ground was near or adjacent to the white folks' family cemetery.

Besides funerals, there were other occasions when the slaves were given an opportunity to celebrate and enjoy social intercourse. Usually their holidays followed the "laying by" or the finishing of the plantation crops. Christmas was a much-longed-for season of rest and respite from work, and was eagerly awaited by both young and old. How greatly the slaves enjoyed the merry yuletide is related by an Ohio traveler, W. H. Venable, who was visiting in Montgomery County, Kentucky, during the winter of 1858:

"On Christmas day, the streets of Mt. Sterling were thronged with colored folks, dressed in their Sunday apparel, and bent on pleasure. We were told that it had long been the custom in Kentucky to grant the slaves absolute freedom from duty on Christmas and, indeed, to allow them large liberty during the entire holiday week." [31]

Another traveler, the Englishman, James S. Buckingham, has recorded a characteristic picture of the Kentucky slave at rest and in gala attire:

"We remained at Henderson the greater part of the day, it being a holiday with the negro slaves on the estate . . . some of the female slaves were gaily dressed, and many of them in good taste, with white muslin gowns, blue and pink waists, ribbons, silk handkerchiefs or scarfs, straw bonnets and a reticule for the pocket handkerchief held on the arm. In talking with them and inquiring the reason for the holiday, one said she believed it was Easter, another said it was Whitsuntide and a third thought it was midsummer. They were chiefly the household slaves, who are always better treated, better dressed and more indulged than the field laborers."

Of the men slaves seen at Henderson on this occasion, this traveler reported that they appeared "to be more cheerful in their general aspect and behavior than the field slaves" he had seen in the South, and there was no doubt that "in Kentucky their condition is much better than in most other [slave] states, their work lighter, their food and clothing better, and their treatment more kind and humane." [32]

It is doubtful if any description written today could adequately portray the importance, in its relation to the affairs of the community, which the old-fashioned

31. "Down South before the War," *Ohio Arch. & Hist. Quarterly,* II, 461.

32. *Op. cit.,* III, 41. Slaves in Kentucky numbered: 1790, 12,430; 1800, 40,343; 1810, 80,561; 1820, 126,732; 1830, 165,213; 1840, 182,258; 1850, 210,981; 1860, 225,483. During 1830 the slaves and free Negroes (4,917) constituted 24.7 per cent of the entire population, the greatest percentage during the history of the institution.

corn shuckings assumed during the ante-bellum era. During these years they were chiefly the means by which a large part of the social life of the community, both for master and slave, was carried on. These corn shuckings and their attendant gatherings were the one big event of the farming season, and their arrivals were eagerly awaited by the inhabitants of all ages.

In many sections of Kentucky there were a number of small farmers or planters who had but a few slaves, or field hands. These farmers generally raised large crops of corn and could, with their limited force, do all their work in due season, except the shucking.

"Unless corn is gathered promptly after it is dry enough to crib," explained an old farmer of Madison County, "there is likely to be considerable loss—in fact, the longer the corn remains in the shock the greater the loss." It was the custom, in many parts of the Bluegrass, to send someone around the neighborhood on a horse and pass the word about that there would be a corn shucking on a certain night at some neighbor's plantation, and those notified would be expected to come and shuck out the corn on that night.[33] All the neighbors were invited to be on hand with as many of their slaves as would volunteer or might be persuaded to come. If an invited neighbor could not attend, he was expected to send as many men as he could, for the crop had to be shucked out that night, or not at all.

On Walter Norris' farm, in Madison County, neighboring planters and their slaves were eager to attend the

33. Sometimes, in certain localities, these gatherings were called "shucking bees." "My master," related the ex-slave Fedric, "sent his slaves on horse-back with letters to the other planters around to ask them to allow their slaves to come and help with the corn shuckings."—Fedric, *op. cit.*, pp. 48–49.

corn shucking, which had been set for a certain moonlight night in the fall of the year. "Our negroes are fond of going to corn shuckings," wrote Judge Cabell Chenault in his diary. "I understand that tomorrow night they will set a night to shuck out Colby McKinney's crop, and on that night they will arrange for another crop, and so on until every man who is short of hands will have his corn shucked." Mr. Norris, the host, was expected to be at a little expense, but that was trivial. He would have several gallons of whiskey on hand, costing him but fifty cents per gallon, and would prepare a good supper for the shuckers and his neighbors who might come.

Everything was ready on the appointed night for the big event of the neighborhood. Presently, the host, Mr. Norris, upon hearing a great volume of song several hundred yards off, remarked as he entered the yard: "Those singers are my welcome guests tonight, and I must be out to greet them." Nearer and nearer the singers approached, and the harmony was beautiful. "At first I believed that all the negroes in the community had gotten together, for it seemed to me that there were a hundred voices or more; but on the arrival of the singers, I learned that they were only the men from the Chenault plantation." After a friendly greeting from Mr. Norris, they passed on towards the residence.

"The night was pleasant," continued Judge Chenault, "and the moon by this time was shining brightly. The negroes began to drop around on the grass and joke one another, first about one thing and then another, but all in the best of humor."

Presently there came the sound of voices that appeared to be a half mile or so away. The Negroes sprang to their feet as if by the order of a commander. There was much speculation as to who the Negroes were. Then, one of them, straining his ears, exclaimed: "I catch de voice ov one ov 'em, it's Lariemore's Pleas." At this moment off to the northwest, but much closer, other voices were heard. Nearly everyone present recognized the voice of Noland's Allen. Still farther to the northwest, more singers were heard, and someone said: "That bunch mus' be Marse Jack Martin's niggers." Other groups on their way to the shucking were heard from a distance. One of the slaves ventured: "All ov 'em niggers 'll git togedder out yonder at de forks ov de road; den you'll heah some singin' sho' 'nough."

When the singers had all reached the yard, Mr. Norris greeted them with a friendly "howdy" and then returned to the front porch, rapped for order and said: "Men, you have done me the kindness to come here tonight to shuck my corn. I have only three hundred shocks. I am unable to tell how many there are of you, but I imagine you will not have to shuck over three shocks each if you finish my crop." Upon being asked if they would like something to drink first: "Yas, sah; yas, sah; we all's mighty thursty," came the replies from all over the yard, and, as soon as served, they filed off to the field. It was agreed that the shucking was to be done in pairs; two men to a shock, and the best workers, according to custom, were to receive special mention at the supper.

As the pairs were shortly arranged, the leader gave the command to "start your song," and a hundred voices answered from all parts of the field as each man grabbed a stalk for shucking. As they worked away, their favorite Negro melodies filled the air. Such songs as Foster's

Massa's in the Cold, Cold, Ground and *Old Black Joe* were the most popular.

About nine o'clock, word came to the white folks that the slaves had completed their task. "The field is finished," reported a small boy, "and they'll be here in a few minutes." Soon the corn shuckers began filing into the yard, as merry and cheerful as when they started to work.

Mr. Norris, leaving his guests and neighbors, went to the front of his portico and addressed them: "Boys, I must thank you again for helping me as you have, for I know you are not here by order of your masters." "No, sah; no, sah. We cum 'cause we wanted to he'p you all," came from many voices.

"My wife," further explained Norris, "and her good neighbors have prepared a good supper for you—plenty of chickens, turkey, shoat, and mutton, with a washing tub of custard and enough pound cake for each of you to get a big slice to eat with it; so file around to the rear of the house where you can be served."

Drinks were served from stone jugs, and there was plenty to eat for all; but "the food vanished like dew before the sunshine." Soon the Negroes began to say, "Good night, Marse Norris," and "Thank you, Miss Norris, fur de good supper. Call on us 'gin w'en yo' all got mo' corn to shuck," and off they went towards their homes singing as merrily as when they came.[34]

Not all corn shuckings, however, ended as pleasantly as the one in Madison County, so vividly described by Judge Chenault. Late in the fall of 1850 about forty slaves from neighboring farms assembled for a night-

34. Diary of Judge Cabell Chenault, of Madison County.—Jonathan T, Dorris, *Old Cane Springs*, pp. 42–50.

time corn shucking on the farm of John Runyon, in the northern section of Fayette County. As was the custom, Runyon provided "about 2½ gallons of whiskey for the occasion," and the men in high spirits began shucking around his long corncrib, about nine o'clock, as he stated, working "entirely by star light."

For about an hour the Negroes went about their work, cheerfully vying with one another to see who could turn out the most work within a given time. They were lively and gay and all seemed to enjoy the work, having consumed by this time about a gallon and a half of the liquor. None of the slaves were drunk, as the overseer noted, but in the midst of their merriment, a "rumpus broke out" between Martin and Jim, two of the slaves working side by side.

Martin, after "some abusive quarreling," knocked Jim to the ground, and then, with a fierce thrust of his knife, inflicted "a mortal wound in the left side of his belly to the depth of five inches" and "of the length of two inches," from which wound Jim soon afterwards died. Martin fled through the woods, but, in a few hours, was captured. He was brought to trial and, upon being proven guilty of murder, was duly executed according to the laws of the commonwealth.[35]

All slaves executed by law were valued by commissioners appointed, and their owners were reimbursed by the state. For Martin his owner received six hundred and fifty dollars; but Jim, described as one of the "best field niggers" on the farm, was a total loss to his master.

Sometimes at these corn shuckings the Negro songs

35. Commonwealth of Kentucky *vs.* Martin, a slave, Fayette Circuit Court, File 1194, March 25, 1851.

were gay and rollicking and contributed much to the rhythm and flow of the work:

"Ole Dan Tucker he got drunk,
Fell in de fiah an' kicked up a chunk,
A red-hot coal got in his shoe,
An' oh, Lawd a-Mussy, how de ashes flu."

Another well-known and popular song was often heard:

"I started home, but I did not pray,
An' I met ole Satan on de way;
Ole Satan made one grab at me,
But he missed my soul, an' I went free."

In some of the slaves' refrains, there is a marked resemblance to the modern "swing" songs:

"Shoo, shoo, sugar rag roo—
Show me the hole where the hog went through."

Often in these old melodies, the Negroes delighted in mentioning their white folks:

"Massa an' Missus hab gone far away,
Gone on dey honeymoon a long time to stay,
An' while dey's gone on dat little spree,
I'se gwine down to Charles-Town a purty gal to see."

And another:

"Ole Massa take dat new brown coat,
An' hang it on de wall;
Dat darkey take dat same ole coat,
An' wear it to de ball,
Oh, don't you hear my true love sing?"

Many of the slave songs were more or less local in their origin and use, and in the Bluegrass region these were popular:

"Heave away! Heave away!
I'd radder co't a yaller gal,
Dan work for Henry Clay,
Heave away, yaller gal, I want to go."

"Eliza Jane" was a favorite song with field hands:

"You go down de big road
An' I'll go down de lane,
Ef you gits dar befo' I does,
Good bye, Liza Jane!"

The slaves in the quarters had a life of their own. It was peculiar in its own distinctive way. There was much hospitality and sociability, much dancing, laughing, singing and banjo-strumming when the day's work was done. This was the native home of the plantation melody and clog dance. There was little that was morose or gloomy about the slave, either at work or at rest. He was, under reasonable conditions and treatment, almost invariably happy and contented, polite and respectful to his superiors and visiting strangers.

They loved to dance and often performed without music or other accompaniment except "patting"—that is, patting the hands on the knees or clapping them together, and this they did to perfection, giving and keeping perfect time to the dance. These dances consisted of shuffling of the feet, swinging of arms and shoulders, and swaying of the body in a peculiar rhythm known as the "Double Shuffle," "Heel and Toe," "Buck and Wing" and "Juba." [36] To "pat Juba" and "dance Jim Crow" were truly inspiring:

"Once upon the heel tap,
And then upon the toe,

36. John Anderson, *The Story of the Life of John Anderson, the Fugitive Slave,* pp. 29–30.

An' ev'ry time I turn around
I jump Jim Crow." [37]

While the cheerful and fun-provoking exercises at the "quarters" reveal a brighter side of the slave's life, the more serious side is brought out in their religious songs, which furnished an outlet for aching hearts and anguished souls. Nothing tells more truly what the Negroes' life in slavery was than the dirge-like songs, in which they succeeded, sometimes, in expressing their deepest emotions and feelings. As for example:

"Nobody knows the trouble I've seen,
Nobody knows but Jesus,
Nobody knows the trouble I've seen,
Glory Hallelujah!"

Hope of future life and eternal pleasure often permeated the Negro spirituals:

"We'll walk dem golden streets,
We'll walk dem golden streets,
We'll walk dem golden streets,
Whar pleasure nebber dies."

or:

"I looked over Jordan and what did I see,
Comin' fo' to carry me home,
A band of angels comin' after me,
Comin' fo' to carry me home,
Swing low sweet chariot, comin' fo' to carry me home,
Swing low sweet chariot, comin' fo' to carry me home."

Public opinion was not adverse to the religious training of Negroes, and slaves were given religious instruction on many plantations and farms. Domestic slaves often attended the same services as their masters or mistresses, and on the minute books of many of the churches

37. Bullitt, *My Life at Oxmoor,* p. 72.

of Kentucky appear the names of slaves who were faithful and devout members. The churches usually had a gallery for the black people, and if not, then in some cases, certain rear sections were reserved for their use, where they enjoyed the preached gospel in common with the whites.[38]

Benjamin F. Van Meter, who was reared in a well-to-do slaveholding family in Clark County, related that their old carriage driver, Riddle, had his place in the gallery of the local church with scores of other slaves, "and after the sacramental elements had been dispensed on the lower floor," recounted this observer, "they were taken without fail to the gallery, to be received in the same manner by the faithful Christian slaves." [39]

Although there was never any law passed in Kentucky which prohibited teaching slaves to read and write, public sentiment operated strongly against it. Many of the slave owners were willing that their slaves be taught to read the Bible; yet there was the constant dread of their reading "filthy abolition literature," tending to promote insubordination, an overt uprising, or make them thoroughly dissatisfied with their lot. Also, it was believed that, by the slaves becoming able to read or write, it would be easy for them to forge "free papers" or passes for themselves, and others of their kind. There were, nevertheless, numerous cases of faithful and trusted family servants being privately instructed in the rudiments of reading and writing by their master, his wife or some member of his family. Professor Ivan Mc-

38. Ward Russell, *Church Life in the Bluegrass,* pp. 26–27, 162; William O. Shewmaker, *Pisgah and her People,* pp. 162–68, 227–36.

39. *A Dead Issue and the Live One,* p. 13. "On Sundays we were sent to chapel; all of the slaves being seated in the galleries, apart from the white people."—Fedric, *op. cit.,* p. 27.

Dougle, in analyzing the runaway advertisements of Bluegrass slaves, estimated that at least ten per cent of them could read and write "tolerably well." [40]

Very early in the history of the "peculiar institution" some of the more industrious slaves began to secure personal freedom by purchasing themselves or relatives [41] from benevolent masters who were willing to help the slave free himself from bondage. It was a courageous undertaking for a slave of comparatively little earning power to attempt the purchase, either of himself or some member of his family. This difficulty grew out of several circumstances. The slave had to work most of his time for his master and only his spare time, or overtime at nights, or on Sundays or holidays was his own.[42]

Most masters of the better class afforded their slaves the opportunity for making a little extra, or pocket money. They were allowed small plots of ground, or truck patches, where they cultivated gardens, sweet potatoes, tobacco and melons being their favorite produce. Saturday afternoons were usually given over to them to work their patches, and at nights the more thrifty ones would cobble shoes, make foot-mats and brooms, and

40. *Slavery in Kentucky,* p. 80. This work, a doctor's dissertation, is an excellent treatise on the economic and political history of slavery in Kentucky. First appearing in *The Journal of Negro History,* Vol. III, No. 3, it was later published in book form in 1918.

41. There are many cases on record of free Negroes and slaves buying and manumitting their husbands, wives, children and relatives. One such case is that of Jane Slaughter, a free woman of color of Lexington, who from "motives of benevolence and humanity" purchased her father, a slave, from Dickerson Parish, and set him free.—Fayette County Court, Order Book 12, p. 472, February 12, 1850.

42. "A few instances were mentioned to us on the road [from Frankfort to Louisville], of coloured persons, originally slaves, saving enough money out of their earnings, by over-hour work, raising vegetables and rearing poultry for sale, to purchase their freedom."—Buckingham, *op. cit.,* III, 7.

"shuck-bottom" chairs, which "were very comfortable and quite lasting." They cut cord wood and worked at other odd jobs when the season's crops were well up or harvested, and an industrious slave might in this way lay aside a competence, or even enough in time to purchase his freedom.

William C. Bullitt, the owner of one hundred slaves and a thousand acres of fertile land in Jefferson County, carried on extensive farming operations in the antebellum days and has left us an excellent picture of the slaves' farm work. In the book, *My Life at Oxmoor,* edited by his son, Colonel Thomas W. Bullitt, it is pointed out that "cutting hemp in summer and breaking hemp in winter was the hardest work done on a Kentucky farm. Yet they were the two kinds of work the negroes liked best . . . both were task work, and a reward followed good work. The task of a man in cutting hemp was a 'land' and a half across an eighty acre field. A 'land' was a span of about twelve feet wide, between light furrows. The task of a boy of fifteen or sixteen years was a 'land'—two-thirds of a man's work. When the task was finished, work was done for the day." [43]

After being properly "rotted" by lying on the ground for some time and receiving the fall and winter rains, the hemp was broken in the "hand-brakes"—shattered into short fragments of an inch, more or less. Around these individual brakes each evening,[44] there would be a large pile of "herds" or "shores"—being the shattered fragments of the stalks, from which the fibre had been stripped. About dusk the farm wagon, often pulled by

43. P. 45.

44. The task of a field hand in hemp breaking was one hundred pounds; that of a boy, about sixty pounds. For each pound broken in excess of that weight, the slave was paid one cent, or one dollar per hundredweight. —*Ibid.,* p. 46; John B. Castleman, *Active Service,* p. 55.

four horses, would go around the field to collect the hemp as it lay piled in "hands" or bales.

Before leaving the fields at the end of a good hemp-breaking day, the workers usually set fire to every pile of herds to get rid of them and to light the wagon.[45] When hemp production was in its heyday in the Bluegrass, the burning hemp herds presented a picturesque and beautiful sight in the deepening dusk. Upon every hand could be seen the burning mounds of shives, from the roaring blazes in the near-by fields to the pin points of light on the distant horizon, while silhouetted figures moved to and fro as they ended their labors for the day, and the pungent odor of smoke permeated the cool night air.

"To stand on the front porch or the stile," recounted Bullitt, "to see the fires light up; then hear in the distance, from one-third to a mile off, the voices rise, gently at first, but swelling in volume as they drew nearer; voices always strong, well modulated, and attuned to the spirit of the words; frequently sad, perhaps with a tinge of melancholy, always made a profound impression on me. . . ."[46]

As most of the hemp, the "money crop" of ante-bellum Kentucky, was grown in the Bluegrass counties, Lexington early became the manufacturing center for cotton bagging and bale rope.[47] Much slave labor was

45. *Kentucky Farmer,* Frankfort, March, 1859.

46. *Op. cit.,* p. 44.

47. "The principal manufactures of Lexington [in 1810] are hemp, to which the labor of the black people is well suited, and of which the country yields amazing crops, at the low price of four dollars per cwt; being at the rate of eighteen pounds Sterling per ton. There are eighteen extensive rope-walks, five bagging manufactures, and one duck. The other principal manufactures are eight cotton factories, three woollen factories, and one oilcloth factory."—John Melish, *Travels through the United States, 1806–1811,* II, 186–89.

employed in the manufacture of these hempen products. Besides the demand for these in the cotton states of the Far South, hemp and tow were also needed by the merchant marine and United States Navy for caulking ships.

An Easterner, visiting Lexington in 1830, was much impressed with the numerous bagging and rope-walk factories he saw operating in the city. "At one of the principal bagging and bale rope establishments," observed this traveler, "there are employed from 60 to 100 negro slaves, of all ages—all stout, hearty, healthy, and merry fellows, some of whom contrive to while away the time and drown the noise of the machinery by their own melody.

"On the lower floor of a very large stone building was the kitchen, a room where the hatchelling [or hackling] is done, and in the rear of that a rope-walk.[48] In front, on the second floor, over the kitchen, is the sleeping apartment, where the greater portion of the laborers are accomodated on a sort of long table [or bunk], which extends round two sides of the room. Everything in this apartment appeared to be comfortable, and as neat as could have been expected. In the rear of this room is an apartment, 60 yards long, where the 'warp' for the bagging is spun; the best spinners are selected for this, the labor required of them is moderate, and I was informed that one of the young men had received between eight and nine hundred dollars for his 'overwork.' Each piece of bagging is made 60 yards in length, the wheels for spinning being placed at both ends of the

48. Usually a long narrow room where hemp was made into rope. In this process a man walked backward and forward from the spindles, twisting the hempen fibre into rope as he walked, hence the term, "rope-walk." This operation was somewhat similar to spinning cotton or wool.

apartment, so that the men spin going and returning—thus saving half the time—and when the 'warp' is completed the threads are of uniform length and ready for immediate use.

"In the third story were some dozen men weaving the bagging—a labor which they performed with much expedition, showing more skill in the management of their machinery than I had before supposed the slaves possessed. Still above this was another long apartment, where there were 18 to 20 boys, of from 8 to 15 years old, spinning the 'filling.' Each boy selects his hemp and tow in such proportions as suits himself, weighs it in the presence of an overseer and is obliged to return it of the same weight, in the shape of twine for filling. I have never seen a happier set of workmen than these boys; there was no overseer in their apartment; each boy placed his raw material beside his wheel, spun his thread the length of the room, returned to his place, and after winding his thread upon his reel, went on with his spinning with the utmost regularity and good order, singing the while with great earnestness, and not altogether without melody.

"After it is woven, the bagging goes through another operation, which is called 'callendering,' in which it is trimmed. Every man and boy in this establishment, as I before mentioned, has his allotted portion or his stint to perform, and each one is paid for what he does beyond it. This keeps them contented, and makes them ambitious, and no one, who knows anything of mankind, will doubt but that more labor is obtained from the same number of hands than could possibly be forced from them by severity. There are made at this one establishment fifty-six pieces per week, of from 50 to 60 yards each—something being lost after the 'warp' is spun. Bagging is worth about 16 cents per yard, and the business, if not extensively profitable, at least, is worth carrying on. . . ." [49]

What this Northern visitor, and no doubt semi-abolitionist, saw and wrote of the conditions of Negro bondage in the Bluegrass was substantially the same as that recorded by numerous other travelers of the ante-bellum period. "I have no hesitation in saying," pointed out this observer from the New England states, "that to the best of my knowledge, there is more real freedom of body, and quite as much independence of mind, among the slaves of Kentucky, as there is to be found in any other portion of our country. . . ." [50]

49. *Louisville Daily Journal,* November 29, 1830, quoting from the *Boston Courier,* November 10, 1830.

50. *Ibid.*

CHAPTER IV

TOWN WATCH AND PATTEROLLERS

SLAVE OWNERS throughout the South were never entirely free from the anxiety and fear of a possible slave insurrection. Even in Kentucky, where the slaves were comparatively well satisfied, planters were constantly apprehensive. The beginning of this fear manifested itself as early as 1822; it was ushered in by a premature uprising in South Carolina.

Late in the summer of that year, at Charleston, one Denmark Vesey, a free Negro, and five slaves made an elaborate plan to rise, massacre the white population, seize the shipping in the harbor, and, if hard pressed, sail away to the West Indies. One of the slaves gave the plot away, and Vesey was seized, tried and, with thirty-six others, was publicly hanged.[1] This desperate plot was so nearly successful that it left an ineradicable distrust in the minds of the slaveholding Southerners toward free Negroes.

In Kentucky, though far removed from the scene of Vesey's ill-fated conspiracy, there was much excitement and fear; the abortive attempt opened the eyes of the white population to the dangers and difficulties of simi-

1. *Niles' Weekly Register,* XXIII (September 7, 1822), 10; Joseph C. Carroll, *Slave Insurrections in the United States,* p. 100.

lar slave uprisings. Now and then symptoms of uneasiness and rebellion were noticed among the Negroes of Kentucky, although, even with rabid abolitionists at work among them, no organized outbreak had occurred. However, while Kentucky slave owners were enjoying comparative tranquility, there occurred in the mother state of Virginia a slave insurrection which fairly rocked the nation.

For several years Nat Turner, a little-known slave preacher of Southampton County, in Virginia, had stealthily made preparations to ravage the country, raise the slaves, and take refuge in the great Dismal Swamp. On the night of August 21, 1831, with six desperate companions, he rose and spared not a single white soul on the plantations that they visited. His force quickly grew to sixty men, and would probably have spread like wildfire, but for poor generalship on Nat's part.[2] Before the uprising could be checked, sixty white people—mostly women and children—had been massacred.[3] Within forty-eight hours after the alarm was given, the militia mobilized and United States troops were called out. On the first day of resistance over a hundred blacks were killed, and the bloody retribution continued for some time. Besides numerous floggings, fifty-three Negroes were put on trial, of whom twenty-one were acquitted, twelve convicted and sold out of the state, and twenty, including Nat Turner and one woman, were convicted and hanged.[4]

The Nat Turner insurrection shook slavery to its very foundations and cast sombre shadows over all the slave-

2. *The Liberator,* September 3, 1831.

3. Norfork, Virginia, *Herald,* October 29, 1831.

4. James C. Ballagh, *History of Slavery in Virginia,* pp. 93–94; Carroll, *op. cit.,* p. 139.

holding states. The fact that Nat, though he bore some marks of ill-usage, had not been treated with severe cruelty, proved to the fear-stricken slaveholders that kindness did not always bring contentment. Since the plot went on for months without suspicion, similar movements, it was thought, might be developing in any community. As Turner had been joined by slaves not previously recruited, no one could tell how far such an uprising, once started, might spread. In the excited state of public feeling, it was feared that it might be a part of a wide-spread slave plot, and this created a recrudescence of hostility in Kentucky against free Negroes and emancipationists.

Inasmuch as William Lloyd Garrison's anti-slavery paper, *The Liberator,* began circulation in the South about the time of the Turner insurrection, the cry was raised that the two had a direct connection, although in the prison confession of Turner there is not the slightest reference to either *The Liberator* or *Walker's Appeal.*[5] Garrison himself denied any connection with the insurrection, and there is neither proof nor indirect reference which fixes any share of the blame for the insurrection on the abolitionists, although few slaveholders in Kentucky and the South could be persuaded that it had not been inspired by them.

Rumors of slave plots and uprisings, similar to the Nat Turner affair, continued to put the nerves of Kentucky slaveholders on edge for years thereafter. It was the memory of the 1831 insurrection in Virginia that

5. *Walker's Appeal* was a seditious pamphlet issued in Boston, September, 1829, by David Walker, an obscure free Negro from North Carolina. This rabid anti-slavery publication advocated that the slaves free themselves by acts of violence and strongly hinted of a general slave uprising throughout the South.—Arthur Y. Lloyd, *The Slavery Controversy, 1831–1860,* p. 104.

was chiefly responsible for the state of uneasiness that gripped several of the Kentucky counties along the Ohio River, when news came that a general insurrection was planned to take place at Florence, in Boone County, on the night of November 13, 1838. The plot, however, was nipped in the bud, and nothing came of it; but six of the insurgent Negroes, aided by the abolitionists, managed to escape and successfully made their way to Canada.[6]

As a result of this scare, and with the Turner insurrection still in mind, newspapers warned the populace "to be on their guard—to keep a sharp look-out, and closely observe the movements of negroes."[7] "Every man must guard his own hearth and fireside," warned Senator George W. Johnston, of Shelby County, before the Kentucky legislature, in 1841, as he told of the increasing number of blacks with the attendant fear of slave uprisings. Three years later, in Bullitt County, a certain slaveholder, Albert Stewart, was threatening to punish one of his slaves, when he was turned upon by that slave and two others and beaten to death.[8] News of this episode spread throughout the countryside with exaggerated rumors of an insurrection, but the excitement soon died down without any outward incident.

It was the report or suspicion of concerted action by the slaves which alone served to cause widespread alarm and uneasiness. Several years after the Stewart slaying, citizens of the Bluegrass recalled the truthfulness of Johnston's warning, as they learned of a "Daring Movement," or slave uprising, right in their midst. Sunday morning, August 5, 1848, Fayette County was thrown

6. *Western Citizen,* Paris, November 16, 1838.

7. *Ibid. et seq.*

8. *Paducah Kentuckian,* quoted in the *New Orleans Bee,* April 3, 1844.

into the most intense excitement ever known to central Kentucky. Between dusk and daylight some seventy-five slaves had escaped from their masters and, armed and desperate, they were thought to be heading for the Ohio River.[9] It was soon ascertained that Patrick Doyle, a student of Centre College in the neighboring town of Danville, was the ringleader of the insurrection, and the entire Bluegrass, with threats of summary violence, turned out to apprehend the fugitives. Five thousand dollars was immediately offered as a reward for the capture of the runaway slaves.[10]

"The example of the notorious [Calvin] Fairbank," said the *Lexington Observer & Reporter,* "who is now in our state prison, serving a fifteen years apprenticeship at hard labor, has not, it seems, had the effect of keeping our state clear of these detestable villains who, under the false pretext of philanthropy, and with unexampled audacity are perpetrating their foul practices in our midst. It is time that a more severe example should be made of these wretches, and every citizen should be on the alert to detect and bring them to punishment. That there are abolitionists in our midst—emissaries from this piratical crew—whose business it is to tamper with and run off our slaves, there is not the shadow of doubt. . . ." [11]

All efforts were now directed toward the capture of the slaves. Excitement reached a high pitch when an express messenger from Cynthiana drew up his foam-flecked pony in front of the Lexington courthouse, on the morning of the eighth, and handed a note to some of the assembled and excited slaveholders. Coming from

9. *Lexington Observer & Reporter,* August 9, 1848.
10. *Ibid.*
11. *Ibid.*

"some of the most respectable citizens of Harrison County," this urgent plea for help read:

"This will inform you that your negroes are now supposed to be surrounded about the county line between Harrison and Bracken, some fifteen or eighteen miles short of the Ohio River. About one hundred of our citizens have been after them since Monday morning last. They are worn down, and it is requested that you send a fresh set of men immediately, say 50 to 100 men, well armed; for it seems they are determined to fight every inch of the ground, as they are armed generally with revolvers, commanded by a white man or more. They were encamped and fortified last night, and our Cynthiana boys came upon about forty or more and a battle ensued, and Charles H. Fowler was mortally wounded. We hear one dead negro was found. Send all you can—and speedily, or all will be lost." [12]

Immediately upon the receipt of such alarming news, a hurriedly called mass meeting assembled at the courthouse, when "a large company of volunteers promptly came forward and proffered their services. They left, well armed, under the command of Captain O. H. Beard and reached Cynthiana that evening." [13] With hundreds of possemen scouring the countryside, the capture of Doyle and his band of runaway slaves was merely a matter of time. Even before Captain Beard and his reinforcements reached Harrison County, word came that the fugitives had been surrounded in a hemp field in the northern part of Bracken County, and, after a brisk engagement, the whole band surrendered. Doyle, heavily ironed, was brought back to Lexington,[14] while

12. *Ibid.,* August 12, 1848.

13. *Ibid.*

14. Doyle, after his capture, was brought to Cynthiana, "where there

twenty of the captured slaves were lodged in the jail at Brooksville, the county seat of Bracken County.

Doyle, in his rabidly fanatical mind, believed that it was still possible for him to strike a telling blow at Kentucky slaveholders that would in some way bring public acclaim to himself as well. He had, only the week before, escaped from the county jail in Louisville, where he was confined for attempting to sell several free Negroes whom he had induced to accompany him from Cincinnati.[15]

Judge Walker Reid called a special session of the Bracken Circuit Court, and, on August 30, seven of the slaves thought to have been the ringleaders, with forty other Negroes, were led to the bar in the custody of the jailer.[16] These forty-odd slaves and "several other evil-disposed persons" were charged with having "unlawfully, maliciously, rebelliously and feloniously assembled in a warlike and hostile manner" and "armed with guns, pistols, knives and other warlike weapons" did "most wickedly, seditiously and rebelliously prepare and make public insurrection." [17] Such lawless deeds, according to the indictment, were "against the peace and public tranquility of this Commonwealth." For three days the trial lasted, as Harrison Taylor, attorney for the commonwealth, made urgent pleas that speedy justice be administered to the "wicked and rebellious" slaves. Largely pro-slavery, the jury, swayed in some

was intense excitement and an immense crowd assembled around the jail with angry threats. He was taken from thence that night to Lexington."—*Western Citizen,* August 11, 1848.

15. *Louisville Journal,* August 14, 1848. This paper described Doyle as "undoubtedly a scamp of the first water."

16. Commonwealth of Kentucky *vs.* Slaughter, *et al.,* Bracken Circuit Court, Order Book H, p. 216, August Special Term, 1848.

17. *Ibid.*

degree by the passion and prejudice of the hour, returned a verdict of guilty, which carried the extreme penalty [18] against three of the Negroes—Shadrack, Harry and Prestley—all runaways from Fayette County.

Accordingly, at noon, on October 28, the sheriff of Bracken County pulled a wooden trigger and the condemned slaves plunged feet first through the narrow trap door of the scaffold in the jail yard at Brooksville, where, obedient to the order of the court, they were "hung by the neck until dead." [19]

Patrick Doyle, later identified as Edward J. Doyle, was indicted in the Fayette Circuit Court on seven counts [20] and, pleading guilty to the second charge, was sentenced on October 9, 1848, to "the jail and penitentiary house of this Commonwealth at hard labor for the term of *twenty years.*" [21] "Let us now reflect," proudly remarked the *Observer & Reporter,* "how much better is the peaceful operation of the law, which has for twenty years put him [Doyle] out of the pale of society and out of his power to perpetrate any like enormity upon the community. . . ." [22]

It was inevitable that such outbreaks, inciting as they did, general restiveness among the slaves, should create deep apprehension in the minds of the white population. Anxiety bred suspicion which riveted close attention upon all activities of the blacks and, frequently,

18. *Ibid.* Judge Reid ordered the condemned slaves confined in the local jail "until they shall be taken by the sheriff to a gallows and there be suspended by the neck with a cord until they are dead, and this shall be carried into execution on October 28, 1848, or as near that date as possible."

19. *Maysville Eagle,* November 3, 1848.

20. Commonwealth of Kentucky *vs.* E. J. Doyle, Fayette Circuit Court, File 1164, September 27, 1848.

21. Fayette Circuit Court, Order Book 34, p. 270, October 9, 1848.

22. October 11, 1848.

lent a distorted view to the most innocent occurrences.

Every slave community was subject in a varying degree to nervousness and alarm out of proportion to actual conditions. Major Thomas Speed, a prominent figure of Bardstown during that time, recounted to his grandson, Captain Thomas Speed, an occurrence which was perhaps typical of the unsettled period. "One day," wrote the latter, in telling the story, "a neighbor rode up to the gate and gave my grandfather a report that had come to Bardstown that the negroes were going to 'rise' and were to assemble in a certain quarter, on a given night, and, after having killed all in their master's house, would then move in a body to town and kill everybody there.

"My grandfather had no faith in such reports, but he thought it best to be on guard. He mounted his horse and rode into town, a mile distant, and soon returned with the news confirmed. Preparations for defense were being made, but the excitement was all suppressed, for it was all-important not to let the negroes know they were suspected. Word was sent to every farm-house to take steps for protection. A rallying-point was fixed for the assembling of a force as soon as the insurrection broke out."

What took place in the Speed home on the eve of this dreaded "rising" was, no doubt, practically the same as in many other slaveholding homes in Nelson County. "My grandfather," continued Speed, "had his household prepare for the worst. Ammunition was obtained and the guns put in order. When the dreaded night came, as soon as it was dark, all the axes were taken into the house from the woodpile. The scythes and pitchforks were taken in also. Water was provided to put out fire. The doors were barred and the watchers were stationed.

"It was soon discovered that the dogs did not bark as usual. This was interpreted to mean that the negroes had taken them into their cabins. A horse was heard to neigh, which was unusual. The report of a gun was heard some distance away. These things, and the fact that otherwise the night was especially silent, all betokened something going on. Eleven o'clock came! My grandfather concluded he would go out and reconnoiter. He quietly passed out the side door and made his way in the shadows of the buildings, until he could see the door of Jim's cabin. Jim [a slave] was the one who would take a hand in the business, if any did. A suspicious light shone under his cabin door, and while my grandfather was contemplating that fact, the door opened and Jim stepped out, *and went straight to the grindstone and ground a knife!* As soon as he had returned, grandfather went back quickly, fully impressed that there was danger ahead. His report made the watchers all the more vigilant.

"Twelve o'clock came! Grandfather would reconnoiter again. He was determined to see what was going on in that cabin. Fully armed, he made his way to the back of the cabin where he could look in through a window. The light glimmered as he approached, but he heard no sound; evidently, they were planning with great secrecy and caution. He was near enough to look in, but if he did so he might be seen. He paused a moment, then boldly raised himself up and looked into the cabin. There upon the floor, down before the fire, *sat the dreaded negro, Jim, busily engaged in making a shuck mat!* Grandfather went back full of indignation and ordered the young men to go to bed. . . ." [23]

Movements of Negroes, however, apparently innocent, were not always understood. Scraping fiddles, twanging banjos, strumming guitars and shuffling feet down in the slaves' quarters on Saturday evenings might be a sinister ruse covering preparations for escape or insurrection. With the Bardstown scare just over and the Doyle insurrection still fresh in the public mind, the slavocracy of the Bluegrass clamored loudly for some new form of protection; more severe laws against the assembling of Negroes, against their learning to read and write, and against any form of anti-slavery agitation by white men. That slaves should be restrained from prowling about at night was considered by many to be a necessity, and more rigid discipline, it was felt, should be enforced in preventing the Negroes from congregating after dark in large groups. Special precautions were urged to be taken against fires, for it was commonly believed that discontented slaves often set them.[24]

At the September term, 1848, of the Fayette County Court, a number of "respectable citizens" were appointed "to lay off the county into suitable districts" for the establishment of a more efficient county patrol.[25] These mounted patrols, of "discreet and sober men,"

23. *Records and Memorials of the Speed Family,* pp. 190–92.

24. Sam, a slave of Charles Clark, of Lexington, was charged with "setting fire to and burning the Old & Phoenix Cotton Mills, the property of Andrew Caldwell," on April 1, 1839.—Commonwealth of Kentucky *vs.* Sam, a slave, Fayette Circuit Court, File 1008, May 15, 1839.

25. *Lexington Observer & Reporter,* November 6, 1848. In this issue Fayette County slaveholders were advised "to keep their slaves at home as much as possible, that they may know nothing but their master's farm."

went about at night watching the movements and particularly the gregarious habits of the slaves. It was deemed highly desirable to prevent them from meeting in groups or crowds, where they might air their grievances and hatch plots. Such an institution as the county patrol was based on good Negro psychology, for his superstitious fear of the "sperits" of the night was well known.

Patrols were appointed [26] and they operated in many counties of Kentucky [27] for the "public peace and good order of society." Their duties were to visit Negro quarters; to report and disperse all suspected and unlawful assemblies of slaves; to arrest all slaves found "lurking about" on another's plantation. Likewise, they were empowered to arrest all slaves "strolling from one plantation to another," or those found on highways, roads, or in towns and cities without a written pass from their master or overseer, or slaves found in the possession of any article of property, without such writing. Punishment for these offenses was meted out by the captain of the patrols, varying from "ten to thirty-nine lashes on the bare back." [28]

For every slave apprehended by the patrols, and delivered to jail, so that his master might recover him, there was a reward of twenty-five dollars, and, if taken up by the patrol in another county, the fee for the ar-

26. "On New Year's Day ten white men are chosen, who are called patroles; they are sworn in at the court-house, and their special duty is to go to the negro cabins for the purpose of searching them to see whether any slaves are there without a pass or permit from their masters."—Fedric, *Slave Life in Virginia and Kentucky,* p. 29.

27. In those counties where the slave population was large enough to justify adoption of the patrol system, a poll tax of one dollar for each slave or "black tithable" was levied on each slaveholder to finance this law-enforcing organization.

28. *Revised Statutes of Kentucky, 1852,* p. 521.

rest was fifty dollars. In most cases, the patrols were poor whites who owned no slaves, but they were backed up by all the power necessary to make their whips crack with a dreaded authority. True, these patrols, sometimes appointed by the court, sometimes self-constituted, were often overzealous in performing their duties. They had a very definite part in keeping the slaves confined to their own plantations and properly intimidated. Negro hunting, Negro catching, Negro watching and Negro whipping constituted the favorite sport of many youthful whites.

Some of the colloquialisms bestowed upon the patrols or patrollers were "patrole," "padaroe," "paderole" and "patter-roll," but the sobriquet most used and perhaps best suited was "patteroller." The familiar lines, "Run, nigger, run; run a little faster; run, nigger, run, er de patteroll 'il cotch yer," were literal admonitions to the black man. Many accounts are related by slaves, who, being caught away from their masters' plantations at night without a pass, were seized by the dreaded "patterollers" and given the customary floggings, and, oftener than not, more lashes than the law prescribed.

Now and then one may run across an old slave who still remembers the song of the "patterollers" which they used to sing, with many variations, in the fields and in the cabins. One version runs:

> "Run, nigger, run, de patteroll catch you,
> Run, nigger, run, fo' it's almos' day.
> Massa is kind an' Missus is true,
> But ef you don' mind, de patteroll catch you!"

"The head of the patrol," wrote an old slave, "is called the captain. He sends the men into the slave cabins, waiting outside himself at some distance with the horses, the patrol being a mounted body. If any of the slaves are found without a pass, they are brought out, made to strip, and are flogged—the men receiving ten and the women five lashes." [29] Slaves, as a rule, had a great antipathy for the patrollers, who very frequently were recruited from the ranks of that nondescript class which the Negroes called "pore white trash."

Negroes belonging to prominent and well-to-do planters, or quality folks, looked with a great deal of disdain [30] upon this class of poor white common laborers, who, of course, owned no slaves. On the other hand, racial resentment against Negroes was more marked among these indigent whites than among the upper class of society.

In an effort to strike back at the "patterollers," the slaves, on occasion, were known to stretch wild grape vines or hempen ropes across the roads at night about as high as a horse, "so as to strike a man about his waist." [31] In this way many of the mounted horsemen, while furiously galloping down some dark turnpike road, were oftentimes rudely upset and thrown from their horses. To such an extent was this trick practiced that travel on foot came to be considered the only safe method for the scouting patrollers.

It was known for many years before the Negroes were

29. Fedric, *op. cit.,* p. 29.

30. One Madison County slave, who had felt the lash of the "patterollers," denounced them in bitter terms: "They are the offscouring of all things, the refuse, the ears and tails of slavery, the wallet and satchel of pole-cats, the exuvial, the meanest and lowest and worst of all creatures. Like starved wharf rats, they are out at nights, creeping into slave cabins to see if they have an old bone there; they drive out husbands from their own beds and then take their places."—Lewis Clarke, *Narrative of the Sufferings of Lewis Clarke,* pp. 78–79.

31. Elisha W. Green, *Life of the Rev. Elisha W. Green,* p. 2; Smith, *Fifty Years of Slavery,* pp. 22–25.

SLAVE AUCTION ON CHEAPSIDE, LEXINGTON

PUBLIC SALE
OF SLAVES!!

FRANKLIN CIRCUIT COURT.

JAMES HARLAN'S Administrators, Plaintiffs,
vs. } In Equity.
JAMES HARLAN'S Heirs, Defendants,

The undersigned, as COMMISSIONER of said Court, will, on

Monday, November 16, 1863,

(County Court day,) sell at public auction, the following Slaves, viz:

THREE NEGRO MEN;

ONE NEGRO WOMAN AND A SMALL CHILD, ADOPTED;

ONE NEGRO WOMAN AND TWO CHILDREN.

TERMS---Six months credit, with interest from date, the purchasers giving bond with security, to have the force and effect of replevin bond.

GEORGE W. GWIN,
Master Commissioner.

OCTOBER 30, 1863.

COMMISSIONER'S SALE IN 1863

emancipated that, notwithstanding the patrol system kept up in Kentucky,[32] slaves would secretly travel over a large scope of country at night and manage to be back in their quarters before morning. They had a grapevine telegraph or secret system of communication never known or comprehended by their masters.

There were many reasons why Kentucky masters did not allow their slaves to assemble in clandestine meetings at nights and on Sundays. Such meetings, it was thought, not only tended to make the slaves dissatisfied with their condition, but afforded opportunities for concocting mischief as well. Furthermore, well-behaved slaves were demoralized when brought into contact with the worst slaves of the community, often to the extent of running away and even preparing for insurrection. It was the duty of the "patterollers" to seize and whip every slave found away from home, unless on business or with the permission of his master or overseer, which had to be stated in writing. The passes were usually brief and concise, and the following, issued to Sam, a young slave of Boyle County, is typical:

> "June 13, 1854.
>
> "Pass to Danville & return by sun-down my black boy Sam, age 24 years & stout made. He is sent on my business.
>
> Rich. E. Stewart." [33]

While some of the black religious exhorters were viewed with suspicion by the whites, others were highly esteemed and given unusual privileges. One of these,

32. During the daytime slaves worked under the supervision of the owner or overseer, consequently there was little need for public policing. At night the town watch and "patterollers" played an important part in preventing idle and restless blacks from prowling around, running away, stealing, clandestinely meeting and committing other misdemeanors.

33. Original in author's collection.

for example, an old slave living at Lexington, was always supplied with a pass duly signed by his master, Edward McAllister. One of these passes which showed the implicit confidence of the master in his African preacher, read:

> "Lexington, Ky.
> August 6, 1856
>
> "Tom is my slave, and has permission to go to Louisville for two or three weeks and return after he has made his visit. Tom is a preacher of the Reformed Baptist Church and has always been a faithful servant." [34]

Once in a while, a slave pass from some less exacting master displayed unusual favor. It is difficult to understand why a master would allow such extraordinary liberties as are indicated in the pass of Lago, a slave of Mercer County:

> "Harrodsburg, Ky.
> June 8, 1858
>
> "The Bearer, Willis Lago, a slave belonging to me, is permitted to go to any free state and there remain. He is black, about 47 years old and is tolerably lame. Wm. Thompson."

Evidently aware that this unusual slave pass might not be accepted in Kentucky at its face value, Thompson had three of his neighboring slave owners certify to its genuineness: "The above pass," they wrote, "is all right as it should be and we are well acquainted with the owner and his slave." [35]

All slaves found more than eight or ten miles from their master's messuage or plantation without a pass

34. Original in New York City Public Library.

35. Original in author's collection. This pass may have been designed by Thompson as an adroit method for manumitting the slave Lago.

were considered runaways.[36] The liberty of free Negroes, while they remained at home among their neighbors, was not questioned; but when they began to move about from place to place, they were usually suspected and often taken up and imprisoned as fugitive slaves. All unknown Negroes who could not produce their "free papers" were taken up as runaways. Free Negroes thus arrested were occasionally sold secretly and cheaply by unscrupulous patrollers to the despised "nigger traders." Naturally, both the patroller and the Negro trader kept secret all transactions of this nature, and many a free Negro was clapped back into slavery to remain so for life.

In the counties lying along the Ohio River it was necessary to take very strong precautions against the clandestine movement of Negroes in order to prevent wholesale escapes. "Strong and active patrols" were appointed, of "sober and discreet citizens not exceeding thirty," whose duty it was "to guard and watch the places of crossing the river, and to notice the condition and situation of all water craft upon the Kentucky shore of the Ohio River." [37]

It was charged in certain litigation that "the wanton malice of the patrol" often manifested itself in central Kentucky, the largest slaveholding section of the state. There was living on the Leestown turnpike, "about a mile or three-quarters of a mile out of the town bounds of Lexington," an elderly farmer, Benijah Bosworth,

36. In certain sections of the Bluegrass, where the slaves were well-known and visited only in the immediate neighborhood, they were given tags which took the place of passes. "They let us go visiting on Sundays, or to church, but we were all tagged in case the patteroll got us."—J. C. Meadors, interview with Addie Murphy, an ex-slave residing in Lexington, August 13, 1938.

37. *Revised Statutes of Kentucky, 1852,* p. 521.

whom his neighbors knew as "a very industrious & soberly man." His farm of one hundred and sixty acres contained, among other out-buildings, a two-story stone still-house and malt-house. Being in failing health and too old to tend the still-house operations, Bosworth rented the stone building during the spring of 1830 to an itinerant schoolmaster, Henry Hensley, who opened a country school.

During the following winter Hensley dismissed his little school "in consequence of the big snow," but planned "to resume it as soon as the weather broke." Being somewhat of a musician and having the building rented and not in use, Hensley decided to hold a "negro frolic" there on the night of February 27, 1831. From neighboring plantations and farms some forty-odd slaves slipped away from their masters and assembled at Bosworth's still-house to "frolic, make merry & dance." This apparently innocent form of amusement, however, was against the peace and dignity of the commonwealth, as no slaves were allowed to assemble away from their own plantations at night, and under no circumstances, without their masters' knowledge and consent.

Word came to Levin Young, captain of the patrol, that there was "a nigger frolic down at Bosworth's still-house." [38] He hurriedly assembled his "patterollers" and deputized "divers other citizens, to the number of fifteen or more," to assist him in arresting the wayward slaves who were running afoul of the law.

As they approached the still-house, about eleven-thirty o'clock on that cold February night, they could

38. Brand *vs.* Bosworth, Fayette Circuit Court, File 788, March 5, 1831, Deposition of Levin Young, of Fayette County.

hear the groans of Hensley's fiddle above the rhythmic shuffle of the dancers' feet on the heavy wooden floor. Surrounding the house, Young and his party called upon the Negroes to surrender. Well knowing that they were in for a good whipping and, possibly, more serious punishment, the Negroes refused to surrender and, suddenly extinguishing the lights, made the most of their opportunity to escape.

Two pistol charges of "balls and buck-shot" were "wantonly fired" by the "patterollers" into the darkened room, whereupon the frightened slaves "broke & began jumping out of the windows." Some of the hapless blacks "were caught & tied"; some "broke through the ceiling & hid themselves in the oats." [39] When order was restored, it was found that Charles, the slave of John Brand, had been "shot through the head and died instantly," and several others lying about on the floor were suffering from gunshot wounds.[40]

For the loss of his slave Charles, who "previous to his death was of great value, to-wit, of the sum of $600," Brand sued his neighbor Bosworth at the next term of the Fayette Circuit Court, and obtained a judgment of $500, but, upon the case being taken to the Court of Appeals, at Frankfort, the judgment was reversed, and Bosworth, who had vehemently denied from the first any knowledge of the slave frolic on his farm, was relieved from the payment of damages to his fellow slaveholder, John Brand.[41]

Slaves living in the country were kept in their places

39. *Ibid.*, Deposition of Willis Hickey, of Lexington.

40. *Ibid.*, Deposition of John Cluckston, of Sandersville, Fayette County.

41. Bosworth *vs.* Brand, *Kentucky Reports,* 1 Dana 377, October, 1833.

by the "patterollers," while those in the city were restrained by the town watch,[42] an equally effective law-enforcing organization. In Henderson it was the duty of the town sergeant "to punish with any number of lashes, not exceeding twenty, all or any negro slaves found in a grog shop, grocery or other places where spirituous liquors are retailed . . . or those who may be found on the streets of this town after ten o'clock at night. . . ."[43]

And in Louisville, after the tolling of the bell on the Fourth Street Presbyterian Church each night at ten o'clock, all slaves found away from home were liable for fifteen lashes and imprisonment for the rest of the night, with a possible whipping the next morning "when the watchmen could see how to lay the lashes on well."[44] All slaves caught on the streets of Lexington after the watch-bell rang at seven in the evening were subject to the punishment of "35 lashes well laid on the bare back" at the public whipping post.

In the northeast corner of the Fayette County courthouse yard stood the whipping post "of black locust one foot in diameter, ten feet high and sunk two and a half feet in the ground."[45] Samuel R. Brown, who visited Lexington in those early days, saw this instrument of torture and noted in his journal that the public square was "occasionally the scene of a barbarous practice; for it is here that incorrigible or delinquent negroes are

42. The town watch of Bowling Green, Kentucky, in 1825, consisted of "one Captain, one Lieutenant and as many privates as the Trustees may allot." Ten lashes on the bare back was the penalty for slaves caught on the streets of Bowling Green after 10 P.M.—Minutes, Town Trustees, Bowling Green, September 9, 1825.

43. Edmund L. Starling, *History of Henderson County, Kentucky,* p. 290.

44. J. Stoddard Johnston, *Memorial History of Louisville,* II, 67.

45. Order Book 6, p. 311, Fayette County Clerk's Office.

flogged unmercifully. I saw this punishment inflicted on two of these wretches. Their screams soon collected a numerous crowd—I could not help saying to myself, 'These cries are the knell of Kentucky liberty.' " [46]

Some years later, when Fayette County had grown to be the largest slaveholding county in Kentucky, its Fiscal Court at a special session in May, 1847, ordered that the "three-pronged poplar tree in the court-house yard immediately north of the [Wm. T] Barry monument be and the same is hereby established the public whipping-post of this county." [47] Vigorous floggings at this whipping post were familiar sights to those who passed along the public square, and the occasional visitor could see enough to know that, even in Lexington, slavery had its darker side.

Free Negroes were required to have with them at all times and in all places their certificates of freedom, or free papers, and present them for inspection when called upon by the town watch or "patterollers." Usually written on parchment, the certificate set out the name, age and description of the Negro, together with the date and place of his emancipation. Perry's certificate of freedom, splendidly preserved despite its age and constant handling, reads:

"State of Kentucky }
Jessamine County } Sct.

"I Daniel B. Price, clerk of the County Court for the County afsd. do certify that Nathaniel Dunn, Executor of James Dunn, dec'd, at the November County Court, 1838, produced and acknowledged in open court a deed of Emancipation to Perry, a negro man twenty-three years of age, five feet and

46. *The Western Gazetteer,* p. 92.
47. Order Book 12, p. 61, Fayette County Clerk's Office.

one-half inch high, black complexion with a scar in his left eye-brow, and I do certify that the said boy Perry is entitled to full freedom and all the privileges of a freeman as full as if he were born free. In testimony whereof I have hereunto set my hand and the seal of said Court, this 26th day of November 1838.

[SEAL] Daniel B. Price, C. J. C. C.
By A. M. Poage, D. C." [48]

In some instances, in addition to their certificates of freedom, free Negroes were required to show a certificate of good behavior, signed "by some white person of respectable character," usually from the same neighborhood in which such freedmen resided.

Despite the watchful vigilance of the "patterollers" and the town watch of the cities, there appeared from time to time accounts of intended slave uprisings and insurrections among the largest slaveholding counties of the state. On October 13, 1848, the *Western Citizen* announced, under the caption "Stampede Frustrated!" that "about forty negroes had made arrangements to leave their masters in Woodford County on Saturday night last," but, the Paris paper continued, "the plot was discovered in time to defeat its execution." From some of the Negroes involved it was later learned that they had all been furnished with forged passes at the hands of several abolitionists working in the neighborhood, who had planned for each slave "to steal his master's horse and cross the Ohio River before daylight."

It is not strange, then, in the face of such stirring news as the reported action of the slaves in Woodford

48. Original in author's collection.

County, that steps were taken to further check the movements of slaves. Note this proclamation:

> "TO OWNERS OF SLAVES!
>
> "Notice is hereby given, that from and after this date, no slave will be permitted to come to Paris, day or night, without a written pass from his or her owner, and that no slave will be permitted to sell anything in town, without a written permit specifying the article for sale, and all slaves living in town will be required to retire from the streets at nine o'clock P.M. Any infringement of the above orders will be punished with stripes.
>
> A. D. Sebree,
> James Elliott, Patrols."[49]

Throughout the fall of 1856 a series of startling allegations regarding slave insurrections broke through the habitual reserve maintained on the topic by the Southern press. Wild rumors of an all-embracing slave plot, extending from Delaware to Texas, with its execution set for Christmas Day, spread through the slaveholding states. Kentucky came in for its share of participation in this wide-spread plot.

At Hopkinsville, the county seat of Christian County, the situation was tense. From many lips came the ominous words: "The negroes are marching on us!" Telegraph poles were cut down and communications were severed. About one hundred and fifty armed men left for the settlement of LaFayette, in the southern part of the county, under the command of Captain James Jackson and Sheriff Gowen.[50]

49. *Western Citizen,* Paris, November 19, 1852.

50. A citizen of Pembroke, Christian County, wrote of his forebodings: "I have no doubt but that it [the plot] is a universal thing all over the Southern States and that every negro, fifteen years old, or older, either knows of it or is into it; and that the most confidential house servants

During the first week of December of the same year, rumors of slave plots spread into Henderson County, on the Ohio River, where it was believed that the holidays would unloose open revolt upon the whites.[51] Another Christmas Day plot was revealed by a Negro boy in Campbellsville, in Taylor County, where considerable discontent had existed among the slaves.[52]

At Cadiz, in Trigg County, it was alleged that another center of a slave plot had been discovered. A free Negro preacher, Solomon Young, declared to be the "generalissimo" of the plotters and a notorious character, was hanged on December 19. The responsibility for the plot was attributed to "Locofoco" orators and newspapers. As excitement blazed, a vigilance committee began wholesale arrests of suspects and a special court session was called for Christmas Day.[53]

Similar excitement was betrayed near Russellville, in Logan County, where a Negro, employed in one of the ironworks across the border in Tennessee, was whipped to death after remarking that he knew all about the plot but would not tell.[54] Even in Carter County, in the extreme northeastern part of Kentucky, alleged slave plotters were being caught and subjected to severe whippings.[55]

At Carrollton, in Carroll County, some fifty miles northeast of Louisville on the Ohio River, considerable furor was aroused over the alleged plots engineered by

are the ones to be the most active in the destruction of their [masters'] families."—*Canton Dispatch,* December 13, 1856.

51. *Lexington Observer & Reporter,* December 10, 1856.

52. *Louisville Courier,* December 17, 1856.

53. *Baltimore Sun,* December 20, 1856.

54. *Russellville Herald,* December 20, 1856; *The Liberator,* January 2, 1857.

55. This refers to the plot involving the slaves of William McMinnis, a large planter of Carter County.—*Ibid.,* January 23, 1857.

the Reverend William Anderson, a colored Methodist preacher, who was also accused of aiding fugitive slaves to escape to the North. After a reward of six hundred dollars had been offered for his apprehension, he was captured with documents in his possession implicating "several distinguished Northerners." His examination, however, proved disappointingly innocuous and he was discharged.[56]

Another exciting Christmas plot involving some two hundred Negroes was discovered in Wyoming, a settlement in Bath County. Forty Negroes, fully armed, were arrested at a colored festival. Their plan was to assemble all the slaves at White Oak Creek and then to fight their way to Ohio.[57] It appears from the news items and editorials of the contemporary press that the year 1856 was exceptional for the large crop of individual slave crimes reported, especially those directed against the life of the master. It was estimated that at least ten or twelve alleged leaders of insurrections had been hanged in six Kentucky counties and that many more were awaiting trial who might ultimately share the same fate.[58]

"From every quarter of the South we hear of insurrections and rumors of insurrections among the slaves," remarked the *Observer & Reporter,* in noting the panic spirit prevailing in Kentucky and elsewhere.[59] Much of this unrest, as the editor pointed out, was due to the manner in which the recent presidential election had been managed, and which was such as to awaken hopes of emancipation among the slaves and to encourage the

56. *Baltimore Sun,* December 17, 22, 1856.
57. *Mt. Sterling Whig,* December 26, 1856.
58. *Maysville Eagle,* January 6, 1857.
59. December 20, 1856.

efforts of abolitionists in their attempts to overthrow the institution of slavery.

Even with the tightened restrictions[60] progressively imposed upon the slave population, newspapers in the months that followed carried accounts of "Desperate Runaways!" in Bourbon County, "Slave Insurrection!" in Harrison County, "Stampede of Slaves!" in Boyle County, but these items were trivial in significance compared with the startling news which flashed across the country in the fall of 1859. On the night of October 16 of that year, John Brown, who had taken an active part in the Kansas slave troubles, crossed the Potomac River at Harpers Ferry, Virginia, with a small band of supporters and boldly seized the United States arsenal. He planned to make this the starting point of a slave uprising that would grow as it progressed and spread all over the slaveholding states. Secretly planning this uprising for some time, Brown had brought with him a large number of pikes for use in arming the Negroes against their masters.

Accounts of Brown's raid were carried in practically all of the Kentucky newspapers, and the excited citizens of the state followed each news report with extraordinary interest. "It was an attempt," reported the *Western Citizen,* "to excite a servile insurrection, conducted by a handful of crazed fanatics, who supposed that the slaves would rise upon their masters and that they could march through the South, gathering strength with their progress and ending in a universal over-

60. In the winter of 1856–57, twenty-six leading slaveholders of Scott County met at Newtown "to devise some plan for the better government of our slaves, in consideration of the fact of the lawless management of our slaves and the contaminating influence exerted upon them by trafficking and trading with white men."—*Georgetown Gazette,* January 3, 1857.

throw of the institution of slavery."[61] Before accurate accounts of this "awful insurrection" could be obtained in Kentucky and while nerves were on edge, rumors were rife that Brown and his accomplices "were being rescued by a foray of 1500 to 2000 armed abolitionists," and this greatly added to the confusion and excitement of the time. Slaveholders in Kentucky were immensely relieved in a day or so, when definite information arrived that Colonel Robert E. Lee, with ninety United States Marines, after a brisk engagement, had captured the "half-crazed Brown" and four of his men. Ten others of the attacking party lay dead and four had escaped.[62]

Associated with Brown in his attempted slave liberation were seventeen whites and five free Negroes. "Of these whites," commented the *Kentucky Statesman,* "it may be assumed that all these were broken-down Yankee school-masters, debauched and unfrocked preachers, and others of that class of vermin to be found at the North, too lazy to work, and generally too cowardly to steal, and therefore, who turn to abolition lectures, &c."[63]

Brown's plan to free the enslaved race came to naught—none of the neighboring slaves joined him in his mad undertaking. Brown, after a fair trial, was found guilty "upon every count of the indictment, embracing treason, murder and servile insurrection," and was publicly hanged on December 2, 1859. To thousands of Northerners and abolitionists Brown soon thereafter became a martyr to the anti-slavery cause.

61. Paris, October 28, 1859. "Such men as Brown have lived in all ages and are bound to crop up every now and then."—*Ibid.*

62. Elijah Avey, *The Capture and Execution of John Brown,* pp. 117–24.

63. Lexington, October 25, 1859.

Even though Brown was dead and the insurrection over, the affair did not end there. As might have been expected, considerable uneasiness and excitement spread throughout Kentucky, a border slave state, and awakened the public to the state's defenseless condition in the event of a similar outbreak.

Clashes and disturbances were now taking place in various parts of Kentucky between the anti-slavery advocates and the slaveholding element. These occurrences were traced at the time directly to the John Brown raid. Especially noted at this time was the increased distrust shown toward the free Negroes and the keen hostility exhibited toward the abolitionists.

Thirty-six anti-slavery zealots, after being stripped of their property and every means of livelihood, were driven out of the state from Berea, in Madison County, late in December, 1859, by the incensed slaveholders of that neighborhood.[64] In the preceding October William S. Bailey, of Newport, Kentucky, owner and editor of the anti-slavery newssheet, the weekly *Free South,* was openly attacked for his alleged views on Brown's raid. His office was set on fire and destroyed by an angry mob of slaveholders and slaveholding sympathizers, and the presses were smashed and the type dumped into the Ohio River.[65]

Threats of a servile insurrection in Cynthiana, following the Brown affair, occasioned grave apprehension and "the excitement increased nearly to a panic."[66] Farmers and slave owners of Harrison County were warned "to attend closely to the assembling of their

64. Carroll, *op. cit.,* p. 194.

65. *Cincinnati Gazette,* November 4, 1859; *The Liberator,* November 4, 1859.

66. *Cynthiana News,* November 10, 1859.

negroes" and to prevent any undue gathering of slaves. The growing excitement reached a high pitch, when the postmaster received an anonymous letter warning the citizens that an insurrection was about to break out in their midst, that some eighty slaves from Harrison County, and as many from Bourbon and Fayette, had been furnished with guns and were ready to rise and slay their masters. "This insurrection," further warned the menacing letter, "is about to take place of such a magnitude that the *Brown tirade* is but a flea-bite in comparison." [67] It was rumored about the streets of Cynthiana that the abolitionists planned to burn the town.[68]

Extra police were employed in the cities of the Bluegrass and the ranks of the "patterollers" were swelled with new recruits. Well armed, they rode all night, bringing in many suspected slaves and a few whites who had been talking to the Negroes. After a week, however, of intense strain and frantic excitement, conditions became normal once again, and, after running down all the rumors and clues, it was found that the intended terrible uprising had little basis in fact.

In searching the files of old newspapers and courthouse records, it appears that in Kentucky, and especially in the Bluegrass region, where Negro bondage was of a milder form, there were uprisings and rumors of uprisings [69] throughout the entire period of slavery, all of which goes to prove that, even though Kentucky slaves were given kindness and light work, these things

67. *Kentucky Statesman,* November 22, 1859.

68. *Cynthiana News,* November 10, 1859.

69. *Cincinnati Daily Commercial,* May 11, 1861. In this issue was the stirring news of a Negro insurrection in Owen, Gallatin and Henry counties which, like so many others, came to naught.

did not always bring contentment or reconcile the enslaved Negroes to their lot.

Doubtless more fanatics, like "Patrick" Doyle, would have tried to incite the Negroes of Kentucky to rebel against their masters, had it not been for the ever-vigilant efforts of the town watch and the "patterollers" to restrain and subdue the blacks who, aided and abetted by the irrepressible abolitionists, were constantly looking for opportunities to break their shackles and throw off the galling yoke of bondage.

State of Kentucky
Jessamine County Sct

I Daniel B Price clerk of the County Court for the County afsd do certify that Nathaniel Dunn Executor of James Dunn decd, at the November County Court 1838 produced and acknowledged in open Court a deed of Emancipation to Perry a negro man, twenty three years of age, five feet and one half inch high, black complexion with a scar in his left eye brow and I do certify that the said boy Perry is entitled to full freedom and all the privileges of a freeman as if he were born free. In testimony whereof I have hereunto set my hand and the seal of said Court this 26th day of November 1838.

Danl. B. Price clk
By A. M. Poage D.C.

PERRY'S "FREE PAPERS"

MAIN STREET, ANTE-BELLUM LEXINGTON

CHAPTER V

AUCTION BLOCK

Around the auctioneer's stand near the courthouse door gathered a mixed crowd—prospective purchasers, Negro traders, slaveholders, planters, spectators and hangers-on. On the stand stood the crier of the sale, dressed in a long hammer-tailed coat, fancy vest, broad-rimmed hat, with a raucous voice and mallet in hand calling loudly for bids.

"Step up, Gentlemen! What'll you offer for this sprightly wench—she's warranted sound in mind and body—she'll make you a good cook, washer or ironer. Come, Gentlemen, bid up on this likely gal. What do I hear?"

Huddled near the auction block were groups of slaves—men, women and children—awaiting sale. Their downcast looks and heart-rending cries, as the fall of the hammer tore asunder husbands and wives, parents and children, made them objects of great pity and clearly exhibited the darker side of slavery. Such sales of human chattels were familiar sights to the crowds that gathered on the public square of many Kentucky towns on county court day.

Court day in Kentucky was truly a peculiar and

unique institution. On a set Monday in each month, while the justices of the peace, who made up the county court, assembled in the courthouse to transact the people's business, country folk for miles around took the day off and poured into town for the court day sales and gatherings on the public square.

Livery stables crowded with farmers' rigs and horses did a thriving business, and long rows of buggies and surreys lined up on the streets in front of the stables, with their shafts turned skyward, gave unmistakable indication of the crowds that were in town. Saddle horses and mules of planters and farmers tied to the long rows of wooden hitching posts around the courthouse yard notified shopkeepers and city folks that their "country cousins" had come to town for the all-important day.

These sales and gatherings on court day presented a strange spectacle. Here, on the public square of Kentucky towns, was assembled a motley collection of livestock—lean cows with bawling calves, shaggy mules with tails full of cockle-burs, braying jacks, sway-back brood mares with spindle-legged colts, old knock-kneed plug horses and, occasionally, a blooded animal—all to be traded or offered for sale under the hammers of shrill-voiced auctioneers.

Next to the courthouse yard was lined up, for sale or trade, various articles—worn-out stoves, broken-down beds, old furniture and clothing, axe and plow handles, tools, farming implements, plow gear and buggy harness, jars of pickles and preserves, homemade baskets and chairs, sugar-cane "sweetening," and molasses by the gallon.

Court day made a fertile field for the itinerant vendor

and the petty faker. Here also were gathered on this special day junk dealers, patent menders of glass and tin ware, cheap-jewelry salesmen, "painless" tooth extractors, hucksters with their watermelon carts, and traders of every kind and shade of reputation.

Long haired "doctors" and "professors" in frock-tailed coats and beaver hats held their audiences spellbound as they extolled the wonderful merits of their recently discovered "universal remedy," a lightning cure for all pains and ailments, which, as they significantly proclaimed, was now for sale at the extremely low price of fifty cents per bottle, with a *very* limited supply.

Over near the curbstone could be seen a group of country folk eagerly listening to a blind mendicant, who, with a tin cup around his neck, sang mountain ballads to the halting accompaniment of his squeaky fiddle.

Rich landowners and prosperous tobacco and hemp planters rubbed elbows with the nondescript class which the Negroes called "pore white trash," and men in all walks of life met here on terms of amiable equality. The public square on court day was the trading center and gossiping place for all rural Kentuckians and the talk was free and easy. Here they discussed the weather, Negroes, crops, politics and horses, and every man had his say.

Everyone came to town on court day to see the sights and enjoy himself according to his own fancy, whether it was swapping horses, buying, selling, gossiping, attending slave sales, or meeting friends and relatives, and, perhaps in between times, having a few rounds of his favorite drink before the polished rail of a local bar.

Towards evening, tired and footsore, but fully satisfied that he had seen and heard everything worth while, the countryman gathered his family around him and headed homeward.

Such were the court day scenes and gatherings when livestock and slaves alike were sold to the highest bidder on the public square. Most common of the slave sales were those made in the settlement of estates, runaway slaves sold for their jail fees and, occasionally, Negroes levied on and sold to satisfy the demands of their masters' creditors. Some slave owners, greatly abhorring the practice of public sales,[1] sold their Negroes privately, while there were many families throughout the Bluegrass region who proudly boasted that they had never sold a slave, either publicly or privately.

In a large proportion of local sales the slaves sold were disposed of by the sheriff,[2] court commissioners, or administrators and executors of estates, rather than by their owners. After ample notice had been given through the local press, the sale was usually conducted on the public square, near the courthouse door.[3] Here the slave dealer or his agent was always present to pick

1. Mr. D. C. Wickliffe, editor of the *Observer,* had long been opposed to the sale of slaves at public auction, and contended that, if it was necessary to sell Negroes, other than at private sale, this should be done in the yard at the slave jails.—*Lexington Observer & Reporter,* May 26, 1843.

2. As early as 1821 citizens of Louisville were aroused over the barbarous practice of selling slaves on the streets. In one instance, "a laudable indignation was manifested" over the public sale of a woman and child, who, as the account read, "were as white as any of our citizens."—*Niles' Weekly Register,* XX (June 9, 1821), 240.

3. While traveling through Kentucky in 1824, the German nobleman, Karl Bernhard, witnessed a revolting spectacle in Louisville: "A pregnant mulatto woman was offered for sale at public auction with her two children . . . the auctioneer standing by her side, indulged himself in brutal jests upon her thriving condition, and sold her for four hundred dollars."—*Travels through North America, during the Years 1825 and 1826,* II, 133.

up a good bargain, if the opportunity presented itself.

There were, naturally, some unscrupulous masters who cared little for the fate of their slaves or the division of families:

> "I wish to sell a negro woman and four children. The woman is 22 years old, of good character, a good cook and washer. The children are very likely, from 6 years down to 1½. I will sell them together or separately to suit purchaser.
>
> J. T. Underwood." [4]

Runaway slaves, when apprehended and lodged in the county jails, were advertised in the papers and, when not called for by their owners after six months, were sold for their jail fees. James Harrison, sheriff of Jefferson County, advertised:

> "NOTICE: I will on the first Monday of May, 1846, before the court-house door, in the city of Louisville, sell to the highest bidder, JOHN, a runaway slave, 18 or 19 years of age, rather heavy made, supposed to be the property of Daniel McCaleb, residing on the coast some twenty miles below New Orleans." [5]

Philip Swigert, master commissioner of the Franklin Circuit Court, in the fall of 1838, announced through handbills that, by virtue of a decree of said court in the suit of John Samuel's infant heir against Samuel's adult heirs, he would sell certain slaves at public outcry:

"Look At This! ! !
Public Sale of Land & Slaves!

. . . . .

On Monday, the 8th day of December next,
at the Court-House door, in the town of Frankfort.

. . . . . .

4. *Louisville Weekly Journal,* May 2, 1849.
5. *Ibid.,* March 4, 1846.

Slaves to be sold on a credit of one year.
All of them likely, and some of the boys have
been accustomed to working in a hemp factory.
Philip Swigert, Comm'r." [6]

Under the terms of many wills it was frequently necessary for the executors to sell slave property in order to make proper settlement of the estate involved. The customary procedure is revealed in the "For Sale" notice of John Clark, master commissioner of the circuit court of Kentucky's largest slaveholding county:

> "SALE OF NEGROES. By virtue of a decree of the Fayette Circuit, the undersigned will, as Commissioner, carry into effect said decree, sell to the highest bidder, on the public square in the city of Lexington, on Monday the 10th of March next, being county court day, the following slaves, to wit: Keiser, Carr, Bob, Susan, Sam, Sarah and Ben; belonging to the estate of Alexander Culbertson, deceased. The sale to be on a credit of three months, the purchaser to give bond with approved security. The sale to take place between the hours of 11 o'clock in the morning and 3 o'clock in the evening." [7]

For fear the "nigger traders" would buy their slaves and take them to the dreaded Southern markets, many owners, when forced to part with some of their faithful Negroes, were careful to explain the necessities of the case. They were likewise cautious not to be cast under the suspicion that they were trading in Negroes:

6. Photostatic copy in University of Kentucky Library. Nineteen slaves, "from Reuben, 45 years old down to Jack, aged 1 year," were listed for sale in this handbill.

7. *Lexington Observer & Reporter,* February 27, 1854, *et seq.*

"NEGROES FOR SALE! A yellow negro woman of fine constitution, and two children, from the country and sold for no fault but to raise money. Will not be sold to go down the river. Her husband, a fine man, can be had also. Apply at the store of Jarvis & Trabue—3rd & Main." [8]

Of course, the prices of slaves varied widely in Kentucky according to their physical condition, actual or reputed qualities, age and color. There was no precise standard.[9] For male field hands, or "young bucks," the prerequisites for good bids were youth and strength, reliability and skill; for young "wenches," health and fecundity. Looks counted much, especially in the color of the octoroon and quadroon girls, as Robards called his "choice stock," these "fancy girls" often selling from $1,200 to $2,000 and, in some cases, even more.

But with men and boys a tawny complexion was a detriment, for they could more easily pass for white persons, thereby better enabling them to escape from their masters and elude detection. These qualities were often mentioned in notices for fugitives:

8. *Louisville Weekly Journal*, September 3, 1845.

9. The following figures are based on the appraisals of slaves in the settlement of estates in Fayette County from 1845–1847, from the Fayette County Court, Will Book R, pp. 85, 88, 136, 139, 161, 220, 238:

Male slaves, from 3 to 9 years old	$150–250
" " , from 9 to 13 " "	$250–350
" " , from 13 to 19 " "	$350–475
" " , from 19 to 35 " "	$475–750
" " , from 35 to 40 " "	$750–500
" " , from 40 to 60 " "	$500–200
Female slaves, from 3 to 10 years old	$100–300
" " , from 10 to 16 " "	$300–475
" " , from 16 to 25 " "	$475–600
" " , from 25 to 45 " "	$600–300
" " , from 45 to 60 " "	$300–175

> "$100 REWARD—Ranaway from James Hyhart, Paris, Kentucky, on 29th June last, the mulatto boy NORTON, about fifteen years, a very bright mulatto, and would be easily taken for a white boy, if not closely examined. His hair is black and *straight,* &c." [10]

During the decade and a half prior to the Civil War, slaves brought better prices in Kentucky than at any time in the history of the "peculiar institution." [11] Cotton and sugar planters of the South were realizing enormous returns from their plantations and the demand for Kentucky-born slaves became so great that there were ten purchasers for every slave offered for sale.[12] With this inflated demand for Negroes, prices increased from one hundred to one hundred and fifty per cent for the ten years preceding the outbreak of the Civil War.

An idea of the top prices of the time may be gained by noticing a few sales. In Harrison County, in 1858, slaves were sold by the master commissioner to settle the estate of George Kirkpatrick: Peter, twenty-three years old, brought $1,290; Tom, sixteen years, $1,015; while Emma, aged twelve, was sold for $865.[13] And in Henderson County, in the same year, those attending the public auctions marveled at the keen bidding and high prices paid for sound and likely slaves. There, George, age thirty-five years, brought $1,200, and the

10. *New Orleans True American,* August 11, 1836.

11. Newspapers over the country repeatedly called attention to the relation of cotton and Negroes. In 1859 one paper stated: "It is well-known that the price of cotton regulates the price of slaves in the South, and a bale of cotton and a 'likely nigger' are about well balanced in the scale of pecuniary appreciation."—Richmond, Virginia, *Enquirer,* July 29, 1859.

12. Collins, *History of Kentucky,* I, 74.

13. *Cynthiana News,* January 10, 1858.

PUBLIC SALE

OF

VALUABLE

SLAVES!

As Agent for the Owners I will sell at Public Sale to the highest bidder, on Monday, the 8th day of January, 1855, being County Court day, at the Courthouse door in the City of Maysville, Ky.,

Five likely & valuable

SLAVES,

Viz: One Negro Woman and a Mulatto Boy and Girl, and a Mulatto Woman and her Child.

They will be sold on a credit of Six Months, the purchaser to give Bond with good security, bearing interest from the day of sale, for the price.

ABNER HORD.

December 29th, 1855.

A COURT DAY SALE IN MAYSVILLE

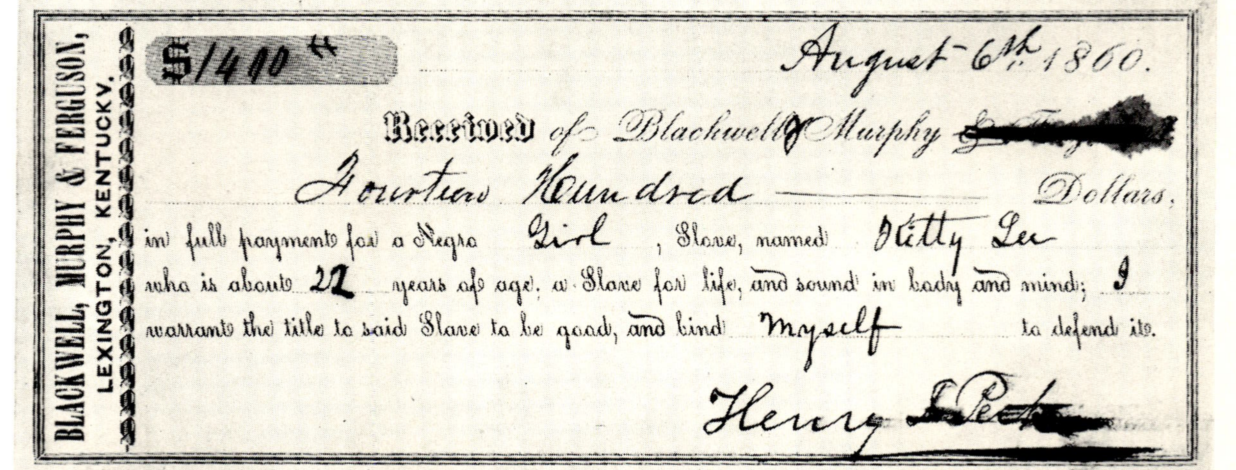

BLACKWELL, MURPHY & FERGUSON,
LEXINGTON, KENTUCKY.

$1400

August 6th 1860.

Received of Blackwell & Murphy

Fourteen Hundred Dollars,

in full payment for a Negro Girl, Slave, named Kitty Lee

who is about 22 years of age, a Slave for life, and sound in body and mind; I

warrant the title to said Slave to be good, and bind Myself to defend it.

Henry

BILL OF SALE FOR KITTY LEE

highest price of several sales was the "likely boy, Andrew, who fetched $1,500." [14]

High prices continued to be paid for slaves in the commissioners' sales in the settlement of estates in Bourbon,[15] Scott,[16] Clark, Franklin and Fayette counties and, probably, the all-time record for high prices was reached the following year (1859) when Negroes were sold at public auction in Lexington, April, 1859, to settle the estate of Spencer C. Graves:

"John	18 years of age	$1500
Dick	21 years of age	$1400
Major	50 years of age	$ 480
Charles	31 years of age	$1155
Billy	18 years of age	$1140
Lucy	18 years of age with infant	$1280
Davidella	31 years of age	$1220
Patience	18 years of age	$1350
Catherine	15 years of age	$1130." [17]

These peak prices for slaves sold in Kentucky were in no wise related to, nor indicative of, the value of slave labor in the state; but were values determined chiefly by the increased demand for Negro cotton hands in the Southern states.

Closely akin to transactions involving purchase or sale was the hiring out of slaves, which was a transfer of their services for a stipulated time. Some small slave owners made it their business to hire out all their slaves, both men and women, at rates varying from $75 to $150 a year and board.[18] Churches were known to own and

14. *Henderson Weekly Journal,* January 29, 1858.
15. *Kentucky State Flag,* Paris, January 5, 1859.
16. *Georgetown Gazette,* December 23, 1858.
17. *Free South,* Newport, April 29, 1859.
18. Samuel G. Jackson, a Fayette County slaveholder, rented out slaves by the year, and during 1854 his ten rented slaves brought him $922.50.—Fayette County Court, Will Book V, p. 102.

hire slaves; in many instances the revenue raised by such means helped pay the pastor's salary and other expenses.

In Henderson, Mt. Sterling and other Kentucky towns, the first day of January usually proved an interesting occasion.[19] Large crowds of slaveholders and would-be slaveholders, as well as inquisitive rustics and idle bystanders, congregated in the county seat, knowing it to be the day for the hiring of Negroes. A block, or box, was usually placed at the most central point of the principal street or public square, and from this improvised stand Negroes—men, women and children—were hired to the highest bidder for the ensuing year.[20]

Many a small farmer, mechanic or country storekeeper, leading away his first hired slave, swelled with pride as he assumed that enviable position in society known as a slaveholder. He was now a member, even though in a small way, of that much respected and influential class who favored the institution.

Because of superior skill or special training, many slaves were hired out, and many were known as "town servants," those hired to work as cooks, washerwomen, ironers, housemaids, hotel waiters, porters, draymen and plain mechanics of all kinds. Slaves of this sort not only were valuable assets to those who hired them, but were equally valuable to their owners. Often they were accorded a considerable measure of liberty and privi-

19. Starling, *History of Henderson County,* p. 196.

20. "By ten o'clock on New Year's morning, the town [Mt. Sterling] was overflowing . . . hundreds came pouring in from every direction. Owner and owned flocked from various parts of the country to readjust their property relations for the ensuing year. It was the day set apart for slaveholders to sell, buy, let and hire human chattels. Many were rented or leased at a rate of from $50 to $200 a year. . . ."—Venable, "Down South before the War," *Ohio Arch. & Hist. Quarterly,* II, No. 1 (June, 1888).

leges.[21] At Thanksgiving and Christmas they were allowed to visit their families and friends on the old plantation, and might by harder work and doing odd jobs earn considerable money of their own besides what they gained for their master. Some slaves in this way saved enough money to purchase their own freedom after years of labor.

Whether the slaves were hired out from the auction block or privately,[22] their "rent papers" were usually drawn in the form of a promissory note, which stated the length of the lease, the consideration and the stipulations for clothes and medical attention:

> "$130. On the 25th day of December 1854, I promise to pay to Mrs. Mary H. Breckinridge, the sum of one hundred and thirty dollars for the hire of her negro man Thomas, as a waiter in a hotel in Lexington for the year 1854. I am not to hire him out without the consent of his owner. I will also treat him well, and board & lodge him comfortably, providing for him whatever is needed during the year in both respects. I am to clothe him comfortably, winter & summer, & return him at the end of the year with a sufficient supply of good & reasonable clothing of all kinds. If he should be sick I am to be at the expense of taking care of him & pay the Doctor bill, but if he should die, the hire to stop from that time. Sanders D. Bruce." [23]

21. W. H. Perrin and J. H. Battle, *Counties of Todd and Christian, Kentucky,* p. 81.

22. In larger cities "general agents" made it a business to hire Negroes on commission, usually varying from 7 to 8 per cent. E. H. Dean, of Louisville, advertised in laconic terms: "Wanted to Hire—five hundred negroes of all ages, sizes and sex, for the ensuing year."—*Louisville Democrat,* December 29, 1859.

23. Mary H. Breckinridge *vs.* Sanders D. Bruce, Fayette Circuit Court, File 1277, January 13, 1855.

And in another case David Marsh and James L. Allen, of Lexington, hired a female slave, Sally, for the year 1853, and carefully specified the clothing they would furnish:

> "$61.80. On or before the 25th day of December 1853, we or either of us promise to pay Charles D. Carr, or order, sixty-one dollars 80/100 cents for the hire of a negro woman Sally, and promise to give her the following clothes; two shirts, two summer dresses, one plaid linsey dress, two pairs of stockings, two pairs of shoes, one winter dress and one blanket and pay her physician's bill and return her at said time. In case of death, her hire to cease from that date. Witness our hands this 19th day of January, 1853." [24]

Sometimes, in the rental contract, mention was made of giving the slave himself a small sum of money, as was the case with Blythefield: "We are to clothe him with all necessary winter & summer clothing & pay his taxes & Doctor's bill & will give the boy twelve dollars for himself." [25] Now and then it was provided in some of the contracts of hire that Negroes under the lease should be insured "payable at the Branch Bank of Kentucky in this city." [26]

Even with good treatment promised their slaves in the rental contracts, owners were occasionally in litigation over the loss of their blacks by death, which, as they charged, was due to improper medical attention during sick spells or from ruthless overwork.[27] However, the courts of Kentucky usually upheld the renter's

24. C. D. Carr *vs.* David Marsh, *et al.*, Fayette Circuit Court, File 1278, June 17, 1854.

25. John Curd *vs.* A. & J. McCoy, *ibid.*, File 1278, January 9, 1855.

26. Sanders D. Bruce *vs.* John C. Chiles, *ibid.*, File 1276, January 19, 1855.

27. Thos. Scott *vs.* David Sutton & Son, *ibid.*, File 779, March 13, 1833.

side of the case in suits over the death or loss by running away of a hired slave.[28]

Readers of the *Louisville Courier* had their attention called to a very unusual slave sale, which the local papers captioned: "Negro Lawyer at Auction!" which, no doubt, created some amazement among members of the local bar, as well as general discussion:

> "There will be offered to the highest bidder, at the office of J. S. Young, on 5th street, this morning at 9 o'clock. A valuable *yellow man,* supposed to have his blood fully half mixed with the Anglo-Saxon, stout and active and weighing 175 pounds. A very good *rough lawyer;* very healthy, and title good—said negro is not fitted to practice in the Court of Appeals or in the Court of Chancery, but take him in a common law case, or a six-penny trial before a County Magistrate and 'he can't be beat.' Said yellow man can also take depositions, make out legal writings, and is thoroughly adept at brow-beating witnesses and other tricks of the trade." [29]

Thomas N. Allen, an early resident of Clark County, recounts in his *Chronicles of Oldfields* some interesting incidents centered around the old auction block in Winchester. "Directly opposite the court-house on Main Street," wrote Allen, "is a large stile block that was put there for the convenience of women, alighting from or mounting their saddle-horses, but it is also

28. A. McCoy *vs.* Edward McAlister, Fayette Circuit Court, File 1265, August 23, 1853. This suit grew out of the rental of the defendant's slave, Henry, who, as the plaintiff charged, was "a confirmed runaway." McCoy alleged that Henry "repeatedly ran away and was absent a greater part of the time he was hired." The court held in favor of McCoy for damages of $66.95 for "ketching the runaway slave Henry," who was apprehended in Greenup County.

29. November 12, 1849; *The Examiner,* Louisville, November 24, 1849.

used, because of its public location, as a block or platform on which negroes are stood when they are offered for sale to the highest bidder.

"Here, on one county court day, I saw a likely young negro man put up for sale. His master had died, and in settling up his estate it became necessary to sell the property, including all the slaves. Immediately preceding the sale of this boy, his mother had been sold, the purchaser being a daughter of the decedent, whose old 'mammy' the woman had been, and who was greatly attached to her. But, in buying the mother, the lady had expended the only money she possessed, and when the boy was offered she was not able to bid on him, notwithstanding the all but heart-breaking appeals of the old negress, who saw several professional negro buyers standing around ready and eager to purchase, and who, as the poor woman knew quite well, bought for the New Orleans market."

The auction began and the bids were lively from the start. Several hard-faced "niggah-tradahs" contended with one another in the offers, first one and then another bidding on the boy, running him up to twelve hundred dollars. Then someone in the crowd bid twelve hundred and fifty. The Negro traders quit their bidding and the boy was "cried off" to Obadiah Crews, local tavern-keeper. It was a matter of some speculation what the "boniface" would do with his new purchase, bought at such a high figure, because it was generally known that he already had all the servants needed at his tavern.

Crews, who had for years bought butter and eggs from the boy's mother, knew that she "was such a kindly, good old negro" that he was unable to resist her appeal when she hurried down to his tavern[30] before the sale and implored him to save her boy. Squire Israel Buckley, overhearing the pathetic appeal of the old Negro woman, offered immediate aid:

"Go, Obe," urged Squire Buckley, "and buy him in. If you need any money, let me know."

" 'Spose," replied Obe, "them damn nigger traders run him up on me out of all reason?"

"You buy him in," answered the Squire, "if you have to pay more for him than you think he's worth, I'll take him off your hands."

Thus it was, through the timely assistance of Obe Crews and old Squire Buckley, that the boy was saved from the Southern trade, that the young mistress acquired him, and was allowed her own time in which to repay the sale price.[31]

On another occasion, Sam Anderson's slave, George, known as "a great rogue and a nuisance in the community," was put on the block to be auctioned off in Winchester. Well knowing that his chances of securing a good home in the community were small, on account of his reputation, George, in an effort to save himself from the "nigger traders," put "his wits to work" to prevent them from buying him.

As he stood on the block looking around him, he saw several "of those cold-blooded creatures" in the crowd —the Negroes instinctively recognized the traders and shrank away from them in terror.

As was customary at a public auction of slaves, the auctioneer announced that Mr. Anderson, the master, would give a bill of sale for his slave with the usual

30. Finnegan's Tavern, Winchester, corner Main and Cross streets, formerly operated by Dennis Finnegan.

31. Pp. 88–89.

guarantee—"sound in mind and body and a slave for life." While there began a lively bidding among the Negro traders, George suddenly assumed a strange appearance—his head was thrown back, his eyes rolled wildly, his body and limbs began to twitch and jerk in an unheard-of manner.

"What's the matter with your boy, Mr. Anderson?" one of the traders asked the owner, who, astonished and puzzled, drew nearer the block. But Mr. Anderson did not answer the question. George was now foaming at the mouth, and the violent twitching and jerking increased precipitously.

"What's the matter with you, boy?" gruffly demanded the trader. "O, I'se has fits, I has," exclaimed George, whereupon his body doubled up and rolled off the block.[32]

Of course, the auction was hastily terminated. George was hustled off to jail, and a doctor sent for, but, after a careful examination, the medical man was somewhat mystified as to the slave's actual condition. He advised the master to leave George in the jailer's custody for a while, promising to look in on him the next morning. Under his master's instructions, the wily slave was put to bed in the debtor's room, where he soon sank, apparently, into a sound sleep.

Next morning, when the jailer brought in breakfast, he found the bed empty. George was gone, and nothing was heard of him again until word came, several weeks later, that he was safe in Canada.[33]

32. Similar actions were not unknown in slave sales. "Frequently on such occasions, there is a strong indisposition in such creatures to be sold, and that by stratagem, to avoid a sale, they may frequently feign sickness, or magnify any particular complaint with which they are affected."—Brownston *vs.* Cropper, *Kentucky Reports,* 1 Littell 175, June, 1822.

33. Allen, *op. cit.,* pp. 91–92.

While slave sales, as a rule, attracted little more than casual interest, there occurred, early in May, 1843, an event which brought together fully two thousand persons on historic Cheapside,[34] the public square of Lexington. Here, around the old rickety auction block, were gathered the wealth and culture of the Bluegrass, ladies and gentlemen in fashionable attire from Cincinnati, Louisville, Frankfort and even as far south as New Orleans.

There were men and women, slave masters and mistresses, speculators in human chattels and idle bystanders—all anxiously awaiting the sale of Eliza, the beautiful young daughter of her master, only one sixty-fourth African. She was white, with dark lustrous eyes, straight black hair and a rich olive complexion. Yet she was a slave, the daughter of her master, about to be sold to the highest and best bidder to satisfy his creditors.

Reared as a family servant in an atmosphere of refinement and culture in an old Bluegrass home, Eliza had acquired grace, poise, education, "social manners" and other accomplishments rarely found in one of her position. For over a week, while awaiting sale, Eliza had been confined in a crowded, vermin-infested slave jail on Short Street along with the common run of Negroes, but, now, she stood frightened and trembling on the block, facing the gazing multitude.

Beside her stood the old auctioneer, in frock-tailed coat, plaid vest, calfskin boots, with a broad-rimmed white beaver hat pushed on the back of his head. In the most insinuating manner he called attention to the handsome girl, her exquisite physique and fine quali-

34. Named for the London Cheapside, which was an open square, famous in the Middle Ages for its fairs and markets, and later for its fine stores and shops. Court day sales in Lexington were abolished in the fall of 1921.

ties, well suited, as he suggested, for the mistress of any gentleman.

Bids began at two hundred and fifty dollars, and rapidly rose by twenty-fives and fifties to five hundred —seven hundred—a thousand dollars. When twelve hundred dollars was reached, all of the bidders except two had withdrawn from the field, Calvin Fairbank, a young Methodist preacher who had lately arrived in town, and a short, thick-necked, beady-eyed Frenchman from New Orleans.

"How high are you going?" asked the Frenchman.

"Higher than you, Monsieur," replied Fairbank.

Fairbank and the Frenchman continued to bid—slower and more cautiously. The auctioneer on the block raved and cursed. "Fourteen hundred and fifty," ventured Fairbank, with a furtive glance toward his competitor. The Frenchman stood silent. The hammer rose—paused—lowered—rose—fell, and then, the exasperated auctioneer, dropping his hammer, suddenly seized Eliza, jerked open her dress and throwing it back from her white shoulders exposed her superb neck and breast to the startled crowd.

"Look here, gentlemen!" he exclaimed, "who is going to lose such a chance as this? Here is a girl fit to be the mistress of a king."

Through the crowd swept a suppressed cry of disgust and contempt, of anger and grief; women blushed and men hung their heads in shame. But the old auctioneer, callous to such scenes and knowing that he was well within his rights, was not to be intimidated, and again, in his rough voice, called loudly for bids.

"Fourteen, sixty-five," risked the Frenchman.

"Fourteen, seventy-five," responded the preacher.

Then, with the lull that followed, it seemed apparent that the bidder from New Orleans was through. Sickened at the sale, many of the crowd were now leaving, when the auctioneer, who seemed at his wits' end, in a frantic effort to stimulate bidding, suddenly "twisted his victim's profile" to the excited crowd and "lifting her skirts, laid bare her beautiful, symmetrical body, from her feet to her waist."

"Ah, gentlemen!" he exclaimed, slapping her naked thigh with his rough hand, "who is going to be the winner of this prize?"

"Fourteen hundred and eighty," came the Frenchman's bid above the tumult of the crowd. "Are you all done?" cried the man on the block as he waved his gavel in the air. "Once—twice—do I hear more? Th-r-e-e." A smile of triumph came over the Frenchman's face, while Eliza, knowing who Fairbank was, now turned an appealing and heart-rending glance toward him.

"Fourteen hundred and eighty-five," cautiously bid the preacher.

"Eighty-five, eighty-five, eighty-five; I'm going to sell this girl." Looking at the Frenchman, he asked: "Are you going to bid again?" With an air of indifference the man from New Orleans slowly shook his head.

"Once—twice—th-r-e-e times—sold!" cried the auctioneer, bringing down his gavel with a loud rap, as Eliza crumpled and fainted on the block.

"You've got her damned cheap, sir," said the auctioneer cheerfully to Fairbank. "What are you going to do with her?"

"Free her," exclaimed Fairbank, as a loud cheer rose from the crowd, led by Robert Wickliffe, the largest slaveholder of the Bluegrass. Eliza and her new owner were driven in Wickliffe's carriage to the home of a friend where her "free papers" were made out.[35]

Slaveholders of the Bluegrass had their allegiance to the institution severely shaken by the sale of Eliza. Abolitionists and emancipationists held it up as a signal example of the barbarity of the slave system, while proslavery advocates contended it was a very unusual case and not likely to happen again. For many months Eliza's sale continued to be one of the main topics of conversation; the affair greatly strengthened the cause of the abolitionists, who within a short time gathered many converts into their ranks.

On a fine spring morning in 1852, a crowd gathered around the old auction block on Cheapside, near the western side of the courthouse lawn, to witness and participate in the sale of a Fayette County estate. First to be offered for sale was a girl Lucy, eighteen years old and handsome, who, as "Uncle Billy" [36] related, "wuz jist as white as you are."

Clad in the slave garb of plaid osnaburg, she was led upon the block and there, before the curious gaze of the crowd, was forced to submit to every indignity. The

35. Calvin Fairbank, *During Slavery Times,* pp. 26–34. Fairbank, an ardent abolitionist from New York, was prominently connected with the Underground Railroad in Kentucky, as related in other chapters. Fairbank states in his autobiography that the sale of Eliza was the "most extraordinary incident" of his quarter of a century of abolition activities in this state. In the purchase of Eliza he represented Salmon P. Chase, later Lincoln's secretary of the treasury, and Nicholas Longworth, of Cincinnati, who had authorized him to bid as high as $25,000 if necessary.

36. Lucy was the sister of "Uncle Billy" Anderson, a former slave in Lexington, who was over one hundred years old when he died in 1938. "Uncle Billy" vividly remembered seeing his sister sold to a Negro trader on Cheapside. He and his mother were sold privately to a planter residing near Lexington and remained together, but the sister was taken to the Deep South and never heard from.—Statement to the author, September 15, 1935.

old auctioneer, with his customary sales technique, called attention to her graceful body, her genteel manners, her health and even the color of her eyes. Men came and felt her limbs, thumped her chest, looked in her mouth and turned her around, for, after all, she was but a chattel offered for sale.

Finally, after much haggling with the bidders, Lucy was "cried off" to a Southern slave trader for one thousand dollars, as "Uncle Billy" and his weeping mother stood by, sadly realizing that they would soon be forever separated. Such scenes were common in the antebellum days in Lexington, but those most vividly remembered and longest talked of were sales of quadroon and octoroon girls, whose resemblance to persons of white blood made the scene all the more repulsive.

Not since the sale of Eliza at public auction on Cheapside, in Lexington, some ten or twelve years before, had public attention been so focused as on the approaching sale of a similar nature. There lived in Lexington a well-to-do and highly respected white man, the father of two handsome mulatto girls by one of his quadroon slaves. These girls were almost white and were reared in refinement and comfort in the household of their father and master. When they were old enough to attend school, they were sent to Ohio to be educated and later attended Oberlin College. Occasionally they returned to Lexington to visit their father; yet they were still slaves, for under the slave code of Kentucky all children born of slave women were slaves regardless of their father's color or condition.[37]

These girls readily passed off as children of white

37. All children born of slave mothers were slaves and, under the law, were the property of the master of the slave, who, in many cases, as above, was also the father.

parents and were so taken and accepted by the people among whom they resided in Ohio. Years passed. The girls had grown into early womanhood, young and handsome and full of life. They moved in the best of society in the free territory where they resided.

Then came the time when their father died. He had lived in Lexington all his life and during his latter years had, through bad management and ill luck, piled up a considerable indebtedness on his estate. When the young women from Ohio came to Lexington to attend his funeral, they were seized by the sheriff and ordered to be sold under the auctioneer's hammer to satisfy the creditors of their deceased father and master.

Public indignation reached a high pitch over the thought of such a sale. There was much speculation and high hopes that a thing of this sort might not happen again in Lexington, the cultural center of the Bluegrass. The sheriff, however, obliged to discharge his duty under the law, pursued his legal course.

At the next county court day, in the middle eighteen-fifties, Thomas W. Bullock, master commissioner of the Fayette Circuit Court, offered these comely females for sale at the rickety auction block which stood on Cheapside, near the courthouse door.

Mingled emotions of disgust and pity swept through the crowd, causing several spectators to leave the scene. Evidently tenderly raised, the handsome girls, with tears of shame and mortification coursing down their cheeks, tried to shrink away from the lascivious looks and indecent remarks of the traders and spectators standing about. The girls were rudely examined by traders, ostensibly for the purpose of determining their physical qualities.

As the sale continued, there was a pause in the bidding. But the auctioneer merely utilized this opportunity to further accentuate and display the fine and beautiful features of the girls. After much spirited bidding, they were "knocked down" at a high price to a gambler from Louisiana who took them South as "fancy girls" and, later, sold them for a good profit as prospective mistresses to a very "discriminating" buyer in old New Orleans.[38]

Senator Orville H. Browning, a Kentuckian who had lived in free territory for a number of years, revisited Lexington in 1854, where he saw "a negro man sold at public auction in the court-house yard." Such a scene was nothing more than an everyday occurrence to most residents of the slaveholding Bluegrass, but to this former Kentuckian it presented a most repellent picture. "Although I am not sensible of any change in my views upon the abstract question of slavery," he wrote, "many of its features that are no longer familiar make a more vivid impression of wrong than they did before I lived away from the influence of the institution." [39] True it was, as Browning found, that living in the midst of slavery and witnessing these sales almost daily caused persons to become hardened to the practice and less conscious of the evils of the institution. To visitors unfamiliar with these happenings, however, they brought out the most inhuman aspect of the whole system of Negro bondage.

There were many curious incidents connected with the auction block on Cheapside. William M. Pratt, a Baptist minister, recorded in his diary the circum-

38. Recollections of Judge George B. Kinkead, of Lexington, statement to the author, March 10, 1938.

39. *The Diary of Orville H. Browning*, I, 138–39, entry of May 8, 1854.

stances surrounding the sale of George DuPuy, the colored minister of the Pleasant Green Baptist Church. George was the slave and property of the late Reverend Lewis Craig, who died in the year 1847, but whose estate was not finally settled until 1856.

George had been permitted to preach at the Pleasant Green Church, in Lexington, after the Reverend Lewis Craig's death, but when the estate of his master was advertised for sale, he was also listed. Members of George's church importuned William Pratt to buy their preacher at the forthcoming sale, the Negroes promising to pay for him in weekly installments.

An agreement was reached between the deacons of the white and colored Baptist churches as to the conditions of the purchase of the thirty-two-year-old colored minister. It was agreed by the white deacons that they would purchase George, provided the sale price did not exceed eight hundred dollars. However, upon examination, this slave preacher was found to be worth more than the sum agreed upon. On the night before the sale, the white deacons argued for a long time with the tenacious auctioneer before they could persuade him to sacrifice George at the stipulated price. Next morning at the auction block, as the auctioneer, one Taylor, was about to terminate the sale at $800, a "nigger-trader" stepped in and ran the bid up. At last, however, the slave preacher was "struck off" to Mr. Pratt for eight hundred and thirty dollars.

George's congregation was much elated over its purchase, a transaction which saved their devoted minister from the Southern trade. Every Monday morning some of his little flock made a journey to the Pratt residence to deposit the collections of the preceding Sunday's services.[40]

On another occasion, several years later, the Reverend William Pratt was approached by Nancy Lee, a slave, who was in great distress because her two daughters were doomed to be sold, and most likely to be taken South. Tony Lee, the father of the girls, had been successful in purchasing their freedom and, just before his death, turned over the papers to them. Negro traders visited Nancy, the mother, and through a ruse secured the daughters' "free papers" and destroyed them. The girls were then offered for sale at public auction on Cheapside at the next county court day, February 13, 1860.

Mr. Pratt noted in his diary that the girls were "17 and 19 years old, handsome and active," and added, with a note of encouragement, that friends of the old Negro woman "had seen negro traders and had persuaded some of them not to bid on the girls."

As Letty, the oldest girl, was first offered for sale, the Baptist preacher opened the bid with $800. Some one bid higher. Pratt continued his bidding until one thousand dollars had been reached. Then, the Baptist divine stepped upon the auction block, explained the situation and begged the bidders to withdraw, but, when the bidding was resumed, the traders ran the price of Letty up to $1700, and the girl was "knocked down" to the Lexington slave-trading firm of Northcutt, Marshall & Company.

When the second girl was put on the block, she was

40. Entry of January 1, 1856, manuscript diary of the Reverend William M. Pratt, pastor of the First Baptist Church, Lexington, in the University of Kentucky Library.

"bid off" in the same manner for $1600 by a slave dealer from Covington. "Such scenes are shocking to our moral natures," lamented Mr. Pratt, "if God's curse does not rest on that concern [Negro traders], then I am no prophet. Negro traders are the greatest curse to our land, and I do wish the city council would impose such a tax as to drive them from our midst. . . ." [41]

Despite adverse public sentiment, however, slave sales continued and "nigger traders" of Kentucky plied their infamous traffic in human beings until well into the Civil War period.[42] As late as the summer of 1864, when it seemed apparent to many that the Confederate States were doomed, there was an occasional slave sale made by some commissioner in the settlement of an estate. Even though slave values had depreciated to almost nothing, there were those, nevertheless, who still believed the institution would survive, or, if emancipation was enforced by law, that compensation would be paid for the liberated slaves, and human chattels were now and then offered on the Lexington market:

> "FOR SALE—8 likely negroes, consisting of two women, both likely and good cooks, one ironer and washer, one boy 13 or 14 years—balance younger children of both sexes—all healthy; of good family and likely." [43]

By the end of 1864, slavery in Kentucky was completely demoralized, although not yet legally abol-

41. Pratt Diary, entry of February 13, 1860.

42. "Negro men are a drug on the market this year. Not one half of them for hire have found homes, and those that were hired out got but low wages compared to the past and former years."—*Mt. Sterling Whig*, January 10, 1862.

43. *Lexington Observer & Reporter*, July 8, 1864.

ished.[44] There was no longer any buying or selling of Negroes. Long coffles of slaves bound for the Southern markets had disappeared forever; iron-barred "coops" and slave pens of the traders stood empty, and the old auction block, for years the scene of many of the darkest spectacles of Kentucky slavery, was no longer a familiar sight to those who passed along the public square.

44. Slavery was not legally abolished in Kentucky until December 18, 1865, when twenty-seven of the thirty-six states ratified the Thirteenth Amendment. Lincoln's celebrated Emancipation Proclamation, issued January 1, 1863, applied *only* to the states in rebellion.

CHAPTER VI

"NIGGAH TRADAHS"

As time went on, it became more and more apparent that the holding of slaves in Kentucky was unprofitable. Slaves had been found useful in clearing the lands, building homes and in other work incidental to the opening of a new country, but cotton, the crop for which slave labor was best suited, was not being produced in Kentucky in merchantable quantities. At the same time the number of slaves increased rapidly, and their disposal without financial loss became the one big problem to the Kentucky slave owner.

Several factors, however, helped to absorb the ever-expanding slave population in Kentucky, which by 1810 numbered fully eighty thousand. After the War of 1812 the Southern states of Mississippi, Alabama and Louisiana underwent a rapid change, and by 1820 much slave labor was needed for clearing the wooded lands preparatory to cane and cotton culture. Along with this rapid development in the South came a decided decline in the price of tobacco, while cotton and sugar prices rapidly rose.[1]

Numerous families of Kentucky, now thoroughly

1. *De Bow's Review,* XI, 69, 70–75.

convinced that slave labor did not pay,[2] moved South to the recently opened up and comparatively cheap lands, where they expected to build their fortunes in the cotton and sugar-cane industry. These planters took their slaves from Kentucky to the lower cotton belt, but in most cases found them to be insufficient in numbers to operate properly the larger plantations, which obviously required an enlarged supply from their home state. When Texas was admitted into the Union, in 1845, it greatly expanded the area of the cotton belt, and caused many wealth-seeking Kentucky families to settle there, and this, of itself, precipitated an increased demand for slaves.

Dr. Jefferson J. Polk, a prominent slaveholder of Boyle County, noted the effects these conditions had upon the extension and perpetuation of slavery. "The love of gain stifled conscience," wrote this Danville physician, "and men professing godliness, who, but a short time before were almost persuaded to emancipate their slaves, emigrated to the newly acquired territories, taking their negroes with them to raise sugar and cotton." [3]

Negro trading in Kentucky was a constantly growing evil, which had begun with the comparatively innocent buying and selling of slaves by the individual owners to satisfy their own needs or desires. By degrees, as the importance of slave labor increased in the South,[4] the

2. Warner L. Underwood, a prominent slaveholder of Warren County, moved to Mississippi in 1833, as he recorded in his diary, "to place my negroes where they could be rendered profitable in cultivating cotton, for they were entirely unprofitable in Kentucky."—Underwood Diary, entry of April 17, 1833, in the Western Kentucky State Teachers College.

3. *Autobiography,* p. 151.

4. The invention and perfection of Eli Whitney's cotton gin enabled cotton planters to realize much larger profits from their crops. Cheap lands

trade grew; men took up slave trading as a business, and slave owners in the border states began to breed slaves for the Southern markets.[5] Although the domestic slave trade was never illegal, it was strongly opposed, mainly on account of the cruelty often attending it and the growing conviction that, unless such traffic was prohibited, slavery would never be abolished.

It is difficult to ascertain how many slave dealers, or "nigger traders" operated during the early years of this commonwealth, for few of them came out in the open and advertised their business. Edward Stone, who lived in the delightful old house known as "The Grange," four miles north of Paris on the old Limestone Road (Maysville), was one of the earliest to notify the public that he was in the "nigger trading" business:

> "CASH FOR NEGROES!
>
> "I wish to purchase TWENTY NEGROES, BOYS & GIRLS from 10 to 25 years of age. A liberal price will be given for those answering the description on early application to the subscriber.
> EDWARD STONE,
> Living on the Limestone Road, 4 miles from Paris leading to Millersburg."[6]

Just when Kentucky's slave trade with the Cotton Kingdom began is not definitely known, but, as early as 1818, Fearon, the English traveler, noted having seen fourteen flatboats loaded with Kentucky slaves on their

---

and the high prices of cotton created an urgent demand for Negro cotton hands.

5. Alice D. Adams, *The Neglected Period of Anti-Slavery in America, 1808–1831,* p. 196. In 1808 Congress outlawed the African slave trade, and after 1820 it was punishable as piracy, but the right to buy and sell slaves within the United States, and to transport them from one state to another, remained unimpaired.

6. *Western Citizen,* July 24, 1816.

way down the Mississippi River to Southern markets.[7] Estwick Evans, while visiting in the South during the same year, observed the growing traffic in slaves: "They are the subject of continual speculation and are daily brought together with other live-stock from Kentucky and other places to Natchez and the New Orleans markets." [8]

Four years later, in 1822, the Reverend James H. Dickey, traveling on the road from Paris to Lexington, encountered a coffle of slaves: "Having passed through Paris, in Bourbon County, Kentucky, the sound of music, (beyond a little rising of ground) attracted my attention; I looked forward and saw the flag of my country waving. Supposing I was about to meet a military parade, I drove hastily to the side of the road; and, having gained the top of the ascent, I discovered, I suppose, about forty black men, all chained together after the following manner: Each of them was handcuffed, and they were arranged in rank and file.

"A chain perhaps forty feet long, the size of a fifth-horse chain, was stretched between the two ranks, to which short chains were joined which connected with the handcuffs. Behind them were, I suppose, about thirty women, in double rank, the couples tied hand to hand. A solemn sadness sat on every countenance, and the dismal silence of this march of despair was interrupted only by the sound of two violins; yes, as if to add insult to injury, the foremost couple were furnished with a violin apiece; the second couple were ornamented with cockades; while near the center waved the republican flag, carried by a hand *literally in chains.*

7. Henry B. Fearon, *Sketches of America,* p. 286.
8. *A Pedestrious Tour,* p. 216.

. . ." [9] These slaves, as the traveling divine later learned, belonged to the "nigger trader" Edward Stone, and were on their way to Paris to be joined with a larger coffle being collected for a shipment to the Southern markets, probably New Orleans.[10]

Writing under the pen name of "Philanthropist," a Bourbon County planter described through the columns of the *Western Citizen* a "revolting spectacle" he had recently witnessed in Paris. "I mean," said he, "the diabolical, damning practice of SOUL PEDLING, or the purchase of negroes and driving them like brutes to [the Southern] market. This is a kind of business commenced at first on a moderate scale, in Kentucky, but now grown so enormously as to become truly alarming. Oh conscience! Has remorse totally lost its sting?" [11]

Court day in Paris, September 17, 1822. Those who visited the county seat on that busy day saw "between seventy-five and one hundred miserable wretches galling under the yoke of despots, doomed to leave their homes, their country and loved ones, rendered dear to them by the strongest ties of nature, from the earliest dawn of life."

Chained and closely guarded, "these slaves," as the account runs, "were paraded on the public square in front of the courthouse, the seat of justice. Over their heads waved the Star-Spangled Banner, the flag of freedom, the Eagle of proud America over a set of poor unhappy slaves, fettered to misery, to despair, who have

9. *Western Luminary,* Lexington, October 4, 1826; Charles Elliott, *Sinfulness of American Slavery,* I, 292.

10. Stone, this early "nigger trader," collected his slaves throughout the Bluegrass, and kept them in the strongly ironed and barred basements of "The Grange" until a sufficient number could be assembled to start out for New Orleans or other Southern markets.

11. September 24, 1822.

From an old print

EDWARD STONE'S COFFLE GANG

GREAT SALE

of

SLAVES

JANUARY 10, 1855

THERE Will Be Offered For Sale at Public Auction at the SLAVE MARKET, CHEAPSIDE, LEXINGTON, All The SLAVES of JOHN CARTER, Esquire, of LEWIS COUNTY, KY., On Account of His Removal to Indiana, a Free State. The Slaves Listed Below Were All Raised on the CARTER PLANTATION at QUICK'S RUN, Lewis County, Kentucky.

3 Bucks Aged from 20 to 26, Strong, Ablebodied
1 Wench, Sallie, Aged 42, Excellent Cook
1 Wench, Lize, Aged 23 with 6 mo. old Picinniny
One Buck Aged 52, good Kennel Man
17 Bucks Aged from twelve to twenty, Excellent

TERMS: Strictly CASH at Sale, as owner must realize cash, owing to his removal to West. Offers for the entire lot will be entertained previous to sale by addressing the undersigned.

JOHN CARTER, Esq.

Po. Clarksburg **Lewis County, Kentucky**

LEWIS COUNTY SLAVES SOLD ON CHEAPSIDE

never known liberty, save in dreams of the night, or the airy visions of the day. . . ." Clearly indicating the strong sentiment[12] against "nigger traders" was the caustic admonition hurled at those operating in Paris: "May the arm of retributive justice soon fall upon the heads of those aliens from refined society, for the heaven-daring, hell-deserving traffic they are engaged in."[13]

Henry Clay, in a speech before the Kentucky Colonization Society, at Frankfort, in 1829, predicted that the slave trader would prosper, for, as he stated: "It is believed that nowhere in the farming portion of the United States would slave labor be generally employed, if the proprietor were not tempted *to raise slaves by the high price of the southern market which keeps it up in his own* [*state*]."[14]

No aspect of slavery was more objectionable to the great majority of the people than that of buying and selling slaves for profit. To be known as a "nigger trader" was about "the last word of opprobrium" that "could be slung at a man."[15] This "state of opinion," as Professor Shaler observed, was very general "among the better class of slave owners in Kentucky."

Another writer characterized the Negro traders as "miserable anti-human critters, walking on two legs and looking like men, called *nigger droviers*."[16] The business was brutalizing in the extreme. "Nigger

12. Advertisements of slave sales frequently reflected the strong sentiment against the traders. A typical notice read: "Neither of my slaves will be sold to a trader, or to be removed from the state."—*Lexington Observer & Reporter*, December 19, 1857.

13. *Western Citizen*, September 24, 1822.

14. Speech printed in pamphlet form, original in author's collection.

15. Nathaniel S. Shaler, *Autobiography*, p. 36.

16. Philo Tower, *Slavery Unmasked*, p. 249.

traders" were constantly called upon to engage in the separation of families, to enforce discipline under adverse circumstances over slaves who in many cases were selected for sale precisely because they were unruly or hard to manage. Few high-minded men would engage in such a business,[17] and those who did were usually demoralized by its demands. To succeed among ruthless competitors, the "niggah tradah" soon learned to drive hard bargains and became as adept at covering up the defects of his Negroes as ever was a Yankee horse trader in making light of blemishes in horseflesh. In spite of all this, there were those who were willing to endure the odium that was universally heaped upon the "nigger traders" in order to reap the large and tempting profits derived from the business.

In 1833 the editor of the *Western Luminary* expressed his indignation at the sight of a large coffle of slaves passing through the streets of Lexington on their way to be sold South: "Last week, a number of slaves were driven through Main Street, of our city, among them a number manacled together, two abreast, all connected by and supporting *a heavy iron chain,* which extended the whole length of the line. . . ."[18] This "nefarious traffic" in slaves, as the Presbyterian Church denominated it, was a "flagrant violation of every principle of mercy, justice and humanity." Other religious sects of the Bluegrass strongly voiced similar sentiments against the traders.

Much pressure was now being exerted by the antislavery forces to bring about the passage of the Non-

17. "Their admission into society, however, is not recognized. Planters associate with them freely enough, in the way of business, but notice them no further."—Ingraham, *The Southwest,* II, 245.

18. June 5, 1833.

Importation Act, the movement being strengthened somewhat by a recent "Affray & Murder" in Greenup County. Finally, after several years' agitation, this measure passed both houses and was approved February 2, 1833. This "Negro law of 1833," prohibiting slaves from being brought into Kentucky for purposes of sale,[19] with severe penalties for its violation, dealt a heavy blow to the slave trade. "Nigger traders" now had to rely upon the natural increase of slaves in Kentucky for their shipments to the Southern markets.

Under these conditions, together with the great expansion of cotton culture in the South, there grew an insatiable demand for slaves. Certain slave owners in the border states, as a means of building up their rundown fortunes, now turned to the raising of slaves for the Southern markets. Kentucky, along with Maryland and Virginia, came to be known as a "slave-breeding" state, "where as much attention is paid to the breeding and growth of negroes as has hitherto been given to the raising of horses and mules." [20] There lived some miles above Louisville an old colonel, veteran of the War of 1812, whose large plantation was well stocked with slaves. This old soldier was known far and wide as a very cruel and harsh "slave-breeder," selecting, as was his custom, his healthiest and most vigorous young mulatto girls for breeding purposes, in the same way that the basic livestock of the farm was chosen. With

19. Owners of slaves bringing them into the state were required to make certificates stating that their Negroes were for "their own use" and not for sale. A typical one reads: "I, Tobias Gibson [of Louisiana], do solemnly swear that my removal to the state of Kentucky was with the intention of becoming a citizen thereof and that I have brought with me no slave or slaves with the intention of selling them, so help me God."—Fayette County Clerk's Office, Deed Book 18, p. 233, December 17, 1840.

20. Frederick L. Olmsted, *The Cotton Kingdom,* II, 58 f.; Tower, *op. cit.,* p. 53.

new human stock coming on all the time for the markets, this Kentuckian enjoyed a very profitable business and, no doubt, looked upon it all as quite lawful and customary.

As early as 1833 two Lexington slave traders, Pierce Griffin and Michael Hughes, were doing business at Natchez, the chief slave market of Mississippi. From the tax returns of that year, which represented one per cent of the gross sales of all "transient merchants" and "vendors of slaves," it appears that Griffin sold over six thousand dollars' worth of slaves, and Hughes' sales totaled fifty-four hundred and ninety-two dollars.[21]

During the succeeding years many slave traders came to Lexington, which was centrally located, surrounded by, and well connected with, other slaveholding counties.[22] Robert Wickliffe, familiarly known as the "Old Duke" and the largest slaveholder in the Bluegrass, appeared before the legislature in 1840 and severely denounced Kentucky's growing slave traffic with the Cotton Kingdom and its attendant evils.[23]

"We most ardently hope," concluded Mr. Wickliffe, "that for the honor, as well as the security of our state, our next Legislature will put a stop to the abominable traffic. We believe that, generally speaking, slaves are treated with more humanity in Kentucky than any other state in the Union, and could the horrid practice of *driving them like cattle to market* be broken up, a

21. Tax Return, 1833, Robert Bradley, Collector of Adams County, Mississippi, manuscript report, Department of Archives and History, Jackson, Mississippi.

22. In 1840 the ten largest slaveholding counties of Kentucky were: Bourbon, Christian, Fayette, Jefferson, Madison, Mason, Mercer, Scott, Shelby and Woodford.

23. Robert Wickliffe, *Speech on the Negro Law* (pamphlet, Lexington, 1840), p. 14.

great blot would certainly be wiped off our moral character." Wickliffe's urgent appeal to the General Assembly seems to have met with little success in stamping out the "down the river" traffic in human beings, or dampening the spirits of the "nigger traders," who, in many cases, were secretly financed by some of the most prominent men of the time.

Before, as well as after 1840, there were numerous small traders in Louisville and elsewhere in Kentucky [24] who combined slave trading of different kinds with real estate transactions, money lending and the handling of various sorts of merchandise. They did comparatively little advertising and do not seem to have dealt exclusively in Negroes.[25] According to circumstances, they were called "agents," "general agents," "general commission merchants," or "auctioneers." However, many of these small traders gradually developed into the class known as regular "nigger traders" or "nigger speculators," devoting their whole time and energy to the sale of slaves.[26]

In the fall of 1843 the firm of Hughes & Downing was established in Lexington for the purpose of "buying slaves in Kentucky and selling them in the South." Their first venture was the purchase of thirteen "good & likely" Negroes from the central Bluegrass counties, and these they sent to Natchez and sold during the win-

24. "About that time [1845–1855] and for some years prior to that time, negro traders made frequent visits to Henderson en route South, and would remain two or three weeks selling, exchanging or buying negro slaves."—Starling, *History of Henderson County,* p. 195.

25. Buckles & Heran, who conducted "A General Agency & Commission Business" in Louisville, also had "three or four likely young negroes for sale," which would indicate they also dealt in slaves.—*Public Advertiser,* Louisville, February 4, 1837.

26. *Daily Kentuckian,* Louisville, January 1, 1842, *et seq.*

ter of 1844.[27] What these traders paid for their slaves in Kentucky and what they realized on them at the Natchez market furnish interesting comparisons:

"October 1843 First Cost of All Negroes.

"One girl of R. Taylor of Bourbon [County]	$385.00
One girl of M. Berry of Nicholas [County] .	337.50
One girl of G. Thomas	300.00
One girl of Marsh P	350.00
One girl of Stockwell C	290.00
One girl of Either L	360.00
One boy of McKinney at Rich'md . . .	700.00
One boy of G. Watts	520.00
One boy of Evins of Clark [County] . . .	440.00
One boy of Massie C	450.00
Two boys of Either L	860.00
One boy of J. Carter of Nicholas [County] .	300.00
	$5,292.50" [28]

These slaves were sold by the Kentucky traders at the Natchez market during the winter of 1844 at the following prices:

"1844 Hughes & Downing—Sale of Negroes at Natchez,

Ester & Sealy to McMillen	$1200.00
George, blacksmith for	1500.00
Sam for	690.00
Willis & Nicey for	1200.00
Big Peggy for	600.00
George bricklayer & Little Peggy . . .	1400.00
One boy got of Evins, sold for	540.00
Joe, got of Carter in Nicholas [County] .	500.00
One boy got of Massie C	500.00
Jane, got of Either, sold for	565.00
	$8,695.00" [29]

Thus, it appears that this slave-dealing firm cleared about $3,400 on their first shipment of slaves to the

27. Hughes Admr's *vs.* Salem Downing, Fayette Circuit Court, File 1280, January 12, 1853, Deposition of Salem Downing.

28. *Ibid.*, Exhibit 1.

29. *Ibid.*, Exhibit 2.

South, but out of the profits of this sale came the expenses of the trip from Lexington to Natchez:

"Expenses—Hughes & Downing shipment, 1844

"Jan.	5	Jail Fees at Lexington	$51.00
"	6	Passage to Frankfort	17.50
"	6	Drayage	.75
"	7	Clothing in Louisville	46.50
"	7	Shoes 4 pair, & stockings . . .	7.75
"	7	Tin ware & utensils	2.25
"	7	Spoons, knives, &c	2.75
"	7	3 barrels meal, 1 barrel flour . .	7.75
"	7	Candles & soap	3.35
"	7	Potatoes & bucket	1.37
"	7	Beans, coffee & tin bucket . . .	2.07
"	7	Oysters, vinegar & crackers . .	2.00
"	7	Bacon, Oil & Whiskey	19.42
"	16	Passage on Decater	40.00
"	17	Bread & white sugar	.87
"	17	Storage & Agent's board . . .	9.37
"	18	Doctor's Bill on boat	1.50
"	18	Passage from Vick'sbg to Natchez	15.00
"	18	To wood & sugar	.87
"	23	Bread, wood & sugar	.87
"	23	3 Days house rent	2.00
"	23	Storage	1.00
"	26	Nails & brands	.37
"	27	Bill of Sale	1.25
Feb.	5	Expenses & Fees	2.25
"	10	Nails, Brands, &c	1.02
"	17	Blacking, Tea, Meal & sugar . .	1.02
"	18	Coffee 62, Ferriage 75	1.37
"	24	Drayage & Ferriage	1.50
"	27	Passage up the River	10.00
"	28	Passage to Lexington	3.00
			$257.72[30]

Even with the expense account of $257.72 deducted from the proceeds of their sales, Hughes & Downing cleared more than $3,000—quite a nice sum in those

30. *Ibid.*, Exhibit 3.

days for their first slave trading with the Southern markets.

Generally, the profits were much larger on mechanics, such as blacksmiths, carpenters or bricklayers, than on common field hands—as was the case with George, the blacksmith, who brought $1,500 at the Natchez market. However, such large profits as Hughes & Downing realized on their first coffle of slaves sold South were far above the average. "From $100 to $150 profit per head on each slave carried from Kentucky to Natchez" was considered a fair return on a slave dealer's investment.[31]

While Hughes & Downing were at the Natchez "Forks of the Road" during the winter and spring of 1843–44, disposing of their Kentucky slaves to the Mississippi planters,[32] the firm of Griffin & Pullum, of Lexington, was actively engaged in the trade, but on a larger scale. This concern also consigned slaves to the Southern market where Hughes & Downing were trading.[33]

During the years 1840–48 the slave trade in Kentucky was conducted quietly, and there seems to have been little or no public sentiment exhibited against the business. In its methods slave dealing did not differ greatly from ordinary livestock trading, for, when un-

31. *Ibid.*, Deposition of William A. Pullum, of Lexington.

32. "I was living in Natchez, Mississippi, at that time and saw said Hughes & Downing in the city of Natchez. They were trading in negroes. Downing was at the Forks of the Road, at all times, to attend to the sale of said lot of slaves. Hughes boarded at my house and at the City Hotel, spending most of his time in town."—*Ibid.*, Deposition of William B. Forman.

33. William A. Pullum, of Griffin & Pullum, testified that he carried a much larger group of slaves to the Natchez market in the winter of 1843–44 and there saw Hughes & Downing engaged in the same business.—*Ibid.*, Deposition of William A. Pullum.

able to drive a bargain privately, the trader always had recourse to the public auctions. In 1849 the Kentucky legislature repealed the Non-Importation Act of 1833, and slave dealers and "nigger speculators" in consequence were overjoyed, for it meant that slaves from other states could then be brought into Kentucky and sold either in the markets or out of the state. Having set aside the Non-Importation Act, the legislature went still further and passed an act absolving from punishment all those who had theretofore violated this act. This repeal virtually converted Kentucky into an active slave mart for the Southern states.

New traders were now attracted to the "nigger trading" business, and the profits to be gained therefrom caused the traders to disdain social ostracism and to advertise openly. Lewis C. Robards, the well-known slave dealer of Lexington, now carried a standing advertisement in the local papers: "I wish to purchase a lot of merchantable negroes for which I will pay the HIGHEST CASH PRICE. Persons having negroes can find me at the Phoenix (Chiles) Hotel. L. C. Robards." [34]

Other dealers were now moving to Lexington and opening up their stands; James G. Mathers operated a slave jail on East Main Street and John Mattingly had Negroes for sale at Megowan's jail, corner of Short and Mulberry streets.[35] Traders became bolder and competition keener, while newspaper columns were filled with dealers' announcements. The traders were now making the most of their opportunity: "200 Negroes Wanted! —Men, Women, Boys & Girls, from 12 to 30 years of age," read the want notice of J. M. Heady, a newcomer

34. *Lexington Observer & Reporter,* April 19, 1849, *et seq.*
35. *Ibid.,* January 9, 1849.

to Lexington in the slave-dealing business. He significantly added that he would "at all times pay cash and the highest price." [36]

Citizens of Maysville were surprised and somewhat shocked when they saw the steamer *Herman* from Charleston, Virginia, land at their wharf on November 4, 1849, with forty-four Negroes, men, women and children. According to the local newspaper, "seventeen had handcuffs on one hand and were chained together, two and two," and were being conducted through the streets of Maysville "for the interior of the state, under the charge of two regular [Negro] traders." [37]

It is more than probable that this shipment of slaves was on its way to Lexington, which by 1849 had become the largest slave market in Kentucky. The Bluegrass, with Lexington as its center, was still the largest slaveholding section of the state and was more favorably situated for the slave dealers than the river towns of Louisville, Covington, Paducah or Maysville. In these towns the risk of slaves slipping across the river into free territory was far greater than at the inland city of Lexington.

Many slave owners of Lexington and the Bluegrass were carried off by the cholera epidemic of 1849 before they had a chance to make a final disposition of their estates by will, which, in many cases, would have freed their slaves or provided liberally for their protection and welfare. Under such circumstances, many slaves of the Bluegrass were now seen among the traders' coffles on their way to the Southern markets.[38]

36. *Kentucky Statesman,* August 21, 1850, *et seq.*

37. *Maysville Eagle,* November 6, 1849.

38. Peter Gatewood, of Fayette County, provided in his will that none of his slaves should be sold "to negro traders, who buy to sell again in the Southern States."—Fayette County Court, Will Book S, p. 244, July 8, 1848.

By 1848 Lewis C. Robards had attained the position of the leading "nigger trader" of Lexington, and the following year he rented the slave jail of William A. Pullum, the veteran dealer, who gave notice that, on account of ill health, he had leased out his "old stand" near the Bruen House, which faced Broadway with the slave "coops" fronting on Mechanics Alley.[39] To all of his old friends and customers, Pullum warmly recommended his new lessee, who, as he stated, was now ready to "keep negroes by the day or week for anyone wishing to confine them in jail for sale or for other purposes." [40]

Robards remained at "Pullum's old stand" on Broadway through the years 1849 and 1850, where, in his yard facing Mechanics Alley, he kept the common run of his slaves. Here the Negroes were confined in vermin-infested slave pens or "coops," eight feet square, seven feet high, erected on damp brick floors, with small barred windows near the roof and with heavy, iron-grated doors.

Business continued to grow for Robards, and in the spring of 1849 he leased, as a jail, the old Lexington Theatre on West Short Street, where, in the earlier days, Bluegrass society had witnessed the most popular plays of the time. Within two years he had purchased this property, made extensive improvements, and advertised it as "the largest and best constructed building for a jail in the West." He took particular pride in the rooms, recommending them as "large and airy and

39. *Lexington Observer & Reporter,* May 5, 1849. This two-story red brick building on Broadway was used by Robards as a residence, and he kept his slaves in the rear yard. It was torn down in 1902, and the Elks Club building (now Peerless Laundry) occupies this site at 149 N. Broadway, immediately north of the Opera House.

40. *Lexington Observer & Reporter,* May 5, 1849.

neatly furnished." [41] This establishment under Robards' able management was a busy and select slave market.

In comfortable and well-furnished apartments on the second floor of a two-story brick building adjoining the old theatre site, Robards kept what he called his "choice stock" of female slaves. "After dinner visited a negro jail," wrote Orville H. Browning in describing this exclusive barracoon. " 'Tis a place where negroes are kept for sale—Outer doors & windows all protected with iron grates, but inside the appointments are not only comfortable, but in many respects luxurious. Many of the rooms are well carpeted & furnished, & very neat, and the inmates whilst here are treated with great indulgence & humanity, but I confess it impressed me with the idea of decorating the ox for the sacrifice. In several of the rooms I found very handsome mulatto women, of fine persons and easy genteel manners, sitting at their needlework awaiting a purchaser. The proprietor made them get up & turn around to show to advantage their finely developed & graceful forms—and slaves as they were, this I confess, rather shocked my gallantry. I enquired the price of one girl which was $1600. . . ." [42]

Robards' "choice stock" of beautiful quadroon and octoroon girls, of which Senator Browning speaks, was indeed the talk and toast of steamboat barrooms, tippling houses and taverns, even as far away as old New Orleans. Over the mint julep, planters' punch and other potent beverages which make men reminiscent, many short-necked, beady-eyed Frenchmen and

41. *Kentucky Statesman,* May 28, 1851.
42. *Diary,* I, 139, entry of May 11, 1854.

gangling hawk-faced Kentuckians and Tennesseans swapped vivid stories of the "inspections" in Robards' jail, where the "choice stock," stripped to the skin, dumbly submitted to the leering gaze and intimate examination of traders ostensibly interested only in the physical soundness of prospective purchases.

Obviously Robards' "choice stock" was of the class known everywhere as "fancy girls"—prospective mistresses—common in all large markets, but rarely so advantageously displayed. "Except New Orleans, Lexington was perhaps the best place in all the South to specialize in them, for it was a great center or a favorite resort for prosperous horse-breeders, reckless turfmen, spendthrift planters, gamblers and profligates, whose libertinism was without race prejudice. . . ." [43]

Delphia, a handsome mulatto girl of eighteen, was sold by Robards during the late summer of 1854. This female slave, as was the custom, was subjected to a very rigid physical examination before leaving the jail. Her "small hands, tapering fingers and the beautiful proportions of her body" were "commented upon by those present." [44] Robards, in proof of her inspection before witnesses, warranted her "sound in mind and body, and a slave for life"; but, on the trip to New Orleans, in a gang of eighty slaves, Delphia died of "nigger consumption" at Natchez.[45]

Robards was by far the most unscrupulous of all the

43. Frederic Bancroft, *Slave-Trading in the Old South,* p. 131.

44. Griffin & Pullum *vs.* Robards, Fayette Circuit Court, File 1281, January 10, 1855.

45. In the suit that followed over the loss of Delphia, Robards relied strongly upon the testimony of witnesses who had examined the girl in his jail before purchasing her. "We of the jury find for the defendant" was the verdict rendered in favor of Robards.—Fayette Circuit Court, Order Book 37, p. 578, February 22, 1855.

"nigger traders." He often purchased, with the idea of a quick turnover,[46] slightly diseased Negroes, provided their ailments did not appear too evident. This practice frequently brought him into litigation with purchasers, whose slaves later turned out to be diseased or unsound.

In the fall of 1850 Robards sold an apparently strong, healthy female slave for a "piano & $50 Cash," but the purchaser soon discovered that his "great bargain" was subject to the "most violent fits." [47]

During the spring of 1852 Robards sold a young Negro girl, Isva, to David Smith, of Bryantsville, Garrard County, and gave his customary bill of sale: "Received of David F. Smith One Hundred Dollars in full payment for a negro girl named Isva, about 2 years old, yellow complexion, which negro I warrant sound in mind and body and a slave for life and the title I will forever defend. Bryantsville, Kentucky. May 17, 1852. —Lewis C. Robards." [48] Soon after Robards delivered the slave Isva to Smith, she was "taken violently ill and had a shortage of breath." Becoming alarmed at the condition of his recently purchased Negro, Smith called in Dr. Asel B. Davis, who noted that the slave "was pestered with the phthisic . . . a disease that children is very likely to die from." [49] Witnesses were introduced to prove that Robards was up to his old tricks of selling unsound Negroes to his less suspecting customers.[50]

46. "My instructions from Robards during 1855 were to buy any and all negroes I could on time, and negroes so bought were sold as quickly as possible for cash."—Deposition of Rodes Woods, Morgan *vs.* Robards, Fayette Circuit Court, File 1308, July 16, 1855.

47. Marr *vs.* Robards, *ibid.,* File 1197, December 4, 1850.

48. David F. Smith *vs.* Robards, *ibid.,* File 1213, June 7, 1853.

49. *Ibid.,* Deposition of Dr. A. B. Davis, of Bryantsville, Kentucky.

50. *Ibid.,* Deposition of Asa Shropshire, who testified: "Isva was an unhealthy child—she had a swarthy skin and not a natural color. I would not give anything for such a slave."

In another instance, which occurred the following year, Robards purchased a young "copper-coloured nigger boy" named Tom, who, at the time, was "plagued with short hectic coughs." This condition of "nigger fever" was pointed out to Robards by Dr. Rodes Woods, the jail's physician, but it made little or no difference to the trader, for he hoped to sell the Negro before his condition became generally known.[51] With some twelve or fifteen other slaves from the Lexington jail, Tom was taken to Louisville and there loaded on the packet *Shotwell,* bound for New Orleans, where Robards had instructed his agent to sell the unsound Negro "if it is at all possible."

While in New Orleans, Tom was lodged in Walker's slave jail, which was described as a "dry, pleasant and well-ventilated house"; but the slave was by that time far advanced in the stages of "nigger consumption." [52] He was "sickly and emaciated . . . hollow chested . . . skin an ashy color . . . eyes sunk much in the head and of a pearly whiteness," so much so, that he was never offered for sale nor "put in the show rooms at all, while in New Orleans." [53]

After disposing of the other slaves in the shipment, the agent brought Tom back to Robards' jail in Lexington, where he was "soon afterwards removed from a room upstairs to the dungeon." Here, according to the jail's physician, "he was as well treated as negroes generally are," but lingered only a few days in the "dun-

51. Robards *vs.* Shouse, Fayette Circuit Court, File 1288, July 17, 1853, Deposition of Dr. Rodes Woods, of Lexington.

52. *Cachexia Africana,* or "nigger consumption," was a tubercular condition arising from malnutrition and exposure in damp rooms and sleeping quarters with an inadequate supply of bed clothing.

53. Robards *vs.* Shouse, *supra,* Deposition of Capt. James G. Walker, of New Orleans.

geon" and died of "scrofulous consumption." [54] By this deal, Robards himself was the loser, for he had failed to find a speedy purchaser for the slave who he knew was unsound when he bought him.

At Robards' "nigger jail" on West Short Street, Lexington, which, as the proprietor stated, "was regularly licensed by the city," were other slaves sent there to be sold or hired for their owners. Here at this jail, which was known as "a common receptacle for slaves," were posted these rules:

"NOTICE! NOTICE!

"All slaves taken for Sale or Board will be received on the following terms.
25¢ per day board and lodging of negroes.
Commission charge of 2½% on all sales. Rentals 8%.
Clothes furnished at a moderate charge.
Reasonable care taken to prevent escape or accidents—but will not be responsible should they occur.
All slaves entrusted to my care must be at their owners' risks.
As these rules are posted in my office and yard, the pretense of ignorance will not be a plea!

Lewis C. Robards." [55]

One of the slaves sent to this Lexington jail to be sold was ten-year-old Phebe, from Taylor County, who was described as being "sound and healthy and of a dark colour." Her owner, Palatine Robinson, of Campbellsville, instructed Robards to sell her "for not a cent under $450." Notwithstanding these explicit orders, Robards sold this young slave for four hundred dollars,

54. *Ibid.*, Deposition of Dr. James G. Bush, of Lexington.

55. Bayless Exr's. *vs.* Robards, Fayette Circuit Court, File 1243, September 13, 1852.

WHERE ROBARDS KEPT HIS "CHOICE STOCK" OF SLAVES

L. C. ROBARDS,

DEALER IN NEGROES,

LEXINGTON, KY.

PERSONS wishing to Buy or Sell Negroes, will, at all times, find a market for them by calling at my *NEW JAIL* a few doors below the "Bruen House" on Short street.

N. B. The highest cash price will be paid for Young and Likely Negroes.

july 2–81-y

Negroes Wanted.

THE undersigned wish to purchased a large number of **NEGROES**, of both sexes, for which they will

Pay the Highest Prices in Cash.

Office on Main-street, opposite the Phœnix Hotel, and 2d door above the Statesman Office, Lexington.

SILAS MARSHALL & BRO.

March 15, 1859–50–tf

NEGRO TRADERS' ADVERTISEMENTS

and, sending Robinson only part of the sale price, promised to remit the balance as soon as he was able. For this sale Robinson received a statement of expenses which read:

"Expenses of [Geo. W.] Maraman to Campbellsville	$22.50
Board & lodging for Phebe, 28 days . .	7.00
Dressing Phebe & making dress . . .	2.50
Commission of selling at 2½ per-cent .	10.00
Total . . .	$42.00" [56]

Becoming somewhat worried over the balance due him, Robinson, after waiting more than three months, anxiously wrote Robards: "Sir, I am at a loss to understand the meaning of your treatment to me?" Receiving no satisfaction, Phebe's former master again wrote the dilatory Lexington slave dealer: "You stated in your letter that you was willing to settle up like a gentleman . . . when we meet we can talk that matter all over about honor . . . and where we will neither spend ink nor paper!" Their next meeting, however, was in the Fayette Circuit Court, where damages of $119.81 were awarded Robinson at the spring term, 1855.

Robards was continually in litigation over his slave deals, and, as one reads the records, it appears that he used little discretion in obtaining his fresh supplies of Negroes. When he became a party to a lawsuit, he appeared in court with perfect assurance, numerous alibis and plenty of evidence.

This well-known middleman in the slave traffic, however, who had done more business than any other local "nigger-trader," finally failed to prosper, and to satisfy

56. P. Robinson *vs.* L. C. Robards, Fayette Circuit Court, File 1311, March 7, 1855.

one of his creditors,[57] the sheriff, in 1855, sold his jail and five of his Negroes to Bolton, Dickens & Company, prominent slave dealers of Lexington.[58] This firm, with branch offices in Memphis, Charleston, Natchez, St. Louis and New Orleans, had by this time become the largest and most extensive of the Negro traders in Kentucky. Shortly after the purchase of Robards' jail they advertised in the Lexington papers:

> "NEGROES WANTED!
> "We wish to buy 200 likely YOUNG NEGROES of both sexes. The highest cash price will be given. One of us can always be found at Lewis Robards' old office in Lexington. A liberal compensation allowed all persons giving information in the event of purchase.
> Bolton, Dickens & Co." [59]

As early as 1854, this firm was advertising slaves for sale in Memphis and other Southern cities:

> "We will have a large number of negroes here [Memphis] in the fall from Virginia, Kentucky and Missouri. They will stop here for a short time previous to going farther South in order to give those who wish to buy an opportunity to do so. Bolton, Dickens & Co." [60]

57. John H. Morgan, a prominent hemp manufacturer of Lexington, and later, the great Confederate cavalry leader, had financed Robards to the extent of $6,100. "This money," Robards testified, "was used in the business I was carrying on and was loaned and advanced me by the said Morgan for my accomodations."—John H. Morgan *vs.* Lewis C. Robards, Fayette Circuit Court, File 1308, September 21, 1855.

58. Waller Rodes, Sheriff, to Bolton, Dickens & Co., Fayette County Court, Deed Book 32, p. 328. The First Congregational Negro Church now occupies the site of Robards' "nigger jail" on West Short Street.

59. *Lexington Observer & Reporter,* October 22, 1855. Washington Bolton, Isaac Bolton, Thomas Dickens and Wade H. Bolton were members of the firm of Bolton, Dickens & Company.

60. *Memphis Daily Journal,* July 8, 1854.

Their St. Louis notice read:

> "NEGROES WANTED! I will pay at all times the highest price in cash for all good negroes offered. I am buying for the Memphis and Louisiana markets, and can afford to pay, *and will pay,* as high as any trading man in this state. Also those having negroes to sell will do well to give me a call at No. 210, cor. Sixth and Wash. Streets, St. Louis, Mo.
>
> Thomas Dickens, of the
> firm of Bolton, Dickens & Co." [61]

In 1858 the partnership of A. B. Blackwell of Clark County, G. M. Murphy of Nelson County and George F. Ferguson of Montgomery County, under the name of Blackwell, Murphy & Ferguson, appeared ready to buy "good negroes of all descriptions," and this company announced that they were permanently located at "Pullum's old stand" in Lexington, near the Broadway Hotel.[62]

Another dealer, W. F. White, who came into prominence at this time, gave notice to the public through the Lexington papers that he was in a position to do business on a large scale:

> "TAKE NOTICE! W. F. WHITE & CO. have lately purchased the old stand, formerly occupied by Asa Collins as a NEGRO DEPOT where we will at all times, be found ready to PURCHASE ALL GOOD AND LIKELY YOUNG NEGROES AT THE HIGHEST PRICE. We will also attend to SELLING NEGROES on commission, and will BOARD NEGROES at reasonable rates." [63]

61. *The Daily St. Louis Times,* October 14, 1858.

62. *Lexington Observer & Reporter,* August 11, 1858.

63. *Ibid.,* March 27, 1858, *et seq.* This well-known "nigger jail," with its large auction room near-by, was located on the south side of West Short Street, between Broadway and Spring. The John W. Lell building now occupies this site.

Traders multiplied in Lexington to such an extent that by the end of 1858 there were as many slave dealers as there were mule traders. More than two dozen were advertising regularly in the newspapers. Among the more prominent were: Bolton, Dickens & Company; Robert H. Thompson & Company; Griffin & Pullum; Blackwell, Murphy & Ferguson; A. B. Colwell; P. N. Brent; R. W. Lucas; Silas and George Marshall; Northcutt, Marshall & Company; Neal McCann; W. F. White & Company; J. and T. Arteburn; Robert H. Elam; William F. Talbott; J. M. Heady and John Mattingly.

An English traveler visiting the Bluegrass country during this period described Lexington as "one of the largest slave markets in the United States." He considered this market as "the great place from which the South is supplied." As the business of slave trading was a novelty to this traveler, he closely observed all phases of it. The slave-pens, which he examined minutely, fascinated him. After studying "five of these pens," his attention was directed to "one very large slave-pen," where, he afterwards learned, "about one hundred slaves had been sold a few days before," and these "had traveled [to Lexington] by railway all chained together. . . ." [64]

Although Lexington had the best equipped slave markets in the state, there were in Louisville several "barracoons of slaves and slave markets," where, it was reported, "some of the best quality of slaves may be had on terms low for cash." [65] During the period 1845 to 1860, the more prominent Louisville traders were: John Clark, William Kelley, William F. Talbott,

64. H. Trotter, *First Impressions of the New World,* p. 252.
65. Tower, *Slavery Unmasked,* pp. 249–50.

Thomas Powell, John Mattingly, Jordan and Tarlton Arteburn. The Arteburn brothers aspired to leadership and put out flaring advertisements calling first for one hundred, and then for two hundred and fifty Negroes. These purchases they usually shipped direct to the Southern markets.[66] There were also numerous smaller traders in and around Louisville, less prosperous than some of the above mentioned, who likewise engaged in the "nigger trading" business.

The Reverend Calvin Fairbank, writing from "the market of souls in Louisville" in the fall of 1851, mentioned seeing four slave markets, where "men, women and children are sold like sheep—Garrison's, Powell's, Arteburn's and one other." [67] One of these "nigger traders," Matthew Garrison, was known to "travel through the state of Kentucky," where he bought up "the handsomest mulatto females that he could find, and would take them to New Orleans and sell them for the basest of purposes. . . ." [68]

There was nothing which created as much excitement and fear among the slaves as the appearance of a "niggah tradah" in the neighborhood "prospecting for negroes." Mattie, an eighteen-year-old mulatto of "very fair and beautiful complexion," relates her experiences in Nelson County, Kentucky, during the summer of 1854, when a "speculator" came around gathering up Negroes for his southern shipment.

Word quickly passed down to the quarters that a

66. The Arteburn brothers advertised both in Lexington and Louisville: "100 NEGROES WANTED!"—*Kentucky Statesman,* January 2, 1857, and the *Louisville Democrat,* January 1, 1859, *et seq.* Their office, a slave depot for residents, visiting planters and traders, was located at 12 First Street, between Market and Jefferson, Louisville.

67. *The Liberator,* November 7, 1851.

68. *The Voice of the Fugitive,* February 26, 1851.

"nigger trader" was talking with "Marster." The slaves probably knew from the run-down condition of the farm and their master's ominous financial plight that some of them would soon have to be sold to satisfy his creditors. "Who's gwine to be sole?" the slaves asked one another. "Hope 'taint me," they each exclaimed. Presently all the slaves were assembled in the front yard of the big house. "Here's the gang, and a devilish lookin' set they is," proudly remarked the owner, as the trader began to question some of the Negroes.

After examining some of the prime field hands, the trader made several purchases, and was on his way into the house to receive his bill of sale, when he noticed Mattie, the handsome mulatto house servant. "What'll you take for this yaller gal?" inquired the trader, casting a lascivious look toward her. "I ain't much anxious to sell her," replied her owner, "she is my daughter Jane's waiting maid."

"Wal, as she is a fancy article, I'll jist say twelve hundred dollars, and that's a damn sight more 'an she's actily worth; but I wants her *fur my own use;* a sorter private gal like, you knows." "Well," drawled her master, reluctant to part with his prime mulatto girl, but with his scruples overcome by the good price she was inviting, finally concluded: "I reckon the bargain is closed." "Sold," exclaimed the trader, as he roughly took hold of the girl. "Here gal," gruffly added her former owner, "that gentleman is your new master. . . ."[69]

Sometimes, in an effort to swell further their purses, slave owners were known to exhibit some of the rascality often attributed to the traders. With feelings of

69. Mattie Griffith, *Autobiography of a Female Slave,* pp. 174–75.

disgust, mingled with pity, Lewis Clarke stood by and witnessed his fellow slave, an old Negro called Paris, cruelly "sold away" from his Kentucky home: "A slave trader came along one day gathering hands for the South," wrote Clarke. "Old master ordered the waiter or coachman to take old Paris into the back room, *pluck out* all his grey hairs, rub his face with a greasy towel, and then had him brought forward and sold for a young man. His wife consented to go with him, upon a promise from the trader that they should be sold together, with their youngest child, which she carried in her arms. The speculator collected his drove, started for the market, and before he left Kentucky he *sold that infant child* to pay one of his tavern bills, and took the balance in cash. . . ."[70]

Another prominent "nigger trader" was about to start from Louisville with a gang of one hundred slaves for New Orleans. Among the Negroes were two women with infants at the breast. "Knowing that these infants would depreciate the value of the mothers, the trader sold them for *one dollar cash!*"[71]

Slave owners, commissioners and agents often decreed in the sale of slaves that they should "not be taken out of the state," but some of the more wily "niggah tradahs" secretly evaded this part of the contract by having a farm, to which they would transfer the purchased blacks, keep them there for several months until the transaction was duly forgotten, and then dispose of them as they saw fit, often sending them direct to the Southern markets.[72]

70. Clarke, *Narrative of the Sufferings of Lewis Clarke,* p. 71.

71. Elliott, *Sinfulness of American Slavery,* I, 287.

72. E. R. Dean, a Jefferson County trader, advertised in the *Louisville Democrat,* January 1, 1859, that he wished to purchase a number of good

There were several methods by which the slave traders obtained their Negroes to make up their coffles for the Southern markets. Their principal means, no doubt, was through their agents who circulated all over Kentucky and bought privately. Washington Bolton, of the firm of Bolton, Dickens & Company, wrote his agent James McMillen, at Maysville, on October 3, 1855, to gather up some Negroes for his shipment which was to leave Lexington in a few days for the South: "We must have negroes if possible. Can't you buy the man and wife in jail? Buy every good negro you can and have them here by Friday. If you believe we can make $150 a head profit on the Peed negroes, buy them; if not, let them runaway, but don't let any of your negroes get away." [73] On another occasion Bolton sent his agent McMillen "eleven thousand, four hundred and sixty dollars in money and Eastern checks" to "lay out in negroes" for his firm in Lexington.[74]

While the traders themselves usually remained in town near their jails or Negro depots, their agents traveled extensively over Kentucky, stopping and chatting at the country stores and taverns, loitering, treating and asking questions at the barrooms and tippling

---

and likely Negroes "for my farm use." Some of these slaves, no doubt, were later sold South. James Bentley, of Madison County, sold his "family negro slave" to Ellis Oldham, a trader, with the understanding that he was to keep the said Negro "for his own use" and was "not to be taken by slave dealers to the South." Several months later this slave was conveyed to Louisiana and sold to a sugar-cane planter (Oldham *vs.* Bentley, *Kentucky Reports,* 6 B. Monroe 428, April, 1846). See Helen T. Catterall, *Judicial Cases,* pp. 345–75, for a number of similar occurrences.

73. Pearce *vs.* Bolton, Dickens & Company, Fayette Circuit Court, File 1311, December 10, 1855.

74. *Ibid.,* Bolton to McMillen, July 17, 1855. "There was very little encouragement given the negro trader here [in Todd County]. His business was generally dispised and while the laws gave it a legal standing, society viewed the man askance."—Perrin, *Counties of Todd and Christian,* p. 79.

houses, looking in at the slave jails and talking shop.

They were ever cordial to the slaveholding planter or farmer, whether in town on court days, on the highways, or in the fields, as if specially concerned about his welfare, but at all times they were hoping that he would be forced to sell some of his Negroes. Perhaps some of them had become too unruly to keep, perhaps the planter was facing financial ruin. Little did the dealer care, for the planter's necessity was the dealer's opportunity.

A "nigger trader" was usually described as a coarse, ill-bred person, provincial in speech and manner, "with a cross-looking phiz, a whiskey-tinctured nose, cold, hard-looking eyes, a dirty tobacco-stained mouth and shabby dress. . . ." [75]

Abraham Lincoln, in one of his first great speeches on slavery at Peoria, Illinois, October 15, 1854, addressing his remarks to the Southern people, graphically described the typical slave merchant and the social ostracism which followed the practice of his trade: "You have among you a sneaking individual of the class of native tryants, known as the 'slave dealer.' He watches your necessities and crawls up to buy your slave at a speculative price. If you cannot help it, you sell to him; but if you can help it, you drive him from your door. You utterly despise him. You do not recognize him as your friend or even as an honest man. Your children must not play with his; they may rollick freely with the little negroes, but not with the slave dealer's children." [76]

Although he had lived many years in free territory,

75. D. R. Hundley, *Social Relations in our Southern States,* pp. 139–42.

76. Louis A. Warren, *The Slavery Atmosphere of Lincoln's Youth* (pamphlet), p. 9.

Lincoln had gained firsthand knowledge of slavery in his native state through his visits with his wife to her old home in Lexington. From the front lawn of the home of his brother-in-law, on Short Street, he could easily see the crowded slave pens at the rear of Pullum's jail on Broadway. Just across the street, he doubtless saw the coffle gangs march in and out of Robards' jail and heard the clamorous biddings which so frequently attended the spirited auctions which were held on the premises.

Such were the slave dealers, referred to in the soft, slurring accent of the South, as "niggah tradahs." It cannot truthfully be said that all of these men were dishonest or that the sale of every slave was tinged with chicanery or sharp practice. But inhumanity necessarily inhered to the traffic in men, women and children, and gradually, but inevitably, the dealers came to symbolize the shame and barbarity of an institution which would be washed away only in the blood and tears of a terrible Civil War.

CHAPTER VII

DOWN THE RIVER

SLAVES OF Kentucky and especially those in the Bluegrass, where the yoke of bondage rested lightly, had an instinctive dread of being sold South by the "nigger traders." To them it was genuine terror and justly so. They knew from tales of horror and overwork, told by old slaves and runaways, that to be sold down the river meant separation from their families and loved ones, and long hours under cruel taskmasters in the cotton and rice fields of Mississippi and Louisiana. By 1820 the trade had assumed recognizable form in Kentucky, since the increase in slaves far surpassed the domestic demand,[1] and the mere threat to "sell South" or "down the river" was often an effective correction for the most unruly slave. Negro traders, in the parlance of the blacks, were derisively termed "soul drivers."

Edward Stone, of Bourbon County, was one of the Kentuckians who engaged early in the profitable slave traffic with the South. As early as 1816, he was engaged in collecting and buying young slaves of both sexes from all over the Bluegrass, stowing them in the large,

1. E. M. Crutchfield, of Lexington, advertised that he had "five likely & valuable negroes for sale . . . the only reason for selling is too great an increase in the stock."—*Kentucky Reporter,* September 9, 1829.

iron-barred cellars of his home, "The Grange," until he had gathered a sufficiently large number to set out for the Southern markets. Then, he would dress the Negroes in good clothes, daub the grey wool of aging slaves with shoe blacking, comb their kinky heads into some appearance of neatness, rub oil on their dusky faces to give them a sleek healthy color, occasionally give each a dram to make him or her sprightly, teach each one the part he or she was to play, and start overland for the boat at Maysville on the first leg of the long trip down the river.

After having taken numerous cargoes of slaves to the Southern markets, from which he derived a substantial sum of money, Stone at length announced to his friends that he was going to give up the business of trading in Negroes. Henceforth, he would lead the life of a Kentucky planter on his rich Bluegrass farm. But, having a few surplus slaves on hand, he purchased additional Negroes, enough to fill out his cargo for one last trip South to dispose of this remaining stock, so that he would then be free to retire.

As Stone's flat-bottomed boat was drifting down the Ohio River, with his last cargo of seventy-seven slaves on the morning of September 17, 1826, there was uneasiness below deck betokening trouble. Closely guarding their plan of escape, the slaves bided their time until the boat reached a point near Stephensport, in Breckinridge County, about ninety miles below Louisville, when suddenly they seized their opportunity and openly revolted.[2]

Armed and desperate, they completely surprised

2. James M. Gray, of Woodville, Mississippi, was a passenger on the boat, returning home after having visited his father and friends in Kentucky.—*Woodville Republican*, October 14, 1826.

Stone and his crew of four men. In the bloody hand-to-hand struggle that ensued, the Negroes, armed with billets of wood, axes and knives, killed all the white men on board, weighted their bodies and cast them into the river, and, "after plundering the boat of about $2000 in specie and other valuable property, they sank her; then landed on the Indiana shore, from whence fifty-six of them marched in a body through the country and were apprehended, and brought across the river to Hardinsburg, in Breckinridge County, Kentucky." [3]

The handling of the story of this uprising gives further proof of the prevailing abhorrence of "nigger traders." One Lexington paper carried a caustic article, styled: "Awful Judgement of Heaven upon Slave-Traders," in which their nefarious practice was severely denounced, and in the concluding paragraph related the stirring news of this mutiny in which Edward and Howard Stone of Bourbon County, David Cobb and Humphrey David, of Lexington, and James M. Gray, of Woodville, Mississippi, were all murdered by the slaves.[4] Trader Stone's "body-servant," a yellow boy, Lewis, with unswerving devotion and in the face of great odds, fought for his master to the last, "and narrowly, and with great injury escaped his fate." He was left beside Stone for dead, but recovered and returned to Paris with some of his master's personal effects. For his valor he was liberated, given a small tract of land with a cabin, where he passed the remainder of his days in sight of his master's old home—"The Grange." [5]

3. *Western Citizen,* Paris, September 30, 1826.

4. *Western Luminary,* Lexington, September 30, 1826.

5. This fine example of Georgian architecture, located four miles north of Paris on the Maysville Road, was built around 1813–1815. Its present owner, Mr. Thomas Drenan, now occupies it. Beneath this house are five

All of the Negroes "that were in the boat when the murders were committed have been apprehended," proudly announced the *Western Luminary*,[6] and five of them, thought to have been the ringleaders, were tried for murder and found guilty at the next term of the Breckinridge Circuit Court.[7] Jo, Duke, Resin, Stephen and Wesley were publicly hanged for their crimes on November 29, 1826; forty-seven of the Negroes were sold down the river as a punishment, while the remainder, thought to have been drawn into the affair with "serious reluctance," were brought back to Bourbon County.

Anti-slavery leaders in Kentucky were now directing their efforts towards influencing public opinion against the importation of slaves. They were prompted by a desire to lessen the evils of the slave system and, if possible, limit the increase of the blacks. Numerous articles discussing every phase of the slavery controversy and letters from individuals advocating gradual emancipation were widely copied by newspapers in all sections of the state. While this widespread anti-slavery agitation was sweeping the state, Negro traders were having a difficult time finding slaves for their Southern shipments.

News of a "most shocking outrage" in Greenup County, in northeastern Kentucky, further inflamed the public mind and clearly exhibited some of the darker aspects of the domestic slave trade. Henry Gordon, a well-known Negro trader of this state, had recently purchased in Maryland about ninety Negroes,

---

or six strongly-barred cellars where Stone used to confine his slaves while awaiting shipment to the South.

6. October 11, 1826. "All of the five men who were murdered have since been found, and decently interred at an old grave yard near the mouth of Sinking Creek, in Breckinridge County, Kentucky."

7. Breckinridge Circuit Court, Order Book 7, p. 194, October 18, 1826.

men, women and children, and was taking them to the Mississippi market. He was assisted by an associate, Gabriel T. Allen and by William B. Petit (or Petett), the waggoner, who conveyed the baggage.

"The men were handcuffed and chained together in the usual manner for driving these poor wretches, while the women and children were suffered to proceed without incumbrance. By means of a file, the negroes, unobserved, had succeeded in separating the irons which bound their hands, in such a way as to be able to throw them off at any moment. About six o'clock in the morning [August 14, 1829], while proceeding on the state road leading from Greenup to Vanceburg, two of them dropt their shackles, and commenced to fight, when the waggoner, Petit, rushed in with his whip to compel them to desist.

"At that very moment every negro was found perfectly at liberty; and one of them seizing a club gave Petit a violent blow on the head, and laid him dead at his feet; and Allen, who had come to his assistance, met a similar fate, from the contents of a pistol fired by another of the gang. Gordon was then attacked, seized and held by one of the negroes, whilst another fired twice at him with a pistol, the ball of which each time grazed his head; but not proving effectual, he was beaten with clubs and left for dead."

Satisfied now that they had "finished off" their white guardians, the insurgent slaves "commenced pillaging the wagon, and with an axe split open the trunk of Gordon, rifled it of the money, about $2400; sixteen of the negroes then took to the woods." Gordon, in the meantime, not being materially injured, "was enabled by the assistance of a woman to mount his horse and flee; pursued however by one of the gang on another horse with a drawn pistol. Fortunately, he escaped with his life, barely arriving at a plantation as the negro came in sight, who then turned about and retreated. The neighborhood was immediately rallied, and a hot pursuit given; which we understand has resulted in the capture of the whole gang and the recovery of the greater part of the money." [8]

Seven of the slaves, six men and one woman, thought to have been the chief perpetrators of the crimes, were tried for the murder of Allen and Petit at the October term of the Greenup Circuit Court, at Greenupsburg. Five of the men—Jesse, John, Hooper, Fisher and Levin—were found guilty [9] and publicly hanged by Sheriff Thomas B. King on November 20, 1829.

Dinah, the slave woman, was found guilty along with the men, but her execution was temporarily respited when it was found by a "female jury of twelve matrons" that she was "pregnant and quick with child." [10] She was therefore allowed to remain in jail for several months until after the birth of her child,[11] but was taken on May 25 of the following year (1830) to the gallows, which had been erected in the courthouse yard at Greenupsburg, and "hanged by the neck until dead." The public indignation aroused by the murders and the trial contributed to the successful passage of the Non-Importation Act in 1833.

Throughout the South the slave markets of this period attracted much attention from the Northern visitors, especially those at Natchez and New Orleans.

8. *Kentucky Reporter,* September 9, 1829.
9. Greenup Circuit Court, Order Book 11, p. 158, October term, 1829.
10. *Ibid.,* pp. 196–97.
11. *Ibid.,* p. 259, April term, 1830, fifth day.

From an old print

SOLD TO GO SOUTH

$1200

TO

1250 DOLLARS!

FOR NEGROES!!

THE undersigned wishes to purchase a large lot of NEGROES for the New Orleans market. I will pay $1200 to $1250 for No. 1 young men, and $850 to $1000 for No. 1 young women. In fact I will pay more for likely

NEGROES,

Than any other trader in Kentucky. My office is adjoining the Broadway Hotel, on Broadway, Lexington, Ky., where I or my Agent can always be found.

WM. F. TALBOTT.

LEXINGTON, JULY 2, 1853.

BUYING FOR THE NEW ORLEANS MARKET

While visiting in Natchez during the winter of 1834, James H. Ingraham, a New England schoolteacher, closely observed the local slave market held at the "Forks of the Road." [12] "A mile from Natchez," wrote Ingraham, "we came to a cluster of rough wooden buildings, in the angle of two roads, in front of which several saddle horses, either tied or held by servants, indicated a place of popular resort." He found that because of runaways, sickness, deaths and an expanding cotton belt there was a continuous demand for slaves, and that many were obtained from the Kentucky and Virginia markets. The "down the river" boats arriving at Natchez and New Orleans, as Ingraham noted, always brought cargoes of slaves, and he estimated that fully seventeen hundred Negroes changed hands that year through the market outside the town of Natchez.[13]

To keep the slaves from escaping while going down the river, extra precautions were taken by the traders and their agents.[14] "On our trips South the negroes were all put on deck of the steamboat . . . they were chained together until we got to the mouth of the Ohio River, when they were unchained." [15] River boats were common and efficient carriers of Kentucky slaves to South-

12. In the early eighteen-thirties this market was known as "Niggerville," but gradually became known as the "Forks of the Road" market. It was located "at the end of St. Catherine Street, in the forks of the Washington and Liberty Roads, and in the early days was almost a mile from Natchez proper."—Letter from Rogers G. Davis, of Natchez, to the author, November 15, 1937.

13. *The Southwest,* II, 244.

14. Jesse Woodruff, of Lexington, wrote "marine risk" insurance on slaves while en route down the river against such losses "as might occur in transit, by death, illness, accident or escape."—*Lexington Observer & Reporter,* July 4, 1855.

15. Hughes Admr's *vs.* Salem Downing, Fayette Circuit Court, File 1280, January 12, 1853, Deposition of S. W. Todd, agent of Hughes and Downing, who carried many cargoes of their slaves from Lexington to the Natchez markets.

ern markets, for once on board a steamboat there was little chance that a slave would be lost from exhaustion or from running away. Although this trade was notorious and the dealers were clouded with social opprobrium, the steamboat companies seemed to have had no scruples against hauling such cargo.

Slaves were well treated and generously fed on their trips, so that they would be in good condition and look their best when they reached the Southern markets. Many shrewd and unscrupulous traders, aware of the fact that younger Negroes were in greater demand, often resorted to various "tricks of the trade" to swell further their purses.

William Brown, a Lexington-born slave, who helped "groom" some of his master's Negroes on their way South, gives an interesting account of their treatment, which, no doubt, was substantially the same as in many other cases. Describing one of his trips down the river on the packet *Enterprize,* he wrote: "There was on the boat a large room on the lower deck, in which the slaves were kept, men and women promiscuously—all chained two and two, and a strict watch kept that they did not get loose—We took on board, at St. Louis, several hundred pounds of bacon, or smoked meat, and corn meal, and the slaves were better fed than at home.

"I had to prepare the old slaves for market. I was ordered to have the old men's whiskers shaved off, and the grey hairs on their heads plucked out, where they were not too numerous, in which case we had a preparation of blacking to color it, and with a blacking brush we would put it on. This was new business to me, and [was] performed in a room where the passengers could not see us. These slaves were also taught how old they were, and after going through the blacking process, they looked *ten years younger;* and I am sure that some of the planters who purchased these slaves were dreadfully cheated, especially in the ages of the slaves they bought.

"We landed at Rodney [Mississippi] and the slaves were driven to the pen in the back part of the village. Several were sold at this place, during our stay of four or five days, when we proceeded on to Natchez. There we landed at night, and the gang was put in the warehouse until morning, when they were driven to the pen. As soon as the slaves are put in the pens, swarms of planters may be seen in and about them. They know when shipments of slaves are expected, as the traders advertise beforehand when they will be in Rodney, Natchez or New Orleans. These were the principal places where they were offered for sale.

"At the end of a week, we left for New Orleans, the place of our final destination, which we reached in two days. Here the slaves were placed in a negro-pen, where those who wished to purchase could see and examine them. The negro-pen is a small yard, surrounded by buildings, from fifteen to twenty feet high, with the exception of a large gate with heavy iron doors. The slaves were kept in the buildings during the night and turned out in the yard during the day. Before the slaves were exhibited for sale, they were dressed and driven out in the yard. Some were set to dancing, some to jumping, some to singing, and some to playing cards. This was done to make them appear cheerful and happy. My business was to see that they were placed in those situations before the arrival of purchasers, and I have often set them to dancing when their cheeks were wet with tears. After the best of the stock was sold at private sale at the pen, the balance were taken to the Exchange Coffee House auction rooms, and sold at public auction." [16] As Kentucky-bred slaves were in good demand, they were soon disposed of, and William and his master left New Orleans to return homeward for another shipment.[17]

Even on their way down South to the much dreaded cotton, rice and sugar-cane plantations, the slaves were usually in excellent spirits and had no difficulty in amusing themselves. This fact is attested by no less an authority than Abraham Lincoln, who spent a part of the summer of 1841 at Farmington, the old Speed home near Louisville, returning to Illinois by water. "We got on board the steamboat *Lebanon* in the locks of the canal, about twelve o'clock M. of the day we left," wrote Lincoln to Mary Speed, "and reached St. Louis the next Monday at 8 P.M. Nothing of interest happened during the passage, except the vexatious delays occasioned by the sand-bars be thought interesting. By the way, a fine example was presented on board the boat for contemplating the effect of conditions upon human happiness. A gentleman had purchased twelve negroes in different parts of Kentucky, and was taking them to a farm in the South. They were chained six and six together. A small iron clevis was around the left wrist of each, and this was fastened to the main chain by a

16. *Narrative of William W. Brown, a Fugitive Slave,* pp. 40–44.

17. Mary B. Harlan, the daughter of a Kentucky slaveholder, in noting these conditions wrote: "The pressing demand for slaves at the Southern markets, and the high prices offered by Southern traders for the more valuable Kentucky slaves, have in many instances led to the hurrying into perpetual slavery those who, if indulged a short time, would have been enabled to purchase their freedom."—*Ellen; or the Chained Mother and Pictures of Kentucky Slavery,* p. 172.

shorter one, at a convenient distance from the others, so that the negroes were strung together precisely like so many fish upon a trot-line.

"In this condition they were being separated forever from the scenes of their childhood, their friends, their fathers and mothers, and brothers and sisters, and many of them from their wives and children, and going into perpetual slavery, where the lash of the master is proverbially more ruthless and unrelenting than any other where; and yet amid all these distressing circumstances, as we would think them, they are the most cheerful and apparently happy creatures on board. One whose offense for which he had been sold was an over-fondness for his wife, played the fiddle continuously, and the others danced, sang, cracked jokes and played various games with cards from day to day. . . ." [18]

Most of the Kentucky slave traders preferred to take their coffles of slaves South in the autumn. The change of climate was generally less injurious at that time; moreover, the slaves reached Mississippi and Louisiana at the end of the planting season, when the plantation owners were better able to purchase, having the funds or credit of their recently gathered cotton or sugar-cane crops.

Slaves were sent South by both land and water.[19] In

18. Nicolay and Hay, *Complete Works of Abraham Lincoln,* I, 177. Lincoln to Mary Speed, September 27, 1841.

19. Mrs. Elizabeth A. Roe, a resident of Lyon County, on the banks of the Cumberland River, witnessed a Kentucky slave trader en route South with a fleet of flatboats loaded with slaves tie up in front of her house and then permit his Negroes, about two hundred in number, to go out on the banks and hold a religious service. "This was a two fold purpose of the trader," writes Mrs. Roe, "to rest up his slaves and give them exercise after having been cramped and chained on board for several days and to make him a popular slave trader throughout the countryside by his act of benevolence!"—*Aunt Leanna, or Early Scenes in Kentucky,* pp. 188–90.

the fall and winter they were usually sent by water; but in the summer they often went overland. The journey afoot, if carefully made, hardened and enabled them to endure the climate of lower Mississippi and Louisiana. Many traders stressed acclimation as an important element in the value of their slaves, since it was generally estimated among dealers that about twenty-five per cent of the slaves "lose their lives when brought from Maryland, Virginia and Kentucky into the cotton plantations and rice swamps of the lower South." [20]

Alfred Wornell, a Bourbon County slave, related his experiences as he went overland from Lexington to Natchez in one of Griffin & Pullum's coffle gangs: "Sixty-three hade [head] of us walked. Dere wuz two wagons an' a amb'lance. Dere wuz only one little chile; de res' wuz men an' women. De oldes' man wuz 'bout 45 and de women 'bout 15 to 25 years. Dey give us meat an' bread an' coffee. Dere wuz plenty of it while we wuz comin'. We started 'fore day an' traveled 'till three o'clock in de ev'nin. We stopped some days to res' up." When asked if the women in the gang were chained, this old ex-slave from Kentucky exclaimed: "De *women* could'n' do nuthin'; had to foller de men. When dey got sick, dey put 'em in de wagon." [21]

On reaching Mississippi, the traders distributed their slaves to the planters by various methods. Some worked through the country and sold privately, while others had fixed headquarters. Outside Natchez was the important slave market already mentioned, known as the "Forks of the Road," with its several low, rough, frame buildings partially enclosing a narrow courtyard. In

20. Elliott, *Sinfulness of American Slavery*, I, 215.

21. Frederic Bancroft interviewed this old ex-slave in Natchez in May, 1902.—Bancroft, *Slave-Trading in the Old South*, p. 287.

front of the market, as Ingraham noted, were usually found the saddle horses of the planters or traders; inside were the Negroes awaiting sale. The entrance of a planter was the signal for the slaves to line up, the men on one side and the women on the other, in approximate order of size. Then they were examined and questioned, but not as minutely as one might expect, for the slave dealers at the "Forks of the Road" were permanently established and warranted their human chattels "sound in mind and body and a slave for life."

At all times and in all markets the price a slave brought depended, in a great measure, upon the general appearance he or she presented to the intending buyer. Slaves may have been well made and physically faultless, yet their value was impaired by a sour look, a vacant stare, or a dulness of demeanor. For this reason they were instructed to look "spry and smart," to hold themselves well up and put on a smiling countenance. They were charged to speak up and recommend themselves, especially when they were getting past the active period of life. A slave had to give his age as his master had told him to state it, or else take the consequences. As a final part of their examination by prospective buyers, they were required to dance, jump, leap and twist about so that the cautious customers might see that they had no stiff joints or other physical defects.

The customary garb in which men slaves were dressed, when in market, consisted of a "fashionably shaped black fur hat, roundabout and trowsers of coarse courduroy velvet, with good vests, strong shoes and white cotton shirts." [22] Female slaves were, for the

22. Charles S. Sydnor, *Slavery in Mississippi,* p. 149. Another observer noted that men slaves sold in Lexington and central Kentucky were dressed in "broad-rimmed black fur hats, old fashioned dress coats with

most part, uniformly clad in plain or striped osnaburg dresses, or in neat calico frocks, with white aprons and fancy kerchiefs on their heads, and, as one eyewitness noticed, "were constantly laughing and chattering with each other in suppressed voices."

Another Kentucky slave related his experiences in reaching the Natchez market: "Jesse Hutsel bought me [in Missouri] an' tuck me back to Kaintucky in 1844. He got in debt an' sol' me to Jake Stone, who lived fo' mile from Lexin'ton. I run'd away from 'im to Bourbon County. I was caught and brought to de Lexin'ton jail. Tom Scott he bought me and put me in his jail in Lexin'ton. Den Billy Pullum he bought me. Him an' Pierce Griffin was niggah-tradahs, an' put me in his jail in Lexin'ton. Pullum brought me down t' Griffin's yahd at de Forks o' de road. . . ." [23]

While many Kentucky slaves enjoyed the benign side of slavery and were well pleased with their lot, they never quite lost sight of the fact that they, too, through some unforeseen circumstances, or the death of their master, might some day find themselves in a trader's coffle gang bound for the Southern markets. Lewis, a Lexington slave, vividly recalled how this haunting fear affected his fellow blacks: "The trader was all around us," wrote Lewis, "and the slave-pens close at hand. We did not know what time any of us might be in them. Then there were the rice-swamps and the sugar and cotton plantations; we had had them before us as terrors, by our masters and mistresses, all our lives. We knew

---

metal buttons, black cloth vests and cottonade pants."—*Lexington Observer & Reporter*, July 4, 1849.

23. Bancroft, *op. cit.*, pp. 306 f.

about them all, and when a friend was carried off, why, it was the same as death, for we could not write or hear, and never expected to see them again." [24]

Then there were the occasional sales of runaway slaves, who, after being confined in the county jail for six months, and not having been called for by their owners, were sold to the highest bidder for their jail fees. Nobody wanted to buy a "runaway nigger," but the slave dealers could take all such into the Southern states, where their traits were not known, and there easily dispose of them along with their other slaves.[25]

While gaily-painted stage-coaches, with their proud and arrogant drivers, plied back and forth over the old Louisville and Nashville turnpike, their passengers often witnessed coffle gangs of weary slaves slowly wending their way to the South. Much of the overland slave traffic between Kentucky and the Southern cotton markets passed over this old highway.

Slave drivers frequently put up overnight with their human cargoes at farm houses en route, and such a scene left a lasting impression upon John Kerrick, who was reared on this public highway in Hardin County. "I remember," he stated, "when I was a boy, one night a gang of slaves were driven up to my father's house at dusk. The slave dealer wanted to put them in the barn for the night, but father was afraid of fire and would not allow it. We had a big haystack outdoors, and all the slaves, men, women and children were chained together

24. Harriet Beecher Stowe, *Key to Uncle Tom's Cabin,* p. 155.

25. William A. Pullum testified: "I think the average expense of buying and selling slaves at the South, including the keeping here [in Lexington] and at the South and clothing and interest on money invested, would be from 45 to 50 dollars per slave."—Hughes *vs.* Downing, *supra.*

and slept on the haystack that night. Some of the women had babies in their arms. . . ." [26]

Many citizens and slaveholders of the Bluegrass must have privately condemned, but gave no indication of being greatly shocked at, the heartless advertisement which ran for a number of months in the local newspaper:

> "TO PLANTERS & OWNERS OF SLAVES!
>
> "Those who have slaves rendered unfit for labor by Yaws, Scrofula, Chronic Diarrhea, Negro Consumption, Rheumatism, &c, and who wish to dispose of them on reasonable terms will address J. King, No. 29 Camp Street, New Orleans." [27]

This notice suggested the awful realities of slavery as it existed in the Far South. In Louisiana, Mississippi and other Southern states many large plantations were operated entirely by hired overseers, whose salaries were regulated by the amount of the net profit on the annual crops. The owners of these large plantations seldom, if ever, visited them, or had any direct contact with the slaves working on them. A shocking practice, inspired by greed, prevailed more or less in these sections. Old, worn-out, broken-down Negroes, suffering from chronic diseases, were purchased in Kentucky for a few dollars and shipped South, where they were mercilessly overworked under the lash of the large plantation overseers,[28] until they literally died in their tracks

26. Dr. Louis A. Warren, interview with John Kerrick, Hardin County, Kentucky, November 30, 1921. Photostatic record in author's collection.

27. *Kentucky Gazette,* Lexington, January 10, 1839, *et seq.*

28. *"Overseers, Read This!*—It will be remembered by the Overseers of Edgefield [S. Carolina], that Colonel M. Frazer has offered a fine English lever watch as a reward to the overseer (working not less than ten slaves) who will report the best-managed plantation, largest crop per hand of cotton, corn, wheat and pork for the present season. Col. Frazer has just returned from the North and laid before us this elegant prize.

in the fields, victims of the absentee landlord system.[29]

It is no wonder then that slaves sold down the river by the "nigger traders" made every possible effort to get back to their Kentucky homes:

> "$100 REWARD—Ranaway from the subscriber living in Cass County, Georgia, a negro man named Jess. He is a dark mulatto, 45 years old, a small piece bit off one of his ears, a scar on one side of his forehead and his right shoulder bone has been broken. The said slave was raised in Lexington, Ky., where he will doubtless endeavor to go." [30]

Another Kentucky-born slave, who had seen the plantation life in the South, escaped, and was thought to be "lurking about" the vicinity of his old home, near Lexington:

> "$200 REWARD—Ranaway from the subscriber in Yazoo County, Mississippi, a negro man named Henry, *his left eye out,* some *scars* from a *dirk* on and under his left arm, and *much scarred* with the whip." [31]

One planter from Mississippi advertised that his slave had run away from him in De Soto County, and that said slave "could read and write tolerably well," and he believed "the negro has returned to Kentucky about forty miles back of Louisville where he was raised." [32]

There was taken up and confined in the McCracken

Remember, then, that the prize is now fairly upon the stake, and that the longest pole knocks down the persimmon. Whip! Whip! Hurrah!!!"—*The Southern Cultivator,* May, 1855.

29. Theodore Weld, *American Slavery As It Is,* pp. 38–40; Clarke, *Narrative of the Sufferings of Lewis Clarke,* p. 84; George W. Weston, *The Progress of Slavery,* p. 77.

30. *Lexington Observer & Reporter,* January 1, 1840.

31. *Ibid.,* July 22, 1838.

32. *Louisville Courier,* August 16, 1859.

County jail, at Paducah, "a negro mulatto man calling himself Jim; says he belongs to Richard Jones, of Marengo County, Alabama . . . he is spare built, yellow color, about 25 years, considerably marked with stripes on his back." This runaway slave, according to the jailer's description, had on "steel-colored cassinet pants, drab waistcoat, cotton shirt, black summer-cloth frock coat, shoes and sox." [33]

Sometimes Kentucky-born slaves, when sold down the river, retained the appellation "Kentucky" to distinguish them from other slaves: "Ranaway from the plantation of James Surgette, the following negroes; Randal, *has one ear cropped;* Bob *has lost one eye;* Kentucky Tom, *has one jaw broken.*" [34] Then there was the light-skinned mulatto slave, Jacob, of Lowndes County, Mississippi, who, as the runaway notice stated, "was raised in Kentucky." He had, like hundreds of others, escaped from some exacting overseer's slave gang in the Deep South and was working his way back to his old home and loved ones. In his efforts to elude capture, Jacob posed as a white man. He wore "a large dark breast pin, blue coat and pantaloons, ruffled shirt, his hair cut in the latest style, light brown, a little kinkey; it is supposed he wears a wig over his hair and has a dirk and pistols about him." [35]

So many slaves brought down from Virginia, Kentucky and Maryland were running off and attempting to reach their old homes that the Woodville, Mississippi, *Republican* and the Concordia, Louisiana, *Intelligencer* published a "Weekly Register," which included

33. *Paducah Journal,* February 27, 1851.
34. *Southern Telegraph,* September 25, 1837.
35. *Lexington Observer & Reporter,* December 1, 1838.

a brief description of every runaway slave in jail in Mississippi, Louisiana and Arkansas. Better facilities were therefore afforded the cotton and rice planters for tracing their fugitive slaves, and in the first issue of the "Register," November 21, 1848, there was a list of forty-eight runaway slaves from three Southern states, a number of whom had doubtless once lived in Kentucky.[36]

Miss Lizzie Hardin, daughter of a prominent planter and slaveholder of Mercer County, near Harrodsburg, relates in her diary the pathetic and gripping story of one of her grandfather's family servants—"that part of his life which I knew was equally dramatic and equally sad." This slave, familiarly known as Uncle Len, "became unendurable to the neighbors," continued Miss Hardin, "and they told my grandfather that unless he was sent away they would kill him. Again the dreaded mysterious sentence 'down the river' was passed."

With sheer devotion to his master, even in the face of the direst calamity that could befall a slave, Uncle Len remained steadfast. "When the negro trader began to bargain for him, he called his attention to his tremendous frame and sinewy limbs and insisted that his master should not be cheated in the price. The sale was made and as Uncle Len went out to meet his unknown fate he picked up a chicken which had been mine and took it with him as a last memento of the family to whom he had given the devotion of his savage nature. Poor Uncle Len! I hope that he found the terrors of those dreaded horrors 'down the river' existed more in his imagination than in reality and that often in the cotton and rice

36. *Woodville Republican,* November 21, 1848.

fields of the South he thought of us as regretfully as we always thought of him. . . ." [37]

Many other slave owners of Kentucky felt the same way when they heard about the sales of old family servants, Negroes who were born and reared on the same farms, who had played and romped together as children and now had grown to be trusted family servants of the household. "It's all wrong, Elizabeth!" exclaimed Mary Todd, "this selling human beings into slavery; think of our selling cross old Aunt Chaney or Mammy or foolish little Mary Jane, or any of our servants. I love them all! It would break my heart. I would feel as if I were selling a member of my own family. . . ." [38]

"So long as the Southern states afford better markets for slaves than even the rich lands of Kentucky," argued Samuel S. Nicholas before the legislature in 1849, "it is in vain to expect that slaves will be generally owned by the small proprietors of our thin lands." [39]

Newspapers of the Lower South carried equally as many advertisements of the slave dealers as did the Kentucky newspapers. Griffin & Pullum, the veteran slave merchants of Lexington, advertised in Mississippi:

> "SLAVES! SLAVES! SLAVES!
> FRESH ARRIVALS WEEKLY!
>
> "Having established ourselves at the Forks of the Road, near Natchez, for a term of years, we have now on hand, and intend to keep throughout the entire year, a large and well-selected stock of negroes, consisting of field-hands, house servants, mechanics, cooks, seamstresses, washers, ironers,

37. Manuscript in possession of Mrs. Blanche B. Bright, of Harrodsburg, Kentucky.

38. Katherine Helm, *Mary, Wife of Lincoln,* p. 51.

39. *Louisville Courier,* March 7, 1849.

> etc, which we can and will sell as low or lower than any other house here or in New Orleans. Persons wishing to purchase would do well to call on us before making purchases elsewhere, as our regular arrivals keep us supplied with a good and general assortment. Our terms are liberal. Give us a call. Griffin & Pullum." [40]

Thomas Foster, of New Orleans, advertised that he was in a position to serve as commission merchant dealing in slaves, and invited his Kentucky friends to visit him at his office, 157 Common Street.[41] Robert H. Elam, of Natchez, was also an importer of slaves from Kentucky, and served as a broker for the small traders from the Bluegrass.[42]

At the "Forks of the Road" another Lexington dealer was doing a thriving business in 1854 and 1855:

> "NEGROES! NEGROES! NEGROES!—We would respectfully state to the public that we have leased a stand in the Forks of the Road, near Natchez, for a number of years, and intend to keep a large lot of assorted A No. 1 NEGROES on hand during the year. We will sell as low or lower than any other trader at this place or in New Orleans. We have just arrived from Kentucky with a very likely lot of field men and women; also, house servants, three cooks and a carpenter. Call and See.
>
> Blackwell, Murphy & Ferguson." [43]

And so, by the eighteen-fifties, the Southern slave trade had reached enormous proportions, heightened to a great extent by the repeal, in 1849, of the Non-

40. *Natchez Free Trader,* October 16, 1852.
41. *Semi-Weekly Creole,* New Orleans, January 10, 1855.
42. *Natchez Daily Courier,* September 8, 1857.
43. *Ibid.,* November 20, 1854, *et seq.*

Importation Act in Kentucky, which threw the gates wide open to the activities of the slave traders. From twenty-five hundred to four thousand slaves were annually being transported from Kentucky to the Southern markets.[44]

The Reverend Elisha W. Green, a slave preacher living on the Lexington and Maysville turnpike in Bourbon County, witnessed a Bluegrass "nigger trader" with "twenty-five or thirty colored men, handcuffed and chained," passing in front of his home, and on another occasion, near Mayslick, he saw "forty to fifty men, chained in the same manner, followed by three or four wagons within which were a host of women and children," all headed for the Southern markets.[45]

"These acts are daily occurring in the midst of us," deplored the Presbyterian Church of Kentucky. "Brothers and sisters, parents and children, husbands and wives are torn asunder, and permitted to see each other no more . . . there is not a village or road that does not behold the sad procession of manacled outcasts, whose mournful countenances tell that they are exiled by force from all that their hearts hold dear. . . ." [46]

It is this feeling of sadness and sorrow at being "sold South" by the traders that permeates Stephen Collins Foster's immortal song, *My Old Kentucky Home*, first published in January, 1853. Foster, who had plenty of opportunity to observe the traffic in slaves, pictures a

44. This figure is at best only a mere conjecture, for the few scattered records extant throw but little light on the volume of this interstate slave traffic. One Kentucky writer, Judge Samuel M. Wilson, places the number of Negroes sold South at five thousand per annum.—Samuel M. Wilson and T. Bodley, *History of Kentucky*, II, 211.

45. *Life of Rev. Elisha W. Green*, p. 2.

46. William Goddell, *The American Slave Code*, p. 39; George W. Carleton, *The Suppressed Book about Slavery*, p. 146.

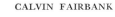

LEVI COFFIN

CALVIN FAIRBANK

Thomas Kennedy House, Garrard County

Marshall Key House, Mason County

WHERE MRS. STOWE GATHERED MATERIAL FOR HER BOOK

poor, luckless old Negro being taken from his home and loved ones and shipped down the river to the large plantations, where:

"A few more days and the trouble all will end,
In the field where the sugar-canes grow.
A few more days for to tote the weary load,
No matter, 'twill never be light,
A few more days 'till we totter on the road,
Then my Old Kentucky Home, good night!"

And, as Foster concludes his song, the old slave, unaccustomed to his new overseer and surroundings, is found despairing of life and pining for his Old Kentucky Home, far away. . . .

CHAPTER VIII

"NIGGER STEALERS"

SLAVEHOLDERS OF the rich Bluegrass section of Kentucky often found themselves in a turmoil with the abolitionists, who "reprobated slavery as the great bane of this fine country." Planters and slaveholders of that fertile section, conscious of the vast amount of money invested in slave property, realized that every abolitionist speech was ominous, and they read the accounts of successful runaways with mounting irritation and dread. Until the early forties, however, slaveholders had experienced little or no trouble with that much despised class, scornfully known as "nigger stealers."

By the latter part of September, 1844, the fall races in Lexington were drawing to a close. Great crowds flocked to the capital of the Bluegrass to see the best horses of the day match their speed and stamina with those of neighboring and distant planters. While gamblers, horse breeders, reckless turfmen and spirited Bluegrass aristocrats mingled at the race track, two antislavery zealots in another part of the city were secretly planning the abduction of Negroes. One of these was Delia A. Webster, a native of Vermont and principal of the Lexington Female Academy; the other a young

Methodist minister, the Reverend Calvin Fairbank, who had recently arrived in town.[1]

Miss Webster, whose school in Lexington stood on the present site of St. Joseph's Hospital, enjoyed a good patronage "of the highest and wealthiest of the city." Here, also, were invited the "humblest and poorest" to participate in the school's advantages "on equal footings with the rich, without money and without price." [2]

Calvin Fairbank, who had preached several times in the city, boarded, as did Miss Webster, with David Glass, Esq., "a gentleman of worth and high respectability," at his home on West Second Street. Here these two abolitionists from the North completed their plans for the stealing and kidnapping of three slaves from their Lexington masters.

As the last race of the fall meet was being run in Lexington on Saturday afternoon, September 28, 1844, Fairbank rented a two-horse hack and driver from Parker Craig, local livery stable operator. About seven o'clock that evening he called for Miss Webster at the Glass residence and, feigning an elopement, they departed in the direction of Paris.[3] But, before leaving Lexington they drove to an unfrequented part of the city, and there, under cover of darkness, picked up three slaves—Lewis, a waiter at the Phoenix Hotel, his wife Harriet, and their ten-year-old son Jo, together with several large bundles of the slaves' clothing.

1. "A man calling himself *Fairbank,* has been about this city and vicinity for two or three weeks past, endeavoring to pass himself off as a Methodist preacher, of which, however, he exhibited no authentic credentials."—*Lexington Observer & Reporter,* October 2, 1844.

2. *Webster Kentucky Farm Association* (pamphlet), pp. 1–3.

3. "We understand that to cover his designs, he induced a young lady of this city to become a partner of his guilt, by a pretense of a runaway matrimonial connection with her, to be consummated at Aberdeen, Ohio." —*Lexington Observer & Reporter,* October 2, 1844.

By hard driving all night, the Methodist preacher and his party reached Washington, in Mason County, about four o'clock next morning, where they remained until the following evening. As darkness set in they drove the four miles to Maysville on the Ohio River and were ferried to the Ohio side by James Helm, operator of the ferryboat plying between that city and Aberdeen, Ohio.

Reaching Ripley, Ohio, some seven or eight miles beyond Maysville, they delivered the three slaves to the Reverend John Rankin, a noted abolitionist and "conductor" of a prominent "station" on the Underground Railroad. Satisfied now that the slaves were in free territory and well on their way to freedom, Mr. Fairbank and Miss Webster retraced their course toward Lexington, hoping to reach that place before they would be missed.

However, news of the abducted slaves traveled fast. Indignant and excited residents of Lexington, alarmed at the loss of valuable slave property by their fellow citizens, set out with determined efforts to run down and capture the elusive "nigger stealers." Miss Webster and Mr. Fairbank were arrested late Monday evening, September 30, as they attempted to pass through Paris on their way home.[4] They were immediately rushed to Lexington and unceremoniously thrown into Megowan's slave jail, located at the corner of Mulberry and Short streets.

There Miss Webster, "defenseless and unprotected," as she claimed, and with "none to extend a friendly hand," was locked in the "debtors' room." On the following morning, in an effort to secure aid in her hour

4. *Western Citizen,* October 4, 1844.

of adversity, Delia Webster, "harassed by persecution" and "assailed by the tongue of slander" asked permission to see "Cash" Clay, noted abolitionist of Kentucky and resident of Lexington. Her request was curtly denied, the jailer's wife scornfully remarking: "You have already had business enough with Mr. Clay in negro stealing. He ought to be in jail himself and will be arrested before night." [5] Mr. Fairbank had the night before attempted to escape from the Lexington jail, but was promptly detected, heavily ironed and thrown into the dungeon of Megowan's stronghold.

Several days later, as the New England schoolteacher looked out of her window in the debtors' room, she saw in the courtyard below old Israel, their hack driver. Stripped to the waist, the old Negro was being unmercifully flogged amid "the most execrable oaths, horrid cursings and awful threats." [6] Begging loudly for mercy as each blow fell on his bare back, the old slave, after fifty or sixty lashes, finally admitted that he had driven the hack from Lexington to Maysville with the prisoners and runaway slaves.

While the prisoners were confined in Megowan's jail, search was made of their rooms in David Glass's residence. Two letters found in the Methodist preacher's trunk gave damaging evidence that he and Delia Webster were secretly engaged in "nigger stealing." One of the letters, signed "Frater" and purporting to be in Fairbank's handwriting, stated: "Miss W will not come away, but will cross the river with us; then I shall have to put these [slaves] on the *daily* or underground line and send them on, till I go back with Miss W." And

5. Delia A. Webster, *A History of the Trial of Miss Delia A. Webster*, p. 18.

6. *Ibid.*, pp. 19–20.

in another letter, Fairbank boasted: "I have been taken up twice, but not here—once by a slave-driver when I was making some discoveries but I pulled the wool over his eyes without telling a lie; and once at Ripley [Ohio] by the abolitionists who suspected me as a spy from Kentucky. . . ."[7]

Evidence as damaging as the letters, together with the confession of old Israel, the hack driver, led to a speedy indictment of the two abolitionists in the Fayette Circuit Court for "aiding and enticing slaves to escape from their masters beyond the state."[8] News of the Webster-Fairbank affair caused considerable excitement throughout the state. Even in Columbus, Ohio, the little Locofoco sheet, *The Ohio Coon Catcher,* in its issue of October 26, 1844, carried the story that "Fairbank and Miss Webster, the negro stealers" are "imprisoned, ironed and manacled *within the shades of Ashland,*" and made it the ground for an impassioned appeal to the abolitionists against Henry Clay.

As Miss Webster reached her twenty-seventh birthday, December 17, 1844, the case for which she and Fairbank stood indicted, was called for trial, with Judge Richard Buckner presiding. Several "first rate lawyers of the highest standing"—General Leslie Combs, Samuel Shy and Madison C. Johnson—represented the Yankee schoolteacher. Fairbank having no counsel of his own, the court appointed William B. Kinkead, of Lexington, to defend him.[9]

This trial attracted more than ordinary notice on ac-

7. *Ibid.,* pp. 53–54.
8. Commonwealth of Kentucky *vs.* Calvin Fairbank & Delia A. Webster, Fayette Circuit Court, Order Book 51, p. 29, October 5, 1844.
9. *Lexington Observer & Reporter,* December 18, 1844.

count of the slavery agitation then fiercely raging in Kentucky, with Lexington as a storm center.[10] Since "nigger stealing" was regarded by the Bluegrass slaveholders as a dastardly and heinous crime, many observers, noting the unusually indignant feelings, predicted that a suitable jury could not be found to give the "vile abolitionists" a fair trial.

On the day of the trial the courtroom of the old brick courthouse was filled with enraged slave owners and curious spectators long before the judge rapped for order. This case was the first of its kind in the history of the county. Led to the bar in the custody of the jailer, Miss Webster, upon being arraigned, "pled not guilty and for her trial put herself upon God and her country." For five days excited men and women packed the circuit court room, crowded the aisles and stood with craning necks in the corridors, as the distinguished lawyers for the defense made a vigorous fight for their two abolitionist clients.

Public sentiment, however, was strongly against the accused. The jury, composed largely of pro-slavery men, finally took the case under consideration and, after remaining together all night,[11] returned into court on Saturday morning with a verdict of "guilty" against the New England schoolteacher and fixed her punishment at two years' confinement in the "penitentiary house of this Commonwealth," at Frankfort.[12]

Mr. Fairbank, who was tried separately, threw himself upon the mercy of the court. In a short address to

10. Cassius M. Clay's fight at Russell Cave Springs, Fayette County, in the year before (August 1, 1843) with Samuel M. Brown, of New Orleans, is related in another chapter.

11. *Lexington Observer & Reporter,* December 25, 1844; *Niles' Weekly Register,* LXVII (December 21, 1844), 256.

12. Fayette Circuit Court, Order Book 31, p. 37, December 21, 1844.

the jury he argued that "he was an abolitionist by education"; that "he had been reared to regard slavery as a crying sin," and furthermore believed that "to relieve men from bondage was a virtue instead of a crime." However, the Methodist divine's views of humanitarianism were at extreme variance with those of the pro-slavery jury, and, as a result, Fairbank was sentenced to serve five years for each of the three stolen slaves, or a total of fifteen years in the state penitentiary.[13]

Soon after the trial Miss Webster began serving her sentence, at Frankfort, and, although efforts were made to secure her pardon, Governor Owsley refused to interfere.[14] "We insist upon her punishment," said the chief executive, "not only on account of the offense she has committed, but because of her sex, which she has desecrated."[15] "Let it be proven," further contended the *Observer & Reporter*, "that the sex of the offender does not alter the character of the crime, or mitigate the punishment. . . ."[16]

However, despite the written protests of one hundred and twenty prominent slaveholders and citizens of Fayette County, Miss Webster, the "petticoat abolitionist," was pardoned by Governor Owsley on February 24, 1845, after having served only six weeks of her two-year sentence.[17] Not unmindful of the charms

13. *Lexington Observer & Reporter*, February 15, 1845.

14. Among the letters received by the Governor was one marked "confidential" from Harry I. Bodley, of Fayette County, who warned him "that the state of public opinion here is strong and decisive against any extension of Executive clemency, *at this time*. The feeling against Miss Webster is *deep & general.*"—Letter dated Lexington, Kentucky, December 26, 1844, original in author's collection.

15. *Lexington Observer & Reporter*, January 11, 1845.

16. *Ibid.*

17. Executive Journal, 1845, I, 73, Kentucky State Historical Society, Frankfort.

of this "pious and much abused woman," Captain Craig, keeper of the penitentiary, felt a strong attraction for her, and there developed, as was charged, a secret "romance" between them. Much capital afterwards was made of this alleged "romance" by Craig's enemies, which resulted, several years later, in his losing the office of warden of the state prison.[18]

While Miss Webster and Mr. Fairbank were awaiting trial in Megowan's slave jail in Lexington, Lewis, the Negro whom they had helped to escape, reached free territory in Massachusetts. Soon afterwards he wrote to his old master, Captain Postlethwait: "I have concluded for the present to try freedom & how it will seem to be my own Master & Manage my own Matters & crack my own whip." [19] Lewis (Hayden) became one of the "busiest station-keepers" of the Underground Railroad, "where he accomodated runaways constantly and sometimes groups of them. . . ." [20]

Two years after the Webster-Fairbank affair, readers of the *Western Citizen* and other Kentucky newspapers had their attention directed to an incident which the anti-slavery advocates of Ohio termed "an outrageous case of kidnapping." [21] For sixteen or eighteen years Jerry Finney, a runaway slave from Frankfort, Kentucky, had lived in Columbus, Ohio, where he posed and was accepted as a free Negro. Jerry's owner, Mrs.

18. In an effort to defend his position, Captain Craig disclaimed any knowledge of an affair with Miss Webster, terming her "a vile wretch, fit for any scheme of villainy, with talent and shrewdness to deceive the most wary."—William C. Sneed, *History of the Kentucky Penitentiary*, pp. 524–25.

19. Original dated October 22, 1844, in possession of William H. Townsend, of Lexington.

20. Wilbur H. Siebert, *The Underground Railroad in Massachusetts*, p. 53.

21. *Western Citizen*, April 10, 1846; *Covington Register*, April 14, 1846.

Thomas Long, of Frankfort, had repeatedly tried to locate him. Finally, word came to her of his whereabouts. She immediately dispatched Alexander C. Forbes and Jacob Armitage to Ohio with orders to bring back, if possible, the long lost and much hunted runaway.

Jerry was "seized without law," complained the Ohio papers, "and gagged and carried away to Frankfort by two Kentuckians." Mrs. Long's agents, Forbes and Armitage, were arrested upon orders issued by Governor Mordecai Bartley, of Ohio, on a charge of "nigger stealing," and taken before the Franklin Circuit Court, of Kentucky, on April 10, 1846. Judge Mason Brown, having been appointed by Governor William Owsley, presided at the hearing and found no evidence that the Kentucky law relating to fugitives from justice had been violated.[22] He therefore promptly discharged the two "nigger-catchers" from Frankfort.[23]

William Johnson, one of the attorneys appearing on behalf of the State of Ohio, argued that encouragement was given, as this trial showed, "to a horde of pirates who infest the waters of the Ohio on both of its banks, and make man-catching a trade. They are to be found on both sides of the water . . . they are the enemies of the human race—men who will steal your slave from you today and sell him to you tomorrow . . . if you were on the southern line of Ohio, you would almost imagine you were on the slave coast of Africa. . . ."[24]

One of the most obnoxious features of the social

22. Judge Brown voiced the opinion that "the prisoners are within the protecting clause of the Act of 1820, and that the warrant of the Ohio Executive does not justify an order for their delivery to the agent of the State of Ohio."—*Frankfort Commonwealth,* April 14, 1846.

23. *Western Citizen,* April 17, 1846.

24. *The State of Ohio vs. Forbes & Armitage* (pamphlet), pp. 19–20.

establishment and relationship in Kentucky was the insecurity of life and liberty among free persons of color. Every Negro was regarded as a slave unless he could produce his "free papers" or other evidences of his freedom. "Color in Kentucky," ruled Judge Walker Reid, "is generally considered *prima facie* evidence of slavery." [25] Taking advantage of these conditions, which they were quick to recognize as a means of evading the law, "nigger stealers" secretly seized and sold back into slavery many free persons of color. And, when thus reduced to slavery, the once free Negroes had little or no recourse through the courts of the land. Although the crime of "nigger stealing" was greatly abhorred and carried with it the penalty of from two to twenty years in the state prison, there were those of unscrupulous principles who were willing to take the risk for the sake of gain.[26]

Levi Coffin, the reputed "president" of the Underground Railroad, lived in Cincinnati just across the river from where slavery prevailed in Kentucky, and he had plenty of opportunity to observe numerous cases of this kind. On one occasion, he writes, in the summer of 1840, a gang of "nigger stealers" stole a light-complexioned free Negro, who had saved his money and recently purchased his freedom. "At night they [nigger stealers] came with a gang of ruffians, burst into his house and seized their victim as he lay asleep, bound him, after heroic struggles on his part, and dragged him away . . . his captors hurried him out of the

25. Commonwealth of Kentucky *vs.* Eliza Jane Johnson, a woman of color, Mason Circuit Court, Order Book 32, p. 129, October Term, 1837.

26. "Look Out for a NEGRO STEALER! $25.00 REWARD! John Birch, sentenced to 2 years in the penitentiary for negro stealing in Trimble County, escaped from the sheriff on the way to the state penitentiary."—*Shelby News,* Shelbyville, October 25, 1849.

neighborhood and took him toward the southern slave markets. To get him black enough to sell without question, they washed his face in tan ooze, and kept him tied in the sun, and to complete his resemblance to a mulatto they cut his hair short and seared it with a hot iron to make it curly. He was sold in Georgia or Alabama to a hard master. . . ." [27]

Although many cases were never known or recorded, the "nigger stealers" continued their nefarious work of seizing and selling free blacks into slavery [28] over most of Kentucky. Proof of this are the numerous advertisements of slaves apprehended and confined as fugitives in the county jails. These notices frequently stated that the Negro "says he is free," or, "claims he is a freeman." Such notices became so commonplace that they attracted little or no attention from the readers of Kentucky newspapers.

William Scott, jailer of Bourbon County, notified the readers of the *Western Citizen* that there was confined in his jail "a negro man, who calls himself Jack Harris, and says he is a freeman." This, as in many other cases, proved correct. Jailer Scott, at the "earnest solicitation" of the fugitive, "wrote on to the Floyd [County] Court where he says he is recorded free," and found Jack's certificate of freedom duly recorded, as he had claimed, in that county.[29]

"Nigger stealing" on both sides of the Ohio River was given a fresh impetus when the Fugitive Slave Law of 1850 went into effect. This law, one of the five passed

27. Levi Coffin, *Reminiscences of Levi Coffin,* pp. 30–31.

28. Even in Biblical times such an act was a grave offense. "He that stealeth a man and selleth him, or if he be found in his hand, he shall surely be put to death."—Exod. 21:16.

29. *Western Citizen,* April 30, May 3, 1848.

by Congress in the celebrated Compromise of 1850, provided that slave owners could go into free territory, claim and seize their fugitive slaves and bring them back into bondage.

Notwithstanding the disposition shown in many parts of the free states of Ohio, Indiana and Illinois to protect fugitive slave settlers, this new law of 1850 spread consternation and distress among these Negroes, causing many to leave the little homes they had established for themselves and renew their search for liberty farther northward, often in Canada. This law wrung from the escaped Negroes a cry of anguish that voiced the distress of the people of this class in all quarters, especially in the free states along the Ohio River. Even legally free Negroes in Ohio, Indiana and Illinois had good reason to fear for their safety, as under the new law, the fugitive, or anyone accused of being a fugitive, was denied the right of trial by jury and his status was determined either by a United States judge or some federal commissioner. This act, moreover, was retroactive or *ex post facto,* for its provisions applied to slaves who had fled from their masters at any time in the past, and it contained what amounted to a virtual bribe, for, if the commissioner decided in favor of the master, his fee was ten dollars, whereas, if for the fugitive, it was only five dollars.

Much abuse of this new law now developed. Seizures of persons across the Ohio River in free territory were taking place almost daily.[30] Operating under the guise of slave catchers searching for fugitive Negroes from

30. Abraham Lincoln wrote his close friend, Joshua F. Speed, in 1855: "I confess I hate to see the poor creatures hunted down and caught and carried back to their stripes and unrequited toil, but I bite my lips and be quiet."—Warren, *The Slavery Atmosphere of Lincoln's Youth,* p. 12.

Kentucky, many "nigger stealers" plied their trade with renewed energy, seizing and carrying back into slavery many Negroes without even going through the formality of appearing before a commissioner to lodge a complaint or obtain a warrant. Many of the fugitives thus seized were persons who had escaped from bondage years before, had married, acquired homes and were rearing their families on free soil in peace and contentment.

Many cases of fugitives thus seized now came to the public attention. In August, 1853, the runaway slave, George McQuerry, of Cincinnati, was "roughly caught up" and returned to slavery in Kentucky, while Addison White, of Mechanicsville, Ohio, was seized almost at the moment he had accumulated enough money to redeem his wife and child out of bondage in Kentucky.

Of all the cases of slave rendition, the saddest and probably the most widely circulated at the time was that of Margaret Garner. Winter was the best time for flight across the Ohio River, for when it was frozen over,[31] the difficulties of crossing were fewer. Simeon Garner, with his wife Margaret and two children, fled from slavery in Kentucky during the cold winter of 1856 and, after crossing the frozen stream at night, made their way to the house of a free Negro in Cincinnati.

Quickly tracing the fugitive Negroes to their hide-out in Cincinnati, the armed pursuers, after some resistance, broke down the door and entered the house. There they

31. Former President Rutherford B. Hayes, who practiced law in Cincinnati as a young man and defended many fugitives, stated that "when the Ohio River was frozen over there was terror among the slaveholders of Kentucky. During the winters of 1850–51, 1852–53 and 1855–56, the river was frozen over and numerous crossings were made, especially at Ripley, Ohio and at Cincinnati."—Wilbur H. Siebert, interview with Hayes in the spring of 1893, record in author's collection.

found Margaret, the mother, who, preferring death to slavery for her children, had striven to take their lives, and one child lay dead on the floor.[32] The case was immediately brought into court, where, despite the efforts made by sympathetic whites, rendition was ordered. On their return to slavery, Margaret in despair attempted to drown herself and child by jumping into the river, but even the deliverance of death was denied her, for she was recovered and soon thereafter sold to a trader who took her to the cotton fields of the Far South.[33]

Numerous instances were recorded in Ohio newspapers where free Negroes of that state were "seized from their own firesides" and carried back into Kentucky slavery. "These biped Kentucky blood-hounds," complained the *Anti-Slavery Bugle,* "traverse our country [Ohio] as they please—search the houses of our citizens without legal warrants—peering even into the chambers of our female inmates. . . ." [34]

During the summer of 1853 handbills were freely circulated on the streets of Covington and Cincinnati warning citizens to be on the lookout for Robert Russell, an "idle, loafish, mulatto," contemptuously described as the "Judas of his race," who, for a small sum of money, was decoying slaves to either side of the Ohio River:

"SLAVE-HOLDERS OF KENTUCKY!
BEWARE THE ROGUE, ROBERT RUSSELL!

"Who absconded from Ripley, Ohio, to evade the strong arm of the law he rightly deserved for misdemeanors in that town. This man is a light mu-

32. *The Cincinnati Gazette,* January 29, 1856.

33. Marion G. McDougall, *Fugitive Slaves,* pp. 46–47; *The Liberator,* February 8, 1856.

34. Quoted in *The Liberator,* December 2, 1852.

> latto, and has betrayed members of his race on numerous occasions. He will as readily take ten dollars from any of your slaves to bring them to Cincinnati, and again take ten dollars to return them to you, as he has no higher purpose than to serve his paltry self." [35]

It was charged in litigation, and not denied, that Lewis C. Robards, the well-known "nigger buyer" of Lexington, was "regularly engaged in the slave traffic, buying and selling slaves and sending them out of the state into the Southern slave states" and "that his jail is the rendezvous for a gang of kidnappers and nigger thieves that operate along the Ohio River, seizing free negroes who live in the extreme southern border of the state of Ohio and sending them to Robards in Lexington." [36]

Martha, five years old and free, lived with her aged uncle near Portsmouth, on the banks of the Ohio River, until one night a band of white "nigger stealers" broke open the door with an ax, and "grasping the wool on the top of her old uncle's head" seized Martha and her six little brothers and sisters and carried them away into captivity, to Robards' jail in Lexington.[37] There they remained to be sold into slavery.

During the winter of 1850 James McMillen, trusted "nigger agent" of Robards, and some of his marauding gang broke open the little log cabin of Arian Belle, a free "woman of color" living in Mason County and, seizing her "secretly and clandestinely in the dead of

35. Laura S. Haviland, *A Woman's Life Work,* p. 136.

36. Martha (Colored) *vs.* Robards, Fayette Circuit Court, File 1285, April 10, 1855.

37. *Ibid.,* Deposition of John T. Wiggington.

night," made off with her and Melissa, her four-year-old child. These unfortunates the agents hurried to Lexington and lodged in Robards' slave pen. Soon thereafter Robards sold them as slaves for life to a sugar planter residing in Louisiana and put them on board the river packet *Sea Gull,* operating between Frankfort and Louisville, on the first part of their long journey down the river. It was only through the assistance of some of Arian's white friends, who learned of her sad plight by the time she reached Louisville, that Robards was prevented from "running her off to some of the Southern states and there selling her into slavery. . . ." [38]

Robards had agents working for him in all the Bluegrass counties and those bordering on the Ohio River —buying and selling slaves, and sometimes stealing and kidnapping free Negroes. Among these were James McMillen, George W. Maraman, Rodes Woods, William Hill, George Payton, Booz Browner, John T. Montjoy, Everett Stillwell, and his own brother, Alfred O. Robards.

Many of the Kentucky slaveholders had their sentiments voiced by the Frankfort *Weekly Yeoman,* which denounced the practices of a gang of Negro thieves and slave dealers who made their headquarters in Maysville, close to the Ohio shore. This gang of "nigger stealers" and kidnappers had connections with the slave dealers in the central part of the state, and unscrupulous dealers like Robards never questioned where the slaves were secured. Once the slave was

38. Arian Belle *vs.* C. C. Morgan, *et al.,* Fayette Circuit Court, File 1196, February 12, 1851. Testimony showed during this trial that Robards, the "nigger buyer," paid his agent $600 to steal the woman and child, later selling them to W. N. Hanna, of Louisiana, for $850.

shackled and loaded on a South-bound boat, he found himself helpless insofar as recourse to the courts was concerned.

On one particular occasion this gang of Maysville Negro thieves broke into a house in Ohio and stole a young mulatto girl. This child told a passer-by in Maysville of her plight and thus aroused the suspicions of the citizens of the town. Upon investigating this story, police found that Lewis Allen and Henry Young, of Maysville, were professional Negro kidnappers. These men threatened to burn the town if the police insisted on making further investigations, and it was necessary to appoint vigilance committees to extinguish numerous fires. During this melee a number of Maysville slaves were spirited away to the central Kentucky market and eventually to the South.[39]

While most of the "nigger stealing" cases were more or less local in scope, there were some, nevertheless, which attracted state and even national interest. Willis Lago, a "free man of color" residing in Cincinnati, Ohio, was indicted in the Woodford Circuit Court in the fall of 1859, for "unlawfully & willfully enticing away" a light-skinned mulatto girl, Charlotte, the property of Claiborne W. Nichols, of Versailles.[40] As was proved, Charlotte agreed to pay Lago fifty dollars for his efforts "in enabling her to escape from her master and out of the bounds of Kentucky." [41]

Governor Beriah Magoffin, of Kentucky, made a demand upon William Dennison, Governor of Ohio, for

39. Frankfort *Weekly Yeoman,* quoted in the Vicksburg *Weekly Sentinel,* December 15, 1854.

40. Commonwealth of Kentucky *vs.* Willis Lago, Woodford Circuit Court, File 415, October 4, 1859.

41. *Ibid.,* Deposition of William Lusby, of Woodford County.

the return of Lago, who stood indicted in Woodford County on the charge of assisting Charlotte to escape. Upon the refusal of Dennison to deliver up Lago, the Commonwealth of Kentucky in 1860 appealed to the United States Supreme Court for a mandamus to compel the Governor of Ohio to surrender the "nigger stealer" to Kentucky authorities. The highest court of the land ruled that, although Negro stealing was a crime in Kentucky where slavery was practiced, such was not the case in Ohio, where man was not recognized as property, nor was it an offense affecting the public safety.[42]

Lago was never remanded to Kentucky, while Charlotte, the twenty-seven-year-old slave of "genteel manners and fine appearance," was never found, and remained to her master in Woodford County a total loss "of the value to-wit, of $800." [43]

All "nigger stealers," however, were not actuated by mercenary motives. Because of purely humanitarian principles, some of them risked their lives and surrendered their own personal liberty that human beings in bondage might be free. John Van Zandt, an elderly farmer "of limited education and slender means," but distinguished "by unquestioned integrity and benevolence of heart," lived on a small farm in Hamilton County, Ohio, several miles north of Cincinnati. As was his custom, Van Zandt drove to the Cincinnati market on May 23, 1842, and spent the night in Walnut Hills, a suburb of the city. At daybreak next morning he met, by prearrangement, a small company of Negroes, consisting of a middle-aged man, his wife, their children,

42. Kentucky *vs.* Dennison, *U. S. Supreme Court Reports,* 24 Howard 717.

43. Commonwealth of Kentucky *vs.* Lago, *supra,* Deposition of Nichols.

the wife's mother, and two or three other persons—nine in all.

This small caravan, the property of Wharton Jones, of Kenton County, Kentucky, had the night before escaped from their master's farm and crossed the Ohio River about daylight. Van Zandt, known to be a great advocate of Negro freedom,[44] loaded the runaway slaves in his covered market wagon and set out for Lebanon or Springborough, some thirty or thirty-five miles northward of Cincinnati.

After traveling about fifteen miles, their progress was arrested "by two bold villains, who, without any legal process, without any authority or request, in broad day, in open breach of the laws of Ohio, seized the blacks and carried them out of the state by force, except as to Andrew, the driver, who leaped from his seat, and escaped." [45]

Jones, the Kentucky owner, promptly brought suit in the United States Circuit Court for the District of Ohio against Van Zandt, the "nigger stealer," for the loss of his slave Andrew, and for the expenses of two professional slave catchers who recovered his eight runaway Negroes.

For the plaintiff, a verdict of twelve hundred dollars was returned as damages on two counts. In addition, Van Zandt was fined five hundred dollars for concealing and harboring a runaway Negro in violation of the federal Fugitive Slave Act of 1793.[46] Finally, after about five years of litigation, the case was reviewed by the

44. John Van Zandt, an important station keeper on the Underground Railroad, was the character of "Van Trompe" in Mrs. Stowe's *Uncle Tom's Cabin*. He had formerly been a slaveholder in Kentucky.

45. Salmon P. Chase, for the defendant Van Zandt, before the United States Supreme Court, December Term, 1846.

46. *Western Citizen*, July 21, 1843.

United States Supreme Court. Justice Levi Woodbury, in rendering the decision, sustained all the judgments against Van Zandt, and further denied that the law of 1793 was opposed to either the Constitution or the Ordinance of 1787.[47]

During the spring of 1850 Thomas Brown, with his wife and family, moved from Cincinnati to Henderson, Kentucky. Here Mrs. Brown kept "a millinery establishment and variety shop," and in addition "made many articles of wearing apparel for both sexes." To all outward appearances her husband contributed to the family support by "peddling his wife's manufactures" on both sides of the Ohio River, for some distance above and below Henderson.[48]

His traveling outfit consisted of "a small spring wagon, drawn by two horses," and equipped "with black oil cloth curtains that could be drawn down tightly," as Brown stated, "to protect his goods from the weather." [49] While the ostensible use of this wagon was the carrying of peddler's supplies, actually the vehicle was employed as a conveyance for running off and stealing slaves.

During the months following Brown's settlement in Henderson County, numerous slaves from that locality and neighboring counties along the Ohio River—Daviess, Union, Hancock—began to disappear in such numbers that the slave owners, alarmed and enraged, banded together for effective action. From the beginning it was believed that "nigger stealers" were re-

47. Jones *vs.* Van Zandt, *U. S. Supreme Court Reports,* 5 Howard 215–32.

48. Thomas Brown, *Brown's Three Years in the Kentucky Prisons,* pp. 1–6. (Pamphlet.)

49. *Ibid.,* p. 7.

sponsible for the missing slaves, but Brown with his innocent-looking market wagon continued to operate, and slaves disappeared just the same.

On May 28, 1854, however, Brown was arrested while on one of his customary peddling excursions, six miles below Henderson, and taken to Morganfield, the county seat of Union County.[50] There he was indicted for stealing five slaves (four women and a child), for, as their owners claimed, "they had disappeared about the time of Brown's last peddling trip through the neighborhood."

At the April, 1855, term of court Brown received a two-year sentence,[51] due largely, perhaps, to the combined efforts of several Kentucky planters, among them Archibald Dixon, who raised five hundred dollars to secure the "nigger stealer's" conviction. Upon entering the "gloomy portals" of the state prison, at Frankfort, Brown found there several other well-known "nigger stealers" from different parts of Kentucky—Doyle who had been sent up for twenty years, Lovejoy for fifteen years, and the Reverend Calvin Fairbank for a like period.

Fairbank, who boasted that he had "liberated forty-seven slaves from hell," was in the penitentiary for the second time, when Thomas Brown, from Henderson, arrived there on May 8, 1855. This Methodist preacher was pardoned by Governor Crittenden[52] after having served a little over four years on the fifteen-year sentence he received in connection with Delia

50. Evansville, Indiana, *Journal,* June 2, 1854.

51. Union Circuit Court, Order Book P, p. 284, May 1, 1855.

52. "On the 23rd, August 1849, the Governor pardoned Calvin Fairbank, a convict in the penitentiary."—Minute Book 1, Governor Crittenden, 1849, p. 138, Kentucky State Historical Society, Frankfort.

Webster, at Lexington. Not satisfied with getting off so lightly, and still believing himself to be an apostle of the downtrodden race, Fairbank again tried his hand at Negro stealing.

He was arrested on November 9, 1851, in Jeffersonville, Indiana, on a charge of having stolen Tamar, a twenty-two-year-old mulatto girl who had been doomed to be sold at auction by her master in Louisville.[53] Henry Bibb, a runaway slave from Kentucky, lamented Fairbank's plight through the columns of his anti-slavery newspaper: "Poor Calvin Fairbank, who suffered several years in the state prison of Kentucky for aiding Lewis Hayden to escape from slavery, has again been seized and is now confined in the same state charged with having aided another slave to escape." [54]

At the February term, 1852, of the Jefferson Circuit Court, this inveterate "nigger stealer" was again convicted, and this time was committed to the state prison for fifteen years at hard labor.[55] There he remained until the Civil War was nearly over, when he was pardoned by Acting-Governor Richard T. Jacobs in the spring of 1864.[56] Calvin Fairbank, Yankee preacher and probably the most notorious "nigger stealer" of his time, with no thought of monetary gain, but, moved solely by fanatical devotion to a cause he thought supreme, served, in all, seventeen years and four months of imprisonment for his abolition activities in Kentucky.

53. *The Liberator,* December 12, 1851.

54. *The Voice of the Fugitive,* December 3, 1851.

55. Commonwealth of Kentucky *vs.* Calvin Fairbank, Jefferson Circuit Court, February Term, 1852.

56. Executive Journal, Governor Bramlette, 1864, p. 53, Kentucky State Historical Society, Frankfort.

CHAPTER IX

FOLLOWING THE NORTH STAR

EVEN THOUGH slavery in Kentucky was known and described as being the mildest form that existed anywhere in the United States, freedom and liberty were often the bondman's uppermost thoughts. After the War of 1812, soldiers returning to Kentucky brought back news that there was freedom beyond the Great Lakes. Many of the slaves catching up these vague bits of information made them the basis of their plans to escape.[1]

For a distance of over six hundred miles the Ohio River bounded Kentucky on the north, separating her from the free states of Ohio, Illinois and Indiana. Once the slaves crossed the Ohio River, they were not only in free territory, but had placed that river between themselves and their pursuers. Most important, however, they were in a region where, for the most part, they could find citizens who sympathized with them and were eager to help them. Because of its geographical location and the many Quaker settlements within

1. Wilbur H. Siebert, *The Underground Railroad from Slavery to Freedom,* p. 27.

it, more slaves escaped through Ohio than any other state in the Union.[2]

As early as 1818 slaves were escaping in appreciable numbers across the Ohio River, headed for Canada.[3] Many of the fugitives knew nothing of Canada or the Northern people. Slaveholders, in an effort to deter their bond servants from flight, talked freely before them about the rigors of the northern climate and the poverty of the soil. They pictured Canada as a cold, barren, uninviting place "where niggers freeze to death." Such talk, however, was wasted on the slaves, who were shrewd enough to discern their masters' real purpose. They remained alert to gather all that was said and interpret it in the light of rumors from other sources.

Despite this gloomy view there were always Negroes with heroic hearts and firm courage determined "to make it for Canada." Many of them had seldom left the farm or plantation on which they were born, and were so completely ignorant of geography and relative distances that they rarely chose the best and quickest way north. The journeys of the fugitives were necessarily long, since unfrequented ways had to be chosen and only part of the day could be used. They traveled by night and were guided solely by the North Star.[4] Every slave who fled from his master in Kentucky learned of the North Star and that by following it he would reach a land of freedom. Trusting to this beacon light before

2. Charles B. Galbreath, *History of Ohio,* II, 214.

3. Coffin, *Reminiscences of Levi Coffin,* p. 107.

4. There was an anti-slavery newspaper called the *North Star* (1847–1863), published at Rochester, New York, by an escaped slave, Frederick Douglass, which gained much favor with the abolitionists.

them as a symbol of liberty, hundreds of slaves successfully made their escape.[5] Hiding by day, the fugitives subsisted on green corn, nuts, berries, fruits, an occasional chicken, a stolen pig or whatever else they could find during their flight.

It is, however, plainly evident that no such numbers could have escaped from Kentucky masters had they relied solely on their own efforts. As Negroes began to disappear and their masters found themselves unable to trace them, they said in bewilderment, "There must be an underground railroad somewhere," and this expression, suiting the popular fancy, became the general name by which the whole system later was known.[6] This Underground Railroad was a highly developed and thoroughly organized transportation system, by means of which hundreds of slaves were surreptitiously spirited northward in their frantic escape to freedom.

Just when the "road" began to operate is not known, but by the early part of the nineteenth century it was beginning to take definite form. Its organization became more complete as the anti-slavery agitation became more outspoken, and by 1830 its members made it their business to receive, forward, conceal and protect fugitives. Its personnel comprised hundreds of men and women who were willing to fight slavery with their lives and property, and, despite the drastic laws which made

5. The Reverend Calvin Fairbank, who helped numerous slaves to escape from bondage, stated: "Forty-seven slaves I guided toward the North Star, in violation of the state codes of Virginia and Kentucky."—*During Slavery Times,* p. 10.

6. The Reverend William Mitchell, self-styled "gentleman of color," related the story of a Kentucky slaveholder who, having lost his slave, pursued him to the banks of the Ohio River, where he disappeared, and exclaimed: "These damned abolitionists must have a rail-road under the ground by which they can run off our negroes."—William W. Mitchell, *The Under-Ground Railroad,* p. 4.

the road illegal, the system grew from an obscure trickle of private humanitarianism into a powerful interstate organization.

As the numbers of runaways increased, new agencies were constantly being established, until from the slave states to Canada a perfect chain of "stations" was arranged, not more than a day's journey apart. These stations were at the homes of discreet sympathizers, many of whom were located in the South. Agents or conductors went to and fro throughout the state, ostensibly in the discharge of business, but really helping slaves to escape, and guiding them with the utmost boldness from station to station on their way to freedom. They devised the most ingenious system for the relief of the weary and disconsolate slave. They knew which riverbanks offered concealment, where the woods were thickest, which hayricks and similar hiding places were farthest from the farm house.

If the worst came, they were prepared to arm the fugitives with an extra pistol or two and fight it out on the spot.[7] They provided them with shelter, protection, clothes and food; gave them surcease from the wintry blasts and escorted them to Canada and to freedom. Such were the workings of the mysterious Underground Railroad.

These stations, located, for the most part, in the homes of sympathetic friends of the slaves, offered more than mere opportunity for a night's rest; they were

7. "On Sunday night last [June 21, 1857] three slaves, belonging to Mr. John Sanford and one to Mr. John Berry, made tracks from Henry County, Kentucky . . . they were tracked to the Ohio River, where the negroes, being armed made a desperate resistance, and one of them, while in the act of shooting one of the pursuers, was shot and instantly killed. The second escaped, while the third was arrested and taken back to Kentucky."—*Cincinnati Commercial,* June 24, 1857.

places where the ill and fatigued might remain and be cared for until strong enough to continue the journey northward. Indeed, some of the stations were elaborate and sensational affairs, with their secret walls, false attics and hidden chambers. The Rothier house in Covington, built in 1815, had an ingenious secret tunnel leading from the cellar to the river, large enough to hide dozens of refugees.[8] Fugitive slaves harbored in this house used the passage to get down to the water's edge and thence across the river into Ohio.

All along the Ohio River were points or stations through which branches of the Underground Railroad passed from Kentucky into the free states of Ohio, Illinois and Indiana. Some of the more important crossing places for fugitive slaves were: Cairo, Evansville, Leavenworth, Jeffersonville, Madison, Rising Sun, Lawrenceburg, Cincinnati, New Richmond, Moscow, Ripley, Manchester, Rome, Portsmouth, Ironton, South Point, Burlington, Gallipolis, Point Pleasant, Marietta, Wellsburg and Steubenville.[9] Crossings were made, too, at other places where the conditions were favorable. At a point midway between Owensboro, Kentucky, and Rockport, Indiana, many slaves crossed over the Ohio River, and went on to the Lakes and Canada.[10]

One of the main routes of the Underground Railroad which traversed Ohio from south to north, and which drew many runaways from Kentucky, began at Ripley,

8. This handsome old mansion at 405 East Second Street is the oldest house standing in Covington, and was nineteen years old when the city was incorporated in 1834.—*Cincinnati Enquirer,* July 1, 1938.

9. From a list compiled by Dr. Wilbur H. Siebert, from his *Underground Railroad From Slavery to Freedom,* letter to the author, August 22, 1938.

10. William M. Cockrum, *Pioneer History of Indiana,* p. 604.

in Brown County, Ohio, on the Ohio River some seven or eight miles below Maysville. The Rankin house on the hill at Ripley was a much patronized station on the railroad for many years before the Civil War, and constantly received fugitives from the south side of the river, sometimes by prearrangement with conductors on that side. The Reverend John Rankin, an itinerant minister, left Nicholas County, Kentucky, after many years of denouncing slavery from the pulpit, and became one of the most rabid abolitionists of his time. It was his home that subsequently became a famous retreat for slaves fleeing from Kentucky. Many a frightened slave, having crossed the river in a skiff under cover of darkness, was hurried by friendly hands into that unsuspected retreat.

Systematic attempts to help fugitive slaves to escape from bondage, cross the Northern states and take refuge in Canada had progressed rapidly, even before 1830.[11] An army of abolitionists co-operated so successfully in running off Kentucky slaves that their masters were, for the most part, completely bewildered and totally unable to trace them. This resulted in arousing and greatly encouraging the slave population as they learned of the successful escapes of their fellows and heard the strong denunciation of Northern abolitionists by their masters, who by this time were sure that the smuggling operations took place underground.

Of course, the most hazardous work of the conductors or agents of the Underground Railroad was performed south of the Ohio River. These field agents,

11. On January 24, 1821, a resolution was presented in Congress from the General Assembly of Kentucky protesting against the kindly reception of fugitives in Canada, and asking for negotiations with Great Britain on the subject.—*Annals of Congress,* 16th Cong., 2nd Sess., p. 94.

who penetrated Kentucky and whispered the magic word "freedom" in the slave's ears, were both daring and resourceful. Some came as peddlers; others posed as schoolteachers, map makers, census takers, real estate promoters, musicians; in fact, any guise that would create a plausible pretext for mingling with the populace, both master and slaves, and at the same time afford a chance to study the topography of the region.

Probably the most common guise was that of a pack peddler carrying a large leather pack on his back with compartments filled with cheap jewelry, gaudy ribbons and miscellaneous articles of wearing apparel, together with a line of pocket cutlery and trinkets that would please the slaves, all priced low enough to enable them to purchase. In addition to these items, the peddler also carried fine linens and fancy dress goods, ribbons, laces and costly handkerchiefs, which were shown to the white people, always visited by him first. Approaching the big house, he asked the master and, if he was not at home, then the mistress, for permission to show his wares to their slaves, usually presenting the lady of the Kentucky farmhouse with some fine handkerchief or choice piece of lace. Generally middle-aged, intelligent and shrewd, the pack peddler had no trouble in getting into the best homes, where he always ostensibly agreed with the opinions or prejudices of the family.

He never failed to pose as an uncompromising advocate of slavery and to all appearances his livelihood depended upon his trade with the white folks. On his trips through the country, which were made every three or four weeks, he became well acquainted with both masters and slaves; likewise with the roads, bypaths, streams and rivers in the territory he covered.

After a while, this agent of the Underground Railroad would cautiously approach an intelligent and trustworthy Negro, and casually question him about his desire for freedom. The Negro, in turn, would be equally cautious, for the mere thought of freedom conjured up visions of pursuit by dogs [12] and armed men, the whipping post and possibly death. But when mutual confidence had been established, the plan of escape covered not only the Negro but as many of his comrades as he could enlist. Traveling long distances at night, the Negro leader conferred with other slaves, and returned to his cabin by dawn with no ripple to break the serene surface of plantation life.

As soon as two or three Negroes were ready to take the risk, a meeting place was arranged for some night during the dark of the moon. From this rendezvous another conductor of the road led them through the woods, fields and beds of streams to the Ohio River, which they endeavored to cross and put behind them as far as possible "before the white folks were up and about." Then these fugitive Negroes would be hidden in an out-of-the-way thicket, corncrib or house of some abolitionist or station on the first leg of their long trip to the promised land.

Next morning when the slaves were found to be mysteriously missing, there would be a great commotion. Everybody, including those Negroes left behind, would be scurrying over the country to find the runaways, and the make-believe peddler with a great outward show of interest would be as busy as any one

12. *The Indianapolis Journal,* May 18, 1856, relates the story of two runaway slaves who "were *hunted by blood-hounds* on the Kentucky side of the river; but in a desperate hand-to-hand fight killed the animals with knives."

hunting for a clue. To avert suspicion he always remained in the neighborhood of the farm or plantation from which the lost Negroes had been spirited away, and would, perhaps, offer false clues for pursuit. In this way a day or so would be spent. Then the master or some professional "slave-catcher" would start an organized pursuit of the fugitives. Seldom, if ever, was a sure clue found, and if it was, the runaway slaves by that time were well within the free confines of Ohio, Illinois or Indiana.

After assisting the conductor or agent to collect all likely Negroes in his community who would take the risk of "making it" for Canada, the same Negro who had brought about the liberation of some ten or fifteen of his fellow slaves would slip off secretly with his wife and children by way of the same underground route.

An elusive and shadowy transportation system for runaway slaves, the railroad was shrouded in a mystery that endures to this day. It bore the aspects of a vast secret service. Codes were used; rigid discipline was maintained; nothing was put into writing that might lead to incrimination or conviction.

"Dear Sir," one of the messages read, "by tomorrow's mail you will receive two volumes of *Irrepressible Conflict,* bound in black. After perusal, please forward and oblige." Or, "Uncle Tom says if the roads are not too bad you can look for those fleeces of wool tomorrow. Send them on to test the market."

Levi Coffin, of Cincinnati, had a secret connection with a certain abolitionist named Jones, in Louisville, who sent him twenty-seven refugees during one spring and summer by way of the river packets plying between

Rankin House, Ripley, Ohio

Rothier House, Covington, Kentucky

STATIONS ON THE UNDERGROUND RAILROAD

A LARGE NUMBER
OF
NEGROES
WANTED!

The undersigned wishes to purchase throughout the year, a large number of

SOUND & HEALTHY
Negroes
OF BOTH SEXES.

FOR which the **HIGHEST PRICE IN CASH** will be paid at his Jail, opposite the County Jail, Short Street, Lexington, Ky., where either himself or his Agents L. C. & A. O. Robards, at all times may be found.

Any letters addressed to me concerning negroes, shall have prompt attention.

Dec. 16–25 6mo. R. W. LUCAS.

Negroes Wanted.

THE undersigned having entered into Partnership under the firm of

NORTHCUTT, MARSHALL & CO.,

For the purpose of dealing in Slaves, and will transact business at the house lately occupied by Jos. H. NORTHCUTT, on **East Main Street, Lexington,** nearly opposite the Woolen Factory of Messrs. Thompson & Van Dalsem. They wish to purchase a large number of

NEGROES, OF BOTH SEXES,

And will pay the highest prices offered in the market. Persons at a distance having Negroes for sale, and finding it inconvedient to bring them to the city, will please address us by mail.

JOSEPH H. NORTHCUTT.
SILAS MARSHALL.
Oct. 21–9–tf GEORGE S. MARSHALL.

LEXINGTON SLAVE DEALERS' ADVERTISEMENTS, 1859

the two cities. When Jones did not accompany the fugitives, he telegraphed Coffin to apprise him of the coming of his human cargo. Sometimes the message read: "Go to box seventy-two at the post-office, and take charge of my letters and papers, which you will find there"; at other times, "Pay forty-three dollars to Dr. Peck on my account"—the numbers indicating the stateroom in which the slaves were stowed away.[13]

Fugitives arrived at the first station ignorant, half-clothed and hungry. Here they were fed, clothed and rested. In order to elude detection from the advertisements circulated through the states, all manner of disguises were provided. Men put on women's clothing; women dressed as boys. For women, the veiled bonnet and plain attire of the Quakeress provided one of the best disguises. Occasionally a light-colored Negro woman, dressed in the garb of her mistress, heavily veiled and gloved, was put into a white railway coach or on a north-bound steamboat. Railway passes, forged or genuine, and tickets marked for recognition by abolitionist trainmen were distributed.

In going from station to station, the men fugitives, unless special caution was needed, were sent forward on foot, and they carried a slip of paper with a word or two that would be recognized at the next stop. Women and children, the more apt to attract attention, were sent along the road in special wagons built with false bottoms, in which they would lie with farm produce spread over them. At the end of a night's journey, another abolitionist was on hand, willing to give food and refuge to the escaping slaves who were fleeing in increas-

13. *Reminiscences of Levi Coffin,* pp. 398–400.

ing numbers by night toward Canada with only the North Star as their guide.[14]

Frank A. Wilmot, self-styled "slave thief and negro runner," relates some interesting views on the Underground Railroad and its methods of selecting various stations along the line. "Agents were appointed," writes Wilmot, "to make collections of money throughout the northern country, to be used in purchasing a series of farms or plantations, lying in a line, known as the 'underground railroad' which ran in a zig-zag course, extending from the northern limits of Alabama, through Tennessee and Kentucky to Ohio. These farms were to be occupied by Northern slaveholders, and were to be the depots whereat the trains of the 'underground railroad' were to lay-to during the day, all travelling on the road being done at night." [15]

While traveling through Kentucky, disguised as "an invalid gentleman seeking health," Wilmot learned that a sufficient sum of money had been collected, that a series of plantations had been purchased, "located at a distance of from twenty to thirty-five miles apart and extending from Alabama to the banks of the Ohio River." The parties located on these depot farms, or stations, were instructed to be as severe as possible on their blacks, to induce the belief among their neighboring slaveholders that, at least on these farms, "there was no sympathy with the negro worshippers." [16] On these

14. William, who ran away from his Kentucky master, stated that on the night of his escape he "knew not which way to go. I did not know North from South, East from West. I looked in vain for the North Star; a heavy cloud hid it from my view. I walked up and down the road until near midnight, when the clouds disappeared, and I welcomed the sight of my friend—truly the slave's friend—the North Star!"—Brown, *Narrative of William W. Brown,* p. 96.

15. *Disclosures and Confessions,* p. 15.

16. *Ibid.,* p. 16.

farms fugitives working their way northward were given shelter and passed off as submissive slaves in order to lull suspicion.

By such means the slaveholders of that community or section of the country were completely blinded as to the true purpose of these camouflaged stations, and whenever Negroes were missing from the neighborhood, none of the parties sustaining the loss ever thought of going to one of the unsuspected stations to find them. "Hundreds of slaves," writes Wilmot, "have thus, at various times, laid hidden in the upper rooms of a depot or plantation house, while the apparently revengeful proprietor of it was in company with the losers, scouring the country in search of the thieves." [17]

The slave drivers and "nigger-catchers," with their whips and handcuffs as evidence of their occupation, were so often seen passing through the country that the underground agents and conductors became familiar with their loud, arrogant and swaggering demeanor and conspicuous style of dress. Their handbills were posted at every village store, crossroads and tavern, picturing the runaway Negro with a bundle of clothes swung from a stick across his shoulder, a description of his age, height and special marks, and offering a reward for his capture. These actions of the Negro hunters more often hastened the flight of the fugitive than assisted in his capture.

As soon as it was known that a slave had escaped, a descriptive advertisement was published by his master in the leading papers of the section of Kentucky in which he lived. Rewards were offered for the capture of the fugitive, sometimes dead or alive; and a vigorous

17. *Ibid.*, p. 15.

search and pursuit immediately followed. Sometimes "nigger-dogs"—bloodhounds—trained especially for this purpose, were put on the trail. Occasionally slaves lost their lives in trying to cross the Ohio River,[18] or in desperate efforts to overcome the hardships of cold, rain and hunger and other obstacles not always known or recorded.

There was Francis Fedric, a dissatisfied slave living on his master's farm "twenty miles back of Maysville" in Mason County, who, thirsting for freedom, made known his desire to one of the underground agents. Later, after arrangements had been made, he met the conductor at a designated spot. "He said but little," wrote Fedric, "and seemed restless. He took some rugs and laid them at the bottom of the wagon, and covered me with some more. Soon we were on our way to Maysville. The horses trotted rapidly, and I lay overjoyed at my chance of escape. When we stopped at Maysville, I remained for some time perfectly quiet, listening to every sound. At last I heard a gentleman's voice, saying 'Where is he, where is he?' and then he put in his hand and felt me. I started, but my benefactor told me that it was all right, it was a friend. 'This gentleman,' he added, 'will take care of you; you must go to his house.'

"I then hid in the garret of this friend's house until midnight the next night. A skiff was obtained and I was rowed across the river, which is about a mile wide

18. "Runaways Drowned! On Friday night last, a party of slaves, six in number, ran away from the neighborhood of Millersburg. One belonging to Mrs. Emily Taylor, of Bourbon, one to Mr. Miller, of Irish Station, in Nicholas County, and the others to persons in the latter county. They crossed the country on foot to East Maysville, where the negroes attempted to cross the river in a skiff about daylight. There was a dense fog upon the river and by some means the skiff was overturned and the three women and child drowned."—*Kentucky State Flag,* Paris, December 17, 1855.

at this point. Shortly after we landed a waggon came up, and I was stowed away, and driven about twenty miles that night, being well guarded by eight or ten young men with revolvers. On and on I went, from one station to another, everywhere being received and lodged as if I were a chosen guest." [19]

Many interesting phases of Negro life are revealed as one reads the runaway advertisements in the yellowing files of the old Kentucky newspapers. Some present pictures of harsh treatment, physical deformities, humorous traits and characteristic dress; but all quite obviously true, as there was nothing to be gained by falsifying the runaway notice. A true picture of the lost slave was always presented as far as possible:

> "LOOK OUT FOR THE RUNAWAY! Ran away from the subscriber in Bourbon County, on the night of the 16th inst, a negro man named Austin. He is about five feet, 10 inches high, sparse made, answers pretty quick when spoken to, several of his front teeth knocked out and a large scar on one of his hips about his hamstrings." [20]

A number of fugitives were identified by scars and several by their ears which had been pierced for rings. Jesse, a Fayette County slave who ran off in 1834, had "his ears bored and generally wears small gold rings in them." [21] Bartlet, a mulatto slave who ran away from Edwin H. Hart, of South Elkhorn, Fayette County, had, as the notice revealed, "a scar in the middle of the fore-

19. *Slave Life in Virginia and Kentucky,* pp. 103–105. This little book of 115 pages is probably the rarest of all Kentucky slave narratives, only two copies being known, one in the Library of Congress and another in the University of Virginia Library.

20. *Western Citizen,* Paris, February 4, 1842.

21. *Lexington Observer & Reporter,* November 12, 1834.

head, in a circle, and near the size of a cut half dollar." [22]

There was confined, as a runaway, in the Mason County jail, "the negro Jim Burke, two or three scars across his neck, a large scar on his right shoulder, and his heels have been much frosted." [23] Likewise in Lincoln County, there had been "caught up" the runaway Bob, "much scarred about the face and body, and has the left ear bit off." [24]

Peculiarities in speech furnished another clue to the identity of the runaway. Bill, as the runaway notice stated, "is pert when spoken to and is fond of drink. He will," his master prophesied, "probably make for Ohio and Indiana." [25] Jesse used "the word submit for permit," and Maria was "freely spoken, but seldom speaks the truth." [26] Emily spoke with "a whine in her voice," and Sam, it was said, "stomps on the ground when the word is hard to get out." [27]

Sometimes the masters in their runaway notices were frank enough to admit they were mystified over their slaves' departure. There was Dublin who ran off in 1833—"if he has left the state, it is likely that some white man has the care of him, as he is not sprightly in making arrangements." [28] Fifty dollars was offered for the return of Daniel, who was "blind in one eye and lame in one leg." [29] Henry, who was known as being "very religious and sometimes preaches or exhorts," ran off, but his master could see "no cause or provocation"

22. *Ibid.*, December 9, 1835.
23. *Maysville Eagle,* November 21, 1838.
24. *The Argus of Western America,* Frankfort, December 1, 1824.
25. *Lexington Observer & Reporter,* November 12, 1834.
26. *Ibid.*, October 3, 1838.
27. *Ibid.*, January 10, 1833.
28. *Ibid.*, January 10, 1833.
29. *Ibid.*, October 28, 1835.

for his act, "as he had not been whipped in 6 or 8 years." [30]

Dissatisfied slaves, in an effort to wreak vengeance upon their owners, were sometimes known to burn or damage their master's property before they started in quest of freedom. An interesting case occurred in Bourbon County in the spring of 1822:

> "$50.00 REWARD. Ran away from the subscriber on the 27th of March last a negro woman named SARAH, about 6 feet high, and very slim; a very long face, with black gums, long teeth, white eyes and platted hair. Had on a white linsey dress and took with her a red changeable silk, and black dress, also a white robe and striped gingham dress. Sarah is the biggest devil that ever lived, having poisoned a stud horse and set a stable on fire, also burnt Gen. R. Williams stable and stack yard with seven horses and other property to value of $1500. She was handcuffed and got away at Ruddles Mills on her way down the river, which is the fifth time she escaped when about to be sent out of the country. I will give the above reward for said negro if taken out of the state, $25 if taken in the state and delivered to me or lodged in jail so that I can get her. Levin Adams." [31]

Many slaves left their homes in Kentucky because of their constant and consuming fear of being sold South or down the river by the hated "nigger traders." Then, too, there was the breaking up of the family life of the slave. Husband could be sold from his wife,

30. *Ibid.,* September 12, 1838.

31. *Western Citizen,* April 16, 1822. In another part of the paper it was reported that Sarah had confessed "to the woman with whom she was handcuffed, that she burnt General Williams' and her master's stable, and that she wanted to poison her mistress, and then she would make straight tracks off."

father and mother from their children with no earthly hope of a later reunion. Many slaves had the hardihood to seek the distant, but friendly, land of liberty, but were restrained solely by the bonds of love and kinship which held them to their families. A severe whipping,[32] a threatened punishment, or the death of "old marster," with the inevitable division of his estate, were enough to put many slaves on the trail of the North Star [33] toward freedom.

Henry Bibb, a slave of W. H. Gatewood, of Bedford, Trimble County, escaped with his family and, after reaching Canada, wrote rather ironically to his old master: "You may perhaps think hard of us for running away from slavery, but as to myself, I have but one apology to make for it, which is this: I have only to regret that I did not start at an earlier period. I might have been free long before I was. . . . I think it very probable that I should have been a toiling slave on your plantation today, if you had treated me differently.

"To be compelled to stand by and see you whip and slash my wife without mercy, when I could afford her no protection, not even by offering myself to suffer the lash in her place, was more than I felt it to be the duty of a slave husband to endure, while the way was open to Canada. My infant child was also frequently flogged by Mrs. Gatewood for crying, until its skin was bruised literally purple. This kind of treatment was what drove me from home and family to seek a better home for

32. Lewis Richardson, one of the slaves of Henry Clay, sought relief in flight after receiving a hundred and fifty stripes from Mr. Clay's overseer.—*The Liberator,* April 10, 1846.

33. "I knew the North Star," wrote Josiah Henson, another runaway slave from Kentucky. "Blessed be God for setting it in the heavens. I knew that it had led thousands of my poor, haunted brethren to freedom and blessedness."—*Father Henson's Story of His Own Life,* p. 103.

them. I remain a friend of the oppressed, and liberty forever. . . ." [34]

Losses became so severe to the slaveholders in the counties bordering on the Ohio River that in 1837 those of Mason County organized themselves into a society "for the purpose of concerted measures for the better security of our slave property." [35] Slave owners of Kentucky continued to feel their losses by the activities of the Underground Railroad. "Already the value of slave property has depreciated twenty per-cent in all the counties bordering on the Ohio River," warned a Lexington paper, and these losses, it was claimed, came "from the facilities offered fugitive slaves by their organized societies." [36]

An event occurred in 1838 which greatly unnerved the people and hotly incensed the Kentucky slaveholders. The Reverend John B. Mahan, noted abolitionist of Sardinia, Brown County, Ohio, and a minister of the Methodist Church, was arrested late in June, 1838, on a charge of "inciting, aiding and abetting slaves to escape" from their masters.[37] A short time before Mahan's arrest, fifteen runaway slaves, two of whom belonged to William Greathouse, of Mason County, were seen "loitering about" the preacher's home in Ohio,[38] where they were sheltered and aided

34. Letter dated Detroit, March 23, 1844.—*Narrative of the Life and Adventures of Henry Bibb,* pp. 177–78.

35. *Maysville Eagle,* July 11, 1837.

36. *Lexington Observer & Reporter,* November 10, 1838.

37. *Maysville Eagle,* November 21, 1838.

38. "For the last six months," complained a committee of citizens from Sardinia, "our neighborhood has been unusually infested with negro-hunters. They have prowled about the neighborhood by night, searched the barns and out-houses, and robbed the grain fields of our citizens. In one case, William Greathouse, a Kentuckian, and his rabble of vile hirelings, about thirty in number, also hunted about Sardinia for five or six miles looking for their fugitive slaves. Not finding them, they dispersed

on their northern journey to freedom. Several weeks later, Mahan was arrested for "running off slaves" and brought from Ohio to the county jail, then located at Washington, the county seat of Mason County, Kentucky. While in the Mason County jail, the minister, who had been indicted for felony, sent several letters to Governor Vance of Ohio and other dignitaries, in all of them strongly protesting his innocence.

On Tuesday, November 13, the trial of Mr. Mahan began in the little courthouse at Washington, with Judge Walker Reid presiding. Despite the tense excitement and strong pro-slavery feelings of the crowds of slaveholders and spectators who filled the courthouse, "the most perfect order and decorum prevailed throughout the trial." [39]

For six days the trial lasted. Counsel for the prosecution attempted to prove that the Methodist divine "did aid and assist a certain slave named John, the property of one William Greathouse, to make his escape out of and beyond the state of Kentucky." [40] It was likewise charged that "there was a connecting chain of *friends,* from Kentucky, running all the way to Canada, of which Mahan was a part," and that "these friends paid the passage of the negroes all the way to Canada." [41]

Evidence was then introduced "that a certain colored man in Maysville, a barber, had sent him [Mahan] all the slaves he could," and "that he had helped along fifteen within a short time past." No one doubted that Mahan was guilty of aiding slaves along the Under-

much enraged, Greathouse threatening to bring back from Kentucky 200 men to burn down Sardinia."—*The Philanthropist,* Cincinnati, December 18, 1838.

39. *Western Citizen,* Paris, November 30, 1838.

40. *Trial of Rev. John B. Mahan* (pamphlet), pp. 12–13.

41. *Ibid.,* p. 16.

ground Railroad, once they were on free soil; but it was seen that he had been shrewd enough to confine his activities to the state of Ohio, and that, as testimony proved, "he had never set foot on the soil of Kentucky," except when he was arrested and taken to Washington for trial.

Following Judge Reid's instructions to find for the prisoner, if it appeared that the crime was not committed in Mason County, the jury retired, and in a few minutes brought in a verdict of not guilty.[42] Amid loud threats and cursings, the Methodist preacher "escaped with his life and limbs" to his farm across the Ohio River.[43]

As a result of the Mahan trial, which brought to light the methods of rendering assistance and the extent of the resultant losses of slaves, two commissioners were hastily despatched to the Ohio legislature, then in session, to seek to induce that body to pass a law calculated to prevent the interference with the slave property of Kentucky "by divers ill-disposed persons of Ohio."[44] Such a law was passed, designed to remedy this evil and to heal the grievances of the Kentucky slave owners, but the matter did not end there. The Underground Railroad kept on; in fact, the number of slaves who annually escaped increased alarmingly.[45]

Along the Ohio River, in the counties of Mason and Bracken, an association was formed to unite in pursuing and recovering fugitive slaves; quite liberal rewards were offered to citizens in the free states for their co-

42. Mason Circuit Court, Order Book 33, p. 329, November 20, 1838.

43. In a civil suit that followed over the loss of his two slaves, Greathouse was awarded $1,600 damages against the Methodist preacher.—Mason Circuit Court, Order Book 36, p. 491, May 12, 1841.

44. *Maysville Eagle,* February 2, 1839.

45. *Frankfort Commonwealth,* February 16, 1839.

operation.[46] As the number of escaping slaves grew, large rewards for their capture enticed unscrupulous bands into the business of slave catching. These villains gathered at strategic transfer centers along the Ohio River, such as Ripley, Portsmouth, Cincinnati, Manchester, Evansville and Jeffersonville, and awaited the agents northward bound to hijack their human cargo, but the ever-faithful conductors were ready to defend their charges, and often pitched battles took place. Then, too, there were those in the free states who, actuated by a desire for gain, made it their business to find out the fugitive's old master, write him, and collect a reward.

Levi Coffin and his wife, Catherine, active Quaker abolitionists and noted "conductors" on the Underground Railroad, lived for a while in Newport, Indiana, and later moved to Cincinnati, where, under cover of a country store, they provided a haven of refuge for fugitive slaves from Kentucky and the South. Mr. and Mrs. Coffin were the Simeon and Rachel Halliday of Mrs. Harriet Beecher Stowe's *Uncle Tom's Cabin.* Coffin, the reputed "president" of the Underground Railroad, helped hundreds of men, women and children to escape, and his experiences gave rise to many dramas and tragedies.

The thrilling escape of Eliza and her babe across the ice blocks of the Ohio River, which stirred tens of thousands of hearts, was aided and engineered by the Coffins. After her dramatic escape from Kentucky, much as Mrs. Stowe describes it, Eliza was concealed for some days in an isolated spot near the home of the Reverend John Rankin of Ripley, Ohio. Her presence being suspected,

46. Mitchell, *The Under-Ground Railroad,* p. 84.

she was spirited away at night to Newport, Indiana, and there concealed in the home of Coffin. Thence she was shipped along with other fugitives to Canada, by way of the Greenville route.

On another occasion, Coffin hired several carriages and a hearse, and loading twenty-eight fugitive slaves in them in broad daylight, he passed nonchalantly down the road with his solemn funeral procession some fifteen or twenty miles to the next station of the Underground Railroad.

Occasionally such depots of the road became suspected, and sheriffs and near-by plantation owners would descend upon them. Some of the farms were seized, but new ones were immediately purchased; communication between the depots became more difficult, but was stepped up and the stream of fugitives increased.

Delia A. Webster, the New England schoolteacher, who was found guilty of "nigger-stealing" with the Reverend Calvin Fairbank, in Lexington during the early forties,[47] returned to Kentucky where she resumed her operations as a conductor and operator of a station on the mysterious railroad. In the winter of 1854 she purchased, with funds supplied by Northern abolitionists, a farm of six hundred acres in Trimble County, Kentucky, lying along the Ohio River, between Cincinnati and Louisville. Here on her farm, situated "on the brow of the hill opposite the city of Madison, Indiana," [48] Miss Webster was joined by several individuals in her

47. Miss Webster was sentenced to two years confinement in the state penitentiary, and Mr. Fairbank for fifteen years for their "nigger-stealing" activities in Lexington in 1844. Their story is related at length in Chapter VIII, "Nigger Stealers."

48. Trimble County Court, Deed Book D, p. 377, February 10, 1854, Norris and Elizabeth Day to Delia A. Webster.

"free labor" enterprise; ostensibly to try free labor in slave territory, but really to aid and assist fugitive slaves from Kentucky and the South on their northward journey to freedom.

It was not long before slaveholders began losing their slaves in considerable numbers, and in less than six weeks Miss Webster was waited upon by fifty enraged slave owners who ordered her to abandon her project and leave the state. On one occasion the excitement ran so high that "four different counties passed resolutions that no Northern man or woman should cultivate that Webster farm." [49] Matters continued to grow worse. Slave property diminished in value, so much so that Miss Webster was dragged before a magistrate's court at Corn Creek, in the spring of 1854, and there placed under a ten-thousand-dollar bond "to leave the state and never return," and upon her refusal to give the required bond, was cast into the Bedford County jail, which was described as "a cold, damp, foul and filthy dungeon." There she was confined for several weeks "until life was nearly extinct." Upon "learning that she was still alive and unsubdued," a circuit judge in a neighboring county granted a writ of habeas corpus, and after her trial "she was most triumphantly discharged." [50]

However, pro-slavery sentiment was strongly against her, and shortly afterwards, in June, 1854, she was indicted in Trimble County "for aiding and abetting slaves to run off and escape into the state of Ohio." [51] While the sheriff, armed with a warrant, was looking for Miss Webster, she escaped across the river into Indi-

49. *Webster Kentucky Farm Association* (pamphlet), pp. 5–8.
50. *Ibid.*, pp. 7–8.
51. Commonwealth of Kentucky *vs.* Delia A. Webster, Trimble Circuit Court, Order Book 1, p. 197, June 16, 1854.

ana, and although pursued by a "posse of bloody hirelings" was not found. During her absence from Kentucky payments accrued and accumulated on her farm, and it was not long before the mortgage holders had sold her out. This was a great relief to the harassed slaveholders of Trimble, Oldham and neighboring counties. Inasmuch as the Yankee schoolteacher remained out of the state for over three years and no longer possessed any land in Kentucky, the indictment against her was finally dropped.

"It is ordered by the court that the case be filed away," wrote the circuit clerk of Trimble County [52] in 1858, thus ending the strange case of the "petticoat abolitionist," whose unsuccessful anti-slavery activities in Kentucky caused her to serve a term in the state penitentiary, forced her to lose her farm or depot on the Ohio River, and as a fitting climax led to her being run out of the state by the irate slaveholders of Trimble County.[53]

Benjamin Drew, who traveled through the colored settlements of Canada and collected narratives from certain members thereof, tells, in 1856, the story of a runaway slave, Henry Morehead, who was then living in London, Ontario. The slave's story, one of supreme sacrifice, is vividly related: "I came from Louisville, Kentucky, where I was born and bred a slave," he recounted. "I left slavery a little more than a year ago. I brought my wife and three children with me, and had not nearly enough to bring us through. I left because they were about selling my wife and children to the South. I would rather have followed them to the grave,

52. Trimble Circuit Court, Order Book 3, p. 242, November 22, 1858.

53. Miss Webster, who was born in Vergennes, Vermont, in 1817, was last heard of in 1869 living alone in Madison, Indiana. She never married.

than to the Ohio River to see them go down. I knew it was death or victory—so I took them and started for Canada. I was pursued—my owners watched for me in a free state, but, to their sad disappointment, I took another road. A hundred miles further on, I saw my advertisements again offering $500 for me and my family. I concluded that as money would do almost anything—I ought to take better care—and I took the Underground Railroad.

"I was longer on the road than I should have been without my burden; one child was nine years old, one two years old and one four. The weather was cold and my feet were frostbitten, as I gave my wife my socks to pull over her shoes. With all the sufferings of the frost and the fatigues of travel, it was not half so bad as the effects of slavery." [54]

Arrivals of fugitive slaves in Canada were frequently mentioned in the little anti-slavery newssheet, *The Voice of the Fugitive,* published semimonthly in Sandwich, Ontario, by Henry Bibb, a runaway slave from Shelby County, Kentucky. In it the activities of the Underground Railroad were oftentimes played up with a vain show of braggadocio. In the issue of November 5, 1851, it boasted much: "We can run a lot of slaves through from almost any of the bordering slave states into Canada within 48 hours and we defy the slaveholders and their abettors to beat that if they can. . . ." And on April 22, 1852, Bibb records the arrival of fifteen slaves "within the last few days" and notes that "the

54. *The Refugee; or Narratives of Fugitive Slaves in Canada,* p. 181. Morehead later stated: "I am making out very well here. I have not been in the country long enough to accumulate any wealth, but I am getting on as well as the general run of my people." See Siebert, *The Underground Railroad from Slavery to Freedom,* pp. 190–234, for an excellent account of how the fugitive slaves fared after they reached Canada.

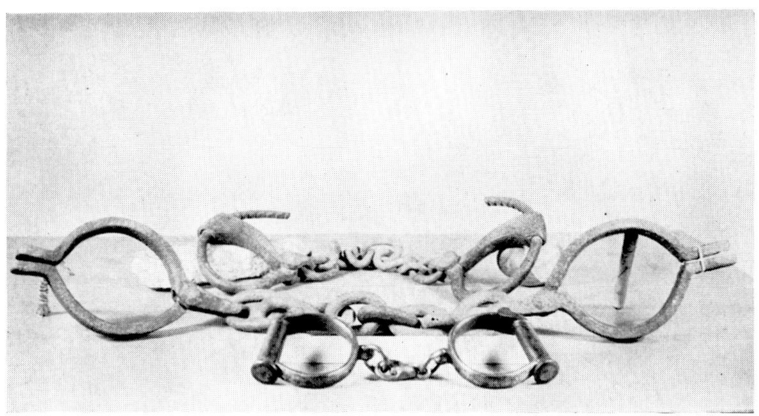

SLAVE HANDCUFFS AND LEG IRONS

$150 REWARD.

RANAWAY from the subscriber, on the night of Monday the 11th July, a negro man named

TOM,

about 30 years of age, 5 feet 6 or 7 inches high; of dark color; heavy in the chest; several of his jaw teeth out; and upon his body are several old marks of the whip, one of them straight down the back. He took with him a quantity of clothing, and several hats.

A reward of $150 will be paid for his apprehension and security, if taken out of the State of Kentucky; $100 if taken in any county bordering on the Ohio river; $50 if taken in any of the interior counties except Fayette; or $20 if taken in the latter county.

july 12-84-tf B. L. BOSTON.

TOM'S RUNAWAY NOTICE

A SLAVE PEN DURING WARTIME

Underground Railroad is doing good business this spring." [55]

While other anti-slavery papers were reticent about the operations of the railroad, the fugitive Bibb seems to have taken great delight in letting the world know how many of his fellow slaves were "making it for Canada" and freedom. "The Underground Railroad," said *The Voice of the Fugitive,* "and especially the express train, is doing a good business just now. We have good and competent conductors—the road is doing better business this fall than usual." [56]

No doubt Bibb was especially overjoyed when news came that some of his fellow slaves and old friends were arriving from his native state. "We are happy to announce the arrival of eight females by the last train of the Underground Railroad from Kentucky," disclosed this anti-slavery journal. "They are all one family consisting of a mother and her daughters . . . and it has scarcely ever been our lot to witness such a respectable and intelligent family of females from slavery . . . they will be an ornament in the future to our social circle in Canada." [57]

Despite the guarded secrecy, upon which the success of the Underground Railroad largely depended, Bibb did not hesitate to give the names of the slaves' old masters back home and, sometimes in an effort at consolation, sent them messages of the well-being of their former slaves: "On June 10th, ten slaves belonging to Robert C. Todd, Colonel James Taylor, Robert Slaughter, Mrs. Mary Winston and Dr. Parker, citizens of New-

55. April 22, 1852.
56. October 29, 1852.
57. *The Liberator,* August 19, 1853, quoting from *The Voice of the Fugitive.*

port, Kentucky, made their escape from that place. We are truly happy," wrote Bibb, "to be able to inform Mr. Todd & Company that the above refugees have arrived safely in Canada, and that they came by way of the Underground Railroad. They are all well, and are likely to do well. They have only one thing to regret, and that is, that they have not known of the Underground Railroad before, so that they might have been in Canada long ago. . . ."[58]

So much of an established institution did the Underground Railroad become[59] that in time it grew rich in songs, stories and poems. Among the songs, probably the best known in this connection is "Away to Canada," the last lines of which reflect the cherished theme of the followers of the North Star:

"Farewell, old Master,
Don't come after me,
I'm on my way to Canada,
Where colored men are free."

—and so, by following the North Star and being assisted in flight by the Underground Railroad, many hundreds of Kentucky slaves[60] escaped from bondage who would never have been able to leave the place where they were born, and, certainly, would never have been able to "breathe the air of freedom" in far-away Canada—the promised land.

58. *The Voice of the Fugitive,* June 16, 1853.

59. "The northern fanatics have so systemized their efforts to steal our slaves, have so organized their underground railroad, that it is impossible for individuals, however vigilant, to frustrate their designs."—*Frankfort Commonwealth,* March 11, 1856.

60. "Hundreds of dollars are lost annually. Kentucky, it is estimated [in 1860] loses annually as much as $200,000."—*Congressional Globe,* 36th Cong., 2nd Sess., p. 356. And the New Orleans *Commercial Bulletin,* December 19, 1860, asserted "that 1500 slaves have escaped annually for the last fifty years, a loss to the South of at least $40,000,000."

CHAPTER X

THE DARKER SIDE

THE MAJORITY of Kentucky slaveholders were men of conscience and sensibility, but, nevertheless, as the uncontradicted records show, some were cruel and brutal in dealing with their slaves. At the same time it must be remembered that some slaves were not only intractable, but even savage and dangerous. For one or another of these reasons, and it is hard to distinguish between them, slaves were now and then rather harshly treated. Consequently, numerous runaways were attributed to excessive toil to which the slaves were subjected or to the rigorous discipline of the farmstead. It is a fact, however, irrespective of the cause, that an excessive amount of whipping indicated a poorly run plantation, and the master of such an establishment was viewed askance by his neighbors, who scornfully said of him—"He's mean to his niggers." [1]

Newspaper advertisements for runaways constitute one of the best sources of information concerning Kentucky slaves; their treatment, motives for escape, birthmarks and blemishes, punishments and other things

1. Recollections of Joseph B. Paxton, who was reared in a large slaveholding community in Lincoln County.—Letter to the author, March 15, 1938.

pertaining to their daily life and physical make-up are therein described. Although these notices were of meager length and leave much untold that we would like to know, they have one great merit as historical material; they were not biased and were all quite obviously true. Here was no cause or occasion for attacking or defending slavery, or falsifying the contents of the advertisements, for it was always the master's object to present, as far as possible, a true picture of his runaway slave. Then too, these notices were written principally for the eyes of other slaveholders and slave catchers.

Readers of the *Lexington Intelligencer* were asked to be on the lookout for Lawson, who was "remarkably well-made, no marks recollected except those [from whipping] on his back, is artful and cunning." [2] Pierce Griffin, of Shelbyville, advertised for his slave Charles, who had "lost several of his fore-teeth, and has considerable marks of the whip on his seat." [3] Then there was Bob, who ran away from Joseph McClaskey, of Nelson County, a "little cross-eyed, bandy-legged and much scarred with the whip." [4] In Fayette County, Henry, "a very ill-natured fellow," ran away from his master, and, as the notice revealed, "has been cut in his back by often whipping." [5]

Numerous other notices revealing severe treatment to slaves are to be seen in the files of the old Kentucky newspapers. James Ferguson, of Jessamine County, offered forty dollars reward for his slave, Daniel, "who was whipped on the day he left for stealing, and proba-

2. *Lexington Intelligencer,* November 13, 1836.
3. *Lexington Observer & Reporter,* December 16, 1835.
4. *Kentucky Gazette,* January 18, 1838.
5. *Lexington Intelligencer,* May 4, 1839.

bly has some marks of the whip on his back." [6] In Warren County, Charles, the runaway slave of Harrison Cooksey, was "very active and sensible" and, as the notice stated, "will no doubt show the marks of a recent whipping, if taken." [7]

While many of the scars were the results of accidents, a number were permanent markings of more or less remote punishments. In Paducah the McCracken County jailer advertised that there was in his care "a negro mulatto man calling himself Jim, who is considerably marked with stripes on his back." [8] At Megowan's slave jail, in Lexington, the keeper announced that there had been apprehended and was now in his custody a "sprightly mulatto wench" who says her name is Callie with a "brand on the cheek, forehead and breast resembling the letter 'H.' " Also a "stout black boy, Mose, who has a burn on his buttock from a red hot iron in the shape of an 'X' and his back is much scarred with the whip." And at another time, there was "Alex, who has had his ears cropped and has been shot in the hind parts of his legs." [9] From Boyle County there ran off the slave Jack, who had "both ears slightly cropped" and was "a pretty shrewd and sensible fellow." [10]

For violation of minor statutory offenses slaves were publicly chastised at the whipping post, erected on the courthouse square of many Kentucky towns and cities. Lexington had its instrument of torture, "of black locust one foot in diameter, ten feet high and sunk two

6. *Kentucky Reporter,* September 1, 1830.
7. *Green River Gazette,* April 13, 1841.
8. *The Paducah Journal,* February 27, 1851.
9. Townsend, *Lincoln and his Wife's Home Town,* pp. 95–96.
10. *Kentucky Tribune,* August 25, 1843.

and one-half feet in the ground," at which incorrigible and delinquent Negroes were flogged severely, and their cries and screams were characterized by an early visitor as the death knell of Kentucky slavery.[11] Ironically enough, the Reverend Jesse Head, who married the parents of the Great Emancipator, erected in May of 1798 the Washington County whipping post "upon the public square in Springfield for the use of this county." [12] Here, as at the other public whipping posts, "39 lashes on the bare back well laid on," constituted the customary amount of punishment for recalcitrant blacks.[13]

While whipping was by far the most usual mode of correction, Negroes were sometimes branded on the chest or body, or had an iron clog or band attached to the ankle. These more severe punishments were usually reserved for habitual runaways. Jefferson County residents in 1848 were requested to be on the lookout for the runaway slave, Jane, "who is branded on the breast something like L blotched." [14] Mary, a fugitive from McCracken County, had "a small scar over her left eye, a good many teeth missing. The letter 'A' is branded on her cheek and forehead." [15]

George Dudley, of Fayette County, advertised that he would give fifty dollars for the return of his Negro, Elijah, who "had on when he left a lock on one of his ankles, a chip hat, and a sleeve jacket of Jeans." [16] Jim slipped away from his Lexington master, but was some-

11. Brown, *The Western Gazetteer,* p. 92.
12. Washington County Court, Order Book A, p. 293, May 2, 1798.
13. John Bradford, *The General Instructor,* pp. 165–68.
14. *The Examiner,* Louisville, October 18, 1848.
15. *The Paducah Journal,* April 27, 1851.
16. *Kentucky Yeoman,* Frankfort, January 14, 1843.

what encumbered by a "ring of iron on his left foot." [17] Cassius M. Clay, who was reared in a large slaveholding community in Madison County, recounts in his *Memoirs* that during his boyhood and early manhood he frequently saw slaves wearing iron collars, sometimes with bells on them, which had been riveted on by a blacksmith,[18] and which could not be taken off without great danger of discovery.

One night during the summer of 1845 Clay heard a disturbance in his chicken house and, upon investigation, found a slave from a neighboring plantation in the act of raiding his hen roost. After capturing the culprit and taking him outside in the moonlight, Clay observed on the Negro "the bright prongs of a steel collar as long, on each side of his neck, as the horns of a Texas steer." [19] In Fleming County the local paper once carried this notice: "Ranaway, the mulatto wench Caroline, had on a collar with one prong turned down." [20]

In Kentucky, and especially in the Bluegrass, where the yoke of bondage rested lightly, events occurred now and then which greatly enraged the public and clearly showed the darker side of slavery. In Lexington during the middle eighteen-thirties, there lived Judge Fielding L. Turner, a wealthy retired jurist, and his wife, Caroline A. Turner, member of a socially prominent family of Boston. In their pretentious household were to be found probably more family servants than in any other home in the city.

17. *Western Monitor,* October 14, 1818.

18. In the files of the Filson Club Library there is a statement rendered to a Jefferson County slaveholder by a blacksmith, Thomas Jefferson, on June 23, 1834: "To making 1 sett Legg fetters, 62¢," and, on July 29: "To repairing Negro Collar, 25¢."

19. *Memoirs,* p. 28.

20. *Flemingsburg Whig,* March 17, 1855, *et seq.*

Mrs. Turner, a woman of strong muscle and fierce temper, frequently whipped her servants with such violence that Judge Turner himself said: "She has been the immediate death of six of my servants by her severities." [21] One morning in the spring of 1837, while vigorously flogging one of her slaves, Mrs. Turner, in a fit of passion, suddenly caught the small Negro boy and deliberately pitched him out of the second-story window to the stone pavement of the courtyard below, seriously injuring his spine, breaking an arm and leg, and rendering him a cripple for life.

Lexington and Fayette County were intensely aroused over such wanton cruelty, and to save his wife from threatened criminal prosecution, Judge Turner had her forcibly removed from his home to the lunatic asylum. After several days' confinement in the institution, Mrs. Turner demanded a hearing on the question of her sanity. On March 31, 1837, a jury of twelve citizens was impaneled "to inquire into the state of mind of Caroline A. Turner," but, before the trial began, the asylum authorities, finding no evidence of mental derangement, released her, and nothing came of the matter.[22]

However, Mrs. Turner seems never to have reformed in her brutal treatment of her slaves, and her husband, who died in 1843, stated in his will: "I have some slaves. I give them to my children. None of them are to go to the said Caroline, for it would be to doom them to misery in life & a speedy death." [23]

But Mrs. Turner renounced the will of Judge Turner

21. Weld, *American Slavery As It Is,* p. 87.

22. Commonwealth of Kentucky *vs.* Caroline A. Turner, Fayette Circuit Court, File 899, April 17, 1837.

23. Will of Fielding L. Turner, Fayette County Court, Will Book P, pp. 503–504, dated October 1, 1843.

and obtained several of these Negroes, including a coachman named Richard, who was described as a "sensible, well-behaved yellow boy, who is plausible and can read and write." In the early morning hours of August 22, 1844, while flogging Richard with her usual zest and severity, the young slave with a great thrust shook off the chains that bound him to the wall and, seizing his mistress by the throat, strangled her to death with his bare hands.[24]

The public, however, now swayed by the passion of the hour, quickly forgot all the cruelties Mrs. Turner had inflicted on her servants, and five hundred dollars was offered for the capture of Richard, who had fled the city. The local press, putting it mildly, stated that Mrs. Turner was only "reproving" her servant for some improper conduct the evening before.[25] Richard was soon apprehended in Scott County and brought to Lexington for trial. His excellent reputation, however, bore but little weight in the case, for under no circumstances could a slave take his master's or mistress's life—not even to save his own—and escape the gallows. Richard was put through the formality of a trial, found guilty of murder in the first degree, and was hanged from a scaffold erected in the Fayette County jail yard, on November 19, 1844.[26]

Another case, much discussed in Lexington at the time, was that of a Mr. and Mrs. Maxwell, charged with brutality to their young female slave. Witnesses testified that they had seen Mrs. Maxwell on a cold winter morning severely whipping the thinly-clad, barefooted slave as she stood on the stone pavement in front of her house,

24. *Lexington Observer & Reporter,* August 24, 1844.
25. *Western Citizen,* August 30, 1844.
26. *Lexington Observer & Reporter,* November 19, 1844.

and was not "particular whether she struck her in the face or not." From such whippings the slave's flesh was greatly lacerated and "one of her eyes was tied up for a week." At other times, Mrs. Maxwell's son was seen vigorously applying the cowhide to the girl, after having stripped her down to the waist. When the girl turned her face toward him, young Maxwell would "hit her across the face with the butt end of his whip to make her turn her back square around to the lash, so that he might get a fair blow at her." From a medical examination made at the time of the trial, the female slave's emaciated body revealed numerous lacerations, bruises and scars resulting from the searing of her flesh with a red-hot iron.[27]

Kentucky masters were compelled by law to maintain the sick, the infirm and the aged; the law itself enacted penalties for inhuman treatment and public opinion sustained it. Notwithstanding the fact that the law was perhaps better than the practice, still it had a general influence for the protection of the slave.

Alpheus Lewis, living with his wife, Margaret, some five or six miles from Paris in Bourbon County, bore the general reputation of "governing his slaves with a sterner discipline than most of his neighbors," for, he boasted, "it is better for them as well as for myself." [28] Thus matters stood until the early spring of 1855, when some of the neighbors complained to the authorities that several of Lewis' slaves "were most severely & cruelly used."

Mentioned in this complaint were two women—Sally, the mother of several children, and Martha, a

27. Weld, *op. cit.,* p. 67.
28. *Western Citizen,* May 11, 1855.

young house girl of twelve years. One day, Mrs. Lewis becoming violently displeased with Martha's work, seized "a good-sized stick about the size of a man's wrist," and struck her several well-aimed blows on the head and shoulders, whereupon the excited girl ran from the house into the yard. As Mrs. Lewis passed through the dining room in pursuit of the young slave, "she caught up the hot tongs from the fire-place, and ran out to the back of the yard, where, coming up behind the girl, she passed one leg of the tongs on each side of the girl's neck and seized her with them." [29] Screaming and kicking, the seared and excited slave broke loose from her mistress and fled to the home of a neighbor, where, upon examination, she showed "burns made with hot irons upon her neck, hands, under both arms, and between her legs, both behind and before; besides bruises upon her head and bleeding at the ears." [30]

Sally, the older of the two females, as was proved by the neighbors, had, at her master's direction, "been tied up naked in the yard with her heels about four feet off the ground." Then Mrs. Lewis, after vigorously whipping her, "stood off a pace and pelted her with stones," forcing another slave to pump water on her, and finally resorted to her more favorite method of torture, the hot iron. When Sally was rescued, there was found on her back a number of scars from burning "that could scarcely be covered with the palm of the hand."

Shortly thereafter, at the next term of the Bourbon

29. *Ibid.*, July 27, 1855. In the same issue of this Paris newspaper there was a card from Mr. and Mrs. Lewis denying charges made in the *New York Tribune* that Martha was "entirely naked" when she reached her neighbors and other accusations of cruelty on their part.

30. Carleton, *Suppressed Book about Slavery*, p. 163.

Circuit Court, held in March, 1855, Alpheus Lewis and his wife were indicted for cruelty to their two slaves, Sally and Martha.[31] Pursuant to an order of the court, which acted on the law governing the inhuman treatment of slaves, the sheriff was directed to seize the badly-treated slaves, confine them in the county jail, and sell them at public auction at the next county court day in Paris.[32]

For several weeks, prior to April second, readers of the *Western Citizen* were informed of the chattels to be offered for sale:

> "Commissioner's Sale of Slaves—As Commissioner, under a decree of the Bourbon County Court, at the March term, in the case of Alpheus Lewis and Margaret, his wife, I will expose to Public Sale, at the Court-House door in Paris, on the 2nd day of April next, County Court day for said County, on a credit of four months, two valuable slaves, to wit: a woman [Sally] aged twenty-five, and a girl [Martha] about twelve. Persons wishing to purchase, can see said slaves by calling on J. Porter. Bond, with approved security will be required, having the force and effect of a replevy bond.
>
> Thomas A. Taylor, Comm'r." [33]

On the day of the sale a large crowd gathered, partly out of sympathy for the ill-treated blacks and partly from idle curiosity. Both slaves found homes in an adjacent county, Sally bringing $575, but Martha, on account of her age and condition, "fetched only $145." After deducting the cost of the prosecution and ex-

31. Commonwealth of Kentucky *vs.* Alpheus Lewis & Margaret, his wife, Bourbon Circuit Court, Order Book NN, p. 48, March 14, 1855.

32. *Ibid.*, p. 126, March 21, 1855.

33. March 22, 1855, *et seq.*

penses of the sale, as well as five per cent for the sheriff, the money resulting from the sale was turned back to the defendants, Alpheus Lewis and wife.

Probably the darkest feature of the so-called black code was the fact that the slave's right of self-defense in the courts of the state amounted to virtually nothing more than mere legal fiction. Slaves of Kentucky could not appear as witnesses against their masters, or the body of society, but could only give testimony for or against Negroes or mulattoes.[34] The subjection of one race to another, coupled with the inability of the subordinate race to testify against the dominant race, made harsh treatment and brutal punishments possible. Some of the outrages perpetrated on the helpless blacks can hardly be classed as punishments.

There lived on "Rocky Point" plantation near Smithland, in Livingston County, during the early part of the nineteenth century, Lilburne Lewis and his younger brother, Isham, nephews of President Thomas Jefferson. As the owners of a considerable number of slaves, the Lewis brothers were known far and wide for their cruel treatment of their blacks, whom they "drove constantly, fed sparingly and lashed severely." [35] In consequence of such harsh treatment, many of their slaves were in the habit of running away.

On the evening of December 15, 1811, these two brothers sat before the open fire in the living room of their log farmhouse, drinking and arguing over their runaway problems. Outside a bitter wind slashed the frozen snow on the wilderness countryside and the turbulence of the wind infected the hearts of the slaves

34. Turner *vs.* Knox, *Kentucky Reports,* 7 T. B. Monroe 88, April, 1828.
35. Carleton, *Suppressed Book about Slavery,* p. 199.

down in the quarters. A grim defiance was growing in every pair of eyes. Among them was George, a fiery, emaciated boy of seventeen, who, some time before, had returned from a skulking spell in the woods. Upon his return he was seized and severely whipped. Again he took to the woods, but, now, after two weeks, had come back in a starved humility, a mere stripling of skin and bones. Such a boy, weak and sick, had lost much of his value as a slave.

Much liquor was consumed from the brown jug which stood on the table in the Lewis home as the fateful evening of December 15 wore on. At length, the two brothers decided to administer, as an example, a new form of cruelty, not to any of the older slaves, but to one with young rebel blood who had not learned the wisdom of submission.

Isham sent one of the old slaves down to the quarters to bring in the boy George. Handing him a beautiful cut-glass pitcher his mother had brought from Virginia, the younger Lewis commanded the frightened boy to fetch some water from the spring at the foot of the hill. With drunken seriousness he impressed the young Negro with the great value, material and sentimental, of the heirloom, and threatened the severest punishment should he even so much as chip it during his errand. Isham followed the slave with his rifle, their figures casting long, weird shadows before them on the moon-flooded hillside.

Lilburne, in the meantime, herded the slaves into the largest Negro cabin on the place, where the frightened slaves took up positions against the wall opposite the fireplace. With drawn pistol, the elder Lewis walked back and forth among them as he nervously tried to read their eyes, seeing mingled there both fear and defiance. Tonight, he told them, they would be taught orders to stay at home, and, since words were of no avail, there would be a demonstration of the kind of punishment a runaway slave would receive in the future.

During these trying minutes the slaves maintained a deathly stillness, which drained from every one of them his former defiance. Suddenly the door opened, and Isham, cursing, jerked the boy George into the room, where he fell on his knees begging loudly for mercy. In his hand was still clutched the arched handle of the pitcher, one side of which, cracked and broken, flashed in the firelight.

Throwing some ropes to several of the nearest Negroes, Isham commanded them to tie up George, while Lilburne dragged a heavy meat block before the open fireplace. Yelling and kicking, the unfortunate slave was bound with frantic haste, and a mournful murmur rose from the slaves as they saw Lilburne reach for his broadaxe. With the first blow he severed the boy's feet, and, after pitching them into the fire, turned to lecture the slaves in a coarse, drunken babble on obedience. Mute with fright they stood dazed and incapable of resistance.

Gradually the boy George was chopped to pieces and his parts thrown into the blazing fireplace. With insane gestures the brothers threatened the assembled slaves with the same fate should any word of their dastardly crime go beyond the bounds of the Lewis plantation. Nothing now remained but to dispose of the flesh and bones of George, and for this purpose the fire was brightly stirred until two hours past midnight, when the gruesome ceremonies ended. Satisfied that their diabolical deed was well done and its secret would be kept inviolate, the crazed brothers, after again warning their slaves, permitted them to disperse.

It was not many days, however, until ugly rumors began to reach the ears of the plain country folk that the missing George had been the victim of foul play. For several months the Lewis brothers held out against their neighbors' suspicions, until one day in March, 1812, a man passing the Lewis home saw a dog gnawing on what he discovered to be a human jawbone. News of this startling discovery swept the countryside and threats of lynching were rife in many parts of the county. The Lewis Negroes, now sensing release from an insufferable tyranny, loosened their fear-frozen tongues as neighbors, digging about the Lewis place, found the remains of the hacked-up slave boy.[36] Lilburne and his brother Isham were soon arrested and taken to Salem, the county seat, where on March 18, 1812, they were indicted for murder by the grand jury of Livingston County:

> "Lilburne Lewis, gentleman, and Isham Lewis, yeoman, not having the fear of God before their eyes, but being moved by the instigations of the devil, on the fifteenth day of December, 1811, at the house of the said Lilburne Lewis, he, with an axe of the value of $2, held in both hands, did wilfully and feloniously and with hate cut a death wound in the neck of one negro boy, George, and

36. One version of this story is that when the horrible deed was about completed, in the early morning hours of December 16, 1811, a terrific earthquake (New Madrid) shook Livingston County and all that part of Kentucky, and the entire back wall of the Lewis slave cabin crumbled, covering the fireplace, which contained the remains of the young Negro. Next morning, as the wall was hastily being reconstructed and the bones of the dissected slave thrown in, a dog, unobserved by all, casually took up one of the bones and slunk slowly off. This was later found by a passer-by, who exposed the crime of the Lewis brothers.—William C. Watts, *Chronicles of a Kentucky Settlement*, pp. 193–95.

WHITE HALL, HOME OF CASSIUS M. CLAY, MADISON COUNTY

KNOW ALL MEN BY THESE PRESENTS, That we, C. M. Clay and M. C. Johnson are held and firmly bound unto the Justices of the Fayette County Court, in the penal sum of $2400 (i.e.) $400 for each Slave. Dollars, current money of Kentucky, the payment of which well and truly to be made, we bind ourselves, our heirs, &c. jointly and severally, firmly by these presents. Sealed and dated this 13 day of January 1845.

The Condition of the above obligation is such, that whereas, the County Court of Fayette, have this day permitted said C. M. Clay to Emancipate his slave,s Scott, Riley, Dave [illegible] David, Polly & Zelia Now, if said Slaves shall not, at any time hereafter, become a County charge, then this obligation to be void, else to be and remain in full force and virtue.

C. M. Clay SEAL

M. C. Johnson SEAL

BOND POSTED BY C. M. CLAY TO EMANCIPATE SIX SLAVES

> did afterwards cause the body of the same to be burned . . . and that the said Isham Lewis then and there was aiding to do and commit the felony and murder aforesaid."[37]

Armed with a warrant for their arrest, the sheriff, accompanied by Joseph Watts, Silas Hovious and several others, set out for the Lewis farm on the morning of April 10, 1812. But the brothers, at liberty on bond since their examining trial, had learned of their impending arrest and the nature of the public feeling. Long before the posse arrived, these proud but perverted descendants of the Virginia aristocracy conceived the plan of finishing the play of life with a still deeper tragedy. Fortified with alcohol, they discussed quickly, but methodically, the details of a suicide pact.

They now agreed that each should kill the other. Isham took down two rifles and began cleaning them, while Lilburne wrote his will, making several bequests to his wife and family, and in a codicil added that he wished "myself & brother to be entered in the same coffin & in the same grave."[38] With rifle in hand, the two nephews of Jefferson walked slowly to the hilltop eminence, to the little family burial ground where their mother had recently been interred.

The brothers, as planned, were to take up their positions on opposite sides of the burial lot, aim their rifles steadily and, at the word, fire together, but, instead of a double killing, Lilburne shot himself while demonstrating how a person could end his own life with the help of a ramrod to set off the trigger of his gun.[39] It had

37. Livingston Circuit Court, Order Book D, p. 290, March 18, 1812.

38. Livingston County Court, Will Book A, p. 34, probated May 9, 1812.

39. There are several conflicting accounts of the death of Lilburne Lewis, but this version seems to be the one most generally accepted. An-

been agreed in the plan that if they did not succeed in killing each other, the survivor should kill himself in that manner. But now, Isham, dazed and panic-stricken at the sight of his brother's contortions, failed to carry out his part of the death pact and fled to the woods. He was soon apprehended and lodged in the county jail at Salem.

News of the murder of the slave George and the tragedy of the Lewis brothers spread far and wide, and the *Kentucky Gazette,* published at Lexington, carried a rather complete account of the affair, but with some minor discrepancies:

> "MURDER! HORRID MURDER! A gentleman from Livingston County informs [us] that the two brothers, Capt. Lilburn and Isham Lewis, who were tried and admitted to bail during the last Circuit court of that county, for murdering a negro boy, (the property of the former) and burning him on a kitchen fire on the night of the 25th [15th] December last, mutually agreed, the week before last, to destroy each other, and met with their rifles for that purpose on the plantation of Capt. Lilburn Lewis. Lilburn stood on his first wife's grave—Isham a few steps from him—Lilburn received a ball through his heart and fell without discharging his gun, which was found cocked and loaded on the ground with him. This shocking affair is said to have been occasioned by the flight of Capt. Lewis' wife, who made her escape to save her life, as it was feared that her evidence would be admitted against Isham, as an aider and abettor of the horrid deed with which

other one has it that Isham, becoming nervous, fired and killed his brother before the word was given. Lilburne's death occurred only a short time before the sheriff and his men reached the Lewis farm on the morning of April 10, 1812.

her husband stood charged. Isham is confined in Salem jail, where it is said he confessed the above particulars, but at present denies them." [40]

On April 11, 1812, John Darrah, coroner of Livingston County, impaneled a jury of twelve "good & honest men truly sworn" to report on the death of Lilburne Lewis, and on the following day they brought in a verdict which read:

> "We the jury are of the opinion that Lilburne Lewis did murder himself on the 10th day of April, 1812, on his own plantation and Isham Lewis [was] present and accessory to the murder." [41]

Isham Lewis, the younger brother, was sentenced to be hanged, at Salem, by the court which sat the following June, but long before the date set, he managed to escape from the log jail. His whereabouts remained a matter of much speculation; one tradition had it that he went down to Natchez, married, later joined Jackson's army and was killed at the battle of New Orleans. Whether this account was true or not, the circuit clerk of Livingston County, on March 20, 1815, entered an order from Judge Benjamin Shackleford relative to the murder charge against Isham Lewis, which read: "Ordered that this case abate, by the death of the defendant." [42] Thus ended one of the strangest and cruelest cases in all the annals of Kentucky slavery.

As a further proof that the enslaved blacks had but very restricted rights in the courts of the state, the Kentucky legislature, when it repealed the age-old law of

40. May 12, 1812.
41. Livingston County, County Court Papers, 1810–1812, Coroner's Report.
42. Livingston Circuit Court, Order Book E, p. 2, March 20, 1815.

"benefit of clergy" in February, 1798, left the law undisturbed insofar as it applied to slaves.[43] This gave them a certain immunity not applicable to the whites. On such charges as murder, rape, barnburning, poisoning, and other felonies punishable by death, the slave might, in the discretion of the presiding judge, claim "benefit of clergy" and by the ancient law be branded in the hand, publicly whipped and set free.

Some slaves, no doubt, being unable to testify against their masters or the body of society, were tried and convicted for crimes they never committed; others, possibly with less justification, took advantage of the technicality of being able to read, claimed the privilege of "benefit of clergy" and, after being branded and whipped, went free.

Preston, a slave of Warren County, in 1845 was accused of burning his master's barn, was tried and convicted, and although he claimed the "benefit of clergy," his plea was denied and he was hung for his crime on November 6 of that year.[44] On the other hand, Bird, a slave of John Hays, a farmer of Barren County, was arrested and accused of "violently & feloniously making an assault on and upon Eliza Syra, a spinster." [45] At the March, 1846, term of the Barren Circuit Court, Bird was tried for rape and found guilty, although the evidence against him was clearly insufficient and the jury was highly prejudiced because the prosecutrix was a white woman.

Judge Richard Buckner, "sympathising with the poor

43. Littell, *Statute Law of Kentucky,* II, 10, Section 44, February 10, 1798. "Slaves are excluded from the provisions of this act," that is, the repeal of the Benefit of Clergy.

44. *Western Citizen,* November 10, 1845.

45. Commonwealth of Kentucky *vs.* Bird, a slave, Barren Circuit Court, June Term, 1845.

wretch," allowed the "benefit of clergy" to be claimed, and, "upon being tendered the United States Constitution and being able to read it," the said Bird was, by order of the court, sentenced to be "branded with a hot iron in the open hand, in the presence of the court by the jailor of Barren County, and thence taken to the public whipping post and there receive on his bare back 39 lashes well laid on by the sheriff." [46] After the infliction of this punishment, the prisoner was set at liberty. This was the last case in which the "benefit of clergy" was granted to a convicted criminal in Kentucky,[47] for the law, unequally and sometimes unfairly applied in the different jurisdictions, was legally abolished at the next term of the Kentucky legislature, on January 16, 1847.[48]

As slaves had little or no chance of taking their grievances to court, numerous cases are on record where the recalcitrant blacks, in an effort to seek redress, conspired against their masters and retaliated in various ways. Probably the most common way for the field or farm hand to wreak vengeance upon his master for harsh treatment, cruel punishment, separation of families or any wrongs, fancied or real, was to burn his house, barn, granary or other buildings. Despite the fact that such an act carried the death penalty, numerous cases of this kind appear in the ante-bellum Kentucky newspapers, in some instances, no doubt, falsely attributed to some sulky slave or a fleeing runaway.

Family servants, on occasion, were known to poison

46. Barren Circuit Court, Civil Order Book, March Term, 1846, p. 225, March 14, 1846.

47. *Kentucky Law Reporter,* VI, 508.

48. *Acts, General Assembly, 1846–1847,* Chap. XXXVII, p. 6, approved January 16, 1847.

the food or drink of their master or some member of his family as a covert means of paying off a grudge or avenging a grievance.[49] In Fayette County, Cassilly, a young mulatto slave, was sentenced to death for "mixing an ounce of pounded glass with gravy" and giving it to her master, John Hamilton, and his wife Martha.[50] Another poisoning, much talked of in the Bluegrass, occurred in the home of Hector P. Lewis, a wealthy planter residing in the northern part of Fayette County. Harriet, his family servant, was likewise subjected to the death sentence for having "mixed and mingled a certain deadly poison, to wit, the seed of the Jamestown weed pulverized, in certain coffee," which she gave to her master, "knowingly, wilfully and of her malice aforethought, with the evil intent that death would ensue to the said Lewis." [51]

In all probability, the strangest case of this kind occurred in the family of Cassius M. Clay, the great champion of Negro freedom and one of the most colorful characters in Kentucky history. Several weeks after Clay's encounter with Brown at Russell Cave Springs, his second son, Cassius Clay, Jr., an infant of three or four years, was taken seriously ill on September 1, 1843. Emily, the boy's nurse and family servant of the Clay family, was strongly accused of poisoning the child, who, despite the best efforts of Doctors Lloyd and Elisha Warfield, "did suffer and languish and languishing

49. Several persons in the household of Mrs. Patrick Pope, of Louisville, were poisoned in July, 1858, with arsenic put in their food by a ten-year-old Negro girl. "She did the deed in revenge," said the local paper, "for a whipping she had received a short time before."—Quoted in the *Western Citizen,* July 16, 1858.

50. Commonwealth of Kentucky *vs.* Cassilly, a slave, Fayette Circuit Court, File 1164, March 16, 1849.

51. Commonwealth of Kentucky *vs.* Harriet, a slave, Fayette Circuit Court, File 744, June 13, 1831.

did live until the 20th of September [1843] next, when he died." [52] Strange and hard to fathom are the motives of Emily, if any, and the fact that the accused slave was not brought to trial until fully two years after the Clay infant had died.

Emily, as charged in the indictment, did "feloniously, wilfully and of her malice aforethought, attempt to kill and murder one Cassius Clay," and "did then and there put, mix and mingle a deadly poison called arsenick, to wit, five grains thereof into a certain quantity of milk, to wit, half a pint, and did then and there, by reason of persuasion, threats and force, induce the said Cassius Clay, an infant of tender age, to drink and swallow down a great quantity of the poison aforesaid, with the evil intent that his death might therefrom ensue." [53]

When the case finally came to trial, on October 14, 1845, the jury, largely pro-slavery and highly prejudiced against an accused slave, could find no evidence sufficient to establish her guilt "beyond a reasonable doubt," the degree required by law, and brought in a verdict, which read: "We the jury find the prisoner Emily *not guilty* of the charge laid in the indictment." [54] Although legally acquitted of the murder charge, there was still a darker side to this strange case.

Clay, the well-known abolitionist, still believing that Emily had taken the life of his infant son, though not proved in her trial,[55] now sought personal retribution and accordingly sold Emily to a "nigger trader," who took her to the torrid cotton fields of Mississippi. While

52. Commonwealth of Kentucky *vs.* Emily, a slave, Fayette Circuit Court, File 1103, April 15, 1845.

53. *Ibid.*

54. Fayette Circuit Court, Order Book 32, p. 15, October 14, 1845.

55. *Lexington Observer & Reporter,* October 18, 1845.

she was awaiting trial in Megowan's slave jail in Lexington, Clay sold her mother, brother and sister likewise into the Southern markets.[56] "I sent them to New Orleans," said Clay, "and sold them there because I knew them to be the abettors of the crime of Emily." [57]

It was but natural that, when transplanted from the wild life of Africa to civilization, the slaves should chafe under restraint and require some discipline. This task was sometimes too great for the master and he had to seek assistance in the person of a hired overseer, usually a middle-aged white man of little property. These overseers were usually employed by the year and had no personal interest in the return of the crops, their sole business being simply the care and management of the plantation and slaves.

William, a Lexington-born slave, relates some rather harsh rules and regulations in force on his master's farm in Fayette County, where about twenty-five or thirty hands worked in the tobacco and hemp fields. Every morning they were summoned to their toil at four o'clock "by the ringing of a bell, hung on a post near the house of the overseer. They were allowed," as William related, "half an hour to eat their breakfast and to get to the field. At half-past four, a horn was blown by the overseer, which was the signal to commence work and every one that was not on the spot at the time, had

56. *Memoirs,* p. 559.

57. Clay was severely criticized by the abolitionists for his sale and separation of Emily's family, and later, Emily herself. To this charge he answered: "I have never at any time in my life sold any slave, except for *crime* or by their *own* desire." He further added that these slaves were held in trust by the will of his father, which provided that if "any of them should behave amiss, they shall be sold, and the money settled in land for the benefit of those [slaves] for whom the trust was created."—*The Liberator,* May 2, 1845.

to receive ten lashes from the negro-whip, with which the overseer always went armed.

"The handle [of the whip] was about three feet long, with the butt-end filled with lead, and the lash six or seven feet in length, made of cowhide, with a platted cracker on the end of it. This whip was put in requisition very frequently and freely, and a small offense on the part of a slave furnished an occasion for its use." [58]

Many of the overseers went about their duties armed with a long whip, both as an emblem of office and a symbol of that rigid discipline to which slaves were expected to conform.[59] On one occasion, a visitor to Henry Clay's estate, "Ashland," near Lexington, while inspecting the blooded cattle, said that he "found the overseer with a long-handled, stout whip which he had broken. This answered both as a cattle whip and, occasionally to 'whip off' the slaves." [60]

Kentucky overseers, as a rule, were kind and considerate and had no other interest in the slaves than to see them perform their required duties, but now and then there crept into the press accounts of cruel overseers in different parts of the state. One of this kind was Jim Kizzie, an overseer of Henderson County, who conformed somewhat to the type of Simon Legree in the famous book, *Uncle Tom's Cabin.* He was much feared by the slaves and took a keen delight in inflicting his innate cruelty upon them. In performing his duties he

58. Brown, *Narrative of William W. Brown,* pp. 14–15.

59. Excessive whipping often broke the slave's spirit, as noted in the appearances mentioned in some of the runaway advertisements. Jim "had a rather down-cast look," and Andy "has a down-cast look when spoken to."—*Kentucky Gazette,* August 2, February 6, 1840.

60. Polk Campaign Pamphlet, entitled: "Christian Voters! Read, Pause and Reflect! Mr. Clay's Moral Character." Original in author's collection, n.p., n.d.

carried a revolver strapped at his waist and, fastened by a loop at the waist, was a long rawhide whip which did frequent duty in whipping the field Negroes.

During the summer of 1862 Kizzie had been particularly active in applying the lash, and the slaves, driven to rebellion, secretly planned to kill him after the next flogging. On the fourth of August the provocative flogging occurred. Biding their time, the long intimidated blacks seized the much-hated overseer as he came to the tobacco field to inspect their work, and, stripping off their cotton suspenders, fastened a noose about Kizzie's neck and, despite his struggles and screams, strangled him to death.[61] Then they dragged his body into the near-by woods and concealed it among the trees.[62]

The utmost excitement prevailed when the news of the killing spread throughout Henderson County. Bloodhounds were called to the scene and five slaves were arrested and charged with the crime.[63] Four of them, Jeff, Joe Daniel, Jim and Stephen were acquitted, but Daniel, the ringleader, was executed for the crime on the sixth day of February, 1863.[64] Numerous slaveholders of that section on the day of Daniel's execution took their Negroes into town to see the hanging in order that it might serve as a salutary lesson to them.[65]

61. Commonwealth of Kentucky *vs.* Moses, a slave, *et al.*, Henderson Circuit Court, Order Book P, p. 252, December 10, 1862.

62. Starling L. Marshall, "Olden Days, A Chapter of Slave History in Henderson County," *Sunday Gleaner and Journal*, Henderson, July 16, 1933.

63. Henderson Circuit Court, Order Book P, pp. 252, 258, December Term, 1862. These five slaves, belonging the estate of A. B. Barret, were charged with killing "James Kissee, by beating, bruising, choking and strangling him with their hands, fists and legs and by choking him with a string or suspenders by tying the same around his neck."

64. *Ibid.*, p. 299, December 22, 1862. Daniel's value was fixed by commissioners at "$800 and allowed to the executors of A. B. Barret, deceased."

65. When Lucy, a slave of Meade County, was hanged in May, 1848,

Not only were slaves known to take the lives of their masters[66] or overseers, but they were now and then charged with the murder of their own children, sometimes to prevent them from growing up in bondage. In Covington a father and mother, shut up in a slave barracoon and doomed to the Southern market, "when there was no eye to pity them and no arm to save," did by mutual agreement "send the souls of their children to Heaven rather than have them descend to the hell of slavery," and then both parents committed suicide.[67]

During the summer of 1847 Theodocia, the mulatto household servant of General Andrew Taylor, of Frankfort, attempted, as was charged, to take the life of her four-year-old daughter. According to the indictment, the said Theodocia, "not having the fear of God before her eyes but being moved and seduced by the instigations of the devil," did "wilfully, feloniously and of her malice aforethought, fix, clasp & press both her hands upon and around the neck of the said female child and did then and there choke, suffocate & strangle her with the evil intent that death would shortly follow."[68]

Upon being tried, Theodocia was acquitted, and here again it was demonstrated that sometimes cases in which slaves were charged with capital offenses, when tried, turned out to have little or no basis in fact. This and other cases of unjust accusations may have been the

---

for the murder of her master, Lewis Hamilton, several thousand people witnessed the execution, and "slave owners for miles around brought their slaves to show them what would happen if they killed their masters."—Ridenour, *Early Times in Meade County,* p. 78.

66. Commonwealth of Kentucky *vs.* Thomas, a slave, Fayette Circuit Court, File 1102, March 21, 1845. This is a typical case of a slave's murdering his master.

67. Carleton, *op. cit.,* p. 138.

68. Commonwealth of Kentucky *vs.* Theodocia, a slave, Franklin Circuit Court, File 713, June 16, 1847.

results of personal grudges, or the attempts of masters to seek unwarranted revenge. Whatever the cause, slaves, as has been pointed out, had but little recourse against their masters, and it can be truthfully said that, even in Kentucky where bondage was of a milder form, slavery had its darker side.

CHAPTER XI

AFRICAN UTOPIA

There were numerous Kentuckians who, through motives of benevolence and humanity, were willing to liberate their blacks, provided a suitable disposal could be made of the manumitted slaves. What to do with the free Negro was a troublesome question in many minds. To turn him loose upon society without means of support was a grave mistake as well as an uncharitable act. Socially and economically the "free nigger" was a misfit in a slaveholding community.

His very presence exerted a bad influence upon the slaves; he might harbor runaways, circulate abolition literature, receive stolen goods, make the black bondsmen discontented with their lot and inspire in them a desire for freedom by revolt. He could neither associate with the whites nor mingle with his enslaved brethren. There was no place for him in Kentucky's industrial system; all the work was done by slaves. Through poverty, ignorance and ostracism by both master and slave the plight of the free Negro was indeed hard and, sometimes, even pitiful. From old age or infirmities, the free Negro was likely to become a public charge. Many persons, though feeling a warm sympathy with those "held to service," believed that immediate emancipation of an excessive number of blacks would surely bring about a state of social and political chaos in slaveholding Kentucky.

By 1810 there were fully seventeen hundred free Negroes in Kentucky, and their problem was a growing perplexity for slaveholders and planters throughout the state. In this period virtually as many abolition and emancipation plans were afoot as there were individuals who opposed slavery. Overshadowing the early efforts of the abolition societies was the movement for colonization—transporting the liberated blacks to distant regions where they could live together and enjoy all the privileges of freedom. Several places were suggested as the haven for this new movement—Haiti, Canada, Santo Domingo, Mexico, Africa and even a district "beyond the Rocky Mountains within the limits of the territory of the United States."

It was, therefore, with eagerness that the American Colonization Society, an organization founded in 1817 principally by Southerners for the purpose of colonizing the free people of color,[1] was seized upon as a means of solving the problem. This organization, composed of slaveholders as well as non-slaveholders, soon gained favor throughout the North and South, and by February, 1819, sufficient money had been raised to send out agents to locate a suitable site for a colony. After several months of investigation a tract of land was selected for this purpose on the western shores of Africa, which was

1. On January 1, 1817, the American Colonization Society was formally organized at Washington, D. C. Its primary purpose was "to ameliorate the condition of the Free People of Colour now in the United States, by providing a colonial retreat, either on this continent or that of Africa." —*National Intelligencer,* January 4, 1817.

significantly named Liberia,[2] "land of freedom," and its capital called Monrovia, in honor of James Monroe.

Late in December, 1820, the first shipload of colored emigrants, eighty-six in number, left New York City for their new home in Africa in the three-hundred-ton sailing ship *Elizabeth,* which was chartered by the government. During the following year the second group of manumitted slaves left the United States on the brig *Nautilus,* followed shortly afterwards in March, 1821, by the schooner *Augusta,* with twenty-five on board.

Many discouragements, however, were met with during these pioneer days of colonization. Contagious diseases frequently broke out on board the slow sailing boats, and tropical fevers took many lives after the colony was reached. Land had to be cleared and the jungle conquered. Dissensions arose from time to time. There was trouble with savage neighbors and with slavers who did not want to see a free colony founded upon the west coast to interfere with their smuggling and well established slave trade.

And yet, despite the many reverses and privations suffered by these early colonists, other expeditions of colored emigrants continued to set out for the new land of promise. On the twentieth of December, 1827, the brig *Dorris* sailed from Baltimore with one hundred and five freed slaves and the *Nautilus* left Norfork a few days later with a cargo of one hundred and eighty manumitted blacks, almost all from North Carolina.

Early in the eighteen-twenties citizens of Kentucky

2. This land, situated south of the British colony of Sierra Leone, was at first leased from native chiefs, but later, on December 11, 1821, in exchange "for gunpowder, tobacco, muskets, iron pots, beads, looking-glasses, cotton, etc.," was acquired by title. This was the nucleus for the colony of Liberia, which afterwards, in 1847, became the Republic of Liberia.—Early L. Fox, *The American Colonization Society,* p. 67.

began to read of the work of the American Colonization Society, and naturally the thought presented itself that this was the sanest plan by which the state could rid itself of slavery and free Negroes. As early as 1823 an independent colonization society was formed, but it was not until 1829 that the Kentucky Colonization Society, composed of five local societies, was organized as an auxiliary to the parent body at Washington. This new adjunct of emancipation, with colonization as its primary object, found favor with many Kentuckians who had heretofore taken little or no interest in the scheme of outright abolition.

Many of the most conservative and respectable citizens of the state belonged to these societies and worked hard for their success. Money had to be raised by subscriptions [3] to finance the expeditions, and benevolent slaveholders found who were willing to liberate their blacks in order that they might be transported back to the land of their ancestors. The movement steadily gained support, and in 1830 the *African Repository* made a very flattering report: "Probably in no State of the Union has the scheme of African Colonization found more decided friends or met with more general approbation than in Kentucky." [4]

Robert S. Finley, agent for the Kentucky Colonization Society, with headquarters in Lexington, made an urgent appeal to Kentuckians to assist the movement and "make donations, either in money or the following

3. Henry Clay in August, 1826, collected and sent to the American Colonization Society, at Washington, $63 from Fayette County—$25 from the First Presbyterian Church, of Lexington; $28 from the McChord [2nd Presbyterian] Church, of Lexington; and $10 from Bethel Church, in Fayette County.—*Western Citizen,* September 6, 1826.

4. *African Repository,* VI, p. 80. This journal was the official publication of the American Colonization Society at Washington.

PUBLIC MEETING!

Since the law of 1833, prohibiting the importation of negroes into our state has been modified, and virtually repealed, and believing that the large importation of refuse negroes which will follow this virtual repeal of the law of 1833, will prove disasterous to the best interests of the State AND BELIEVING THAT SLAVERY IS, IN ITS BEST FORM, A SOCIAL AND POLITICAL CURSE TO THE COUNTRY, AND SHOULD NOT BE MADE PERPETUAL, but should be removed gradually, so as to least interfere with the rights of present slaveholders, we, the undersigned citizens of the County of Boyle, slaveholders and non-slaveholders, being in favor of some system of gradual emancipation with colonization, invite our fellow citizens, friendly to the cause of emancipation, to meet with us at the court-house, in Danville, on Saturday, 17th day of March, 1849, to consult together upon what course should be pursued by the friends of the Cause in the present emergency and to appoint delegates to the State Emancipation Convention, proposed to be held in Frankfort, on the 25th of April next.

BOYLE COUNTY BROADSIDE, 1849

SLAVERY

INCONSISTENT

WITH

JUSTICE AND GOOD POLICY.

By PHILANTHROPOS.

LEXINGTON; PRINTED BY J. BRADFORD.
M. DCC. XCII.

KENTUCKY'S FIRST ANTI-SLAVERY TRACT

articles: bacon, beef, pork, flour, corn-meal, leaf tobacco, salt, nails, hinges, pots, skillets, and all kinds of hard-ware, home-ware, earthen-ware, pound-beans, coarse cotton & calicoes, hemp, linen, etc."[5] These articles, as Finley stressed, were seriously needed in the struggling colony of Liberia.

There were many instances of willingness on the part of the masters to free their slaves for transportation to Africa, but the lack of funds appears to have greatly hampered the work.[6] The Louisville branch of the Kentucky Colonization Society, which appeared to have been more active than any other in the state, raised $805 in 1832, and during the next year the society succeeded in collecting over eleven hundred dollars for the transportation of freed Negroes to Liberia.[7] These sums were obviously very inadequate to take care of the ambitious program, since the cost of transportation was variously estimated to be between twenty-five and forty dollars for each individual given passage to Africa.

It was not until the early part of 1833 that enough money had been raised in Kentucky to outfit the first "expedition" to Liberia. As the prime mover, the Reverend Richard Bibb, of Russellville, Logan County, liberated fifty-one of his slaves and gave the thirty-two who were willing to go in this shipment $444 for their comforts while on the voyage. These thirty-two Bibb Negroes, together with a number of emancipated slaves from over the state, were assembled at Louisville, and on March 22, 1833, this first delegation of liberated

5. *Western Citizen,* September 24, 1831.

6. *The Frankfort Commonwealth,* February 20, 1833, stated that there were a number of prominent slaveholders throughout the state who were ready to liberate their slaves whenever the Kentucky Colonization Society was prepared to transport them to Liberia.

7. Thomas D. Clark, *History of Kentucky,* p. 293.

blacks left the city "in high spirits, having been liberally provided with money and provisions by the people of Kentucky. They were conveyed to New Orleans, free of expense, in the elegant steam-boat Mediterranean, accompanied by the secretary of the Kentucky Colonization Society." [8]

Some time was spent at New Orleans before a suitable vessel could be chartered for the voyage to Africa, and the total number of the colored emigrants was now 150: 107 from Kentucky and 43 from Tennessee. They were described as being "comfortably provided for as circumstances will allow, and, with 3 or 4 exceptions are all in very good health."

At length a vessel was found, and the terms were concluded "by which the emigrants are to be conveyed to Liberia for $3,625," wrote James Birney, a Kentuckian and an early exponent of colonization. Continuing in his description of the boat, he reported: "Everything is to be supplied, except their provisions—the latter is the only expense to which we are to be put. There was only one other vessel which could be had for this purpose. Our vessel is the brig *Ajax,* somewhat smaller than I would have wished, but has been examined by a very skillful sea captain of this place, who pronounced her altogether competent, sound, sea-worthy and a good sailer." [9]

On April 20, 1833, with everything in readiness and the one hundred and fifty emigrants on board in gay spirits, the boat, under the command of Captain William H. Taylor, pulled away from the wharf at New Orleans about five o'clock in the afternoon and

8. *Niles' Weekly Register,* XLIV (April 13, 1833), 98.
9. Dwight L. Dumond, *Letters of James Gillespie Birney,* I, 67.

"dropped down the river a short distance." Then, on the following day, "she was towed out to sea." [10]

With prospects of a pleasant voyage before her, tragedy, however, soon overtook the *Ajax*. In the words of the contemporary press: "We learn with regret that the brig *Ajax,* fifteen days from New Orleans, bound for Liberia, with nearly one hundred and fifty emigrants on board, has been compelled to put back into Key West in distress. She lost her mate and two blacks when only two days out, and the ship's carpenter reported that 30 to 40 persons had died of the cholera, whilst the brig was anchored off the town. They are said to have been as fine a set of emigrants as ever left this country. One hundred of these were from Kentucky, of whom 96 were slaves and had been manumitted upon condition of their deportation to Monrovia." [11]

Of special interest to residents of central Kentucky was the news that among the colored emigrants on board the cholera-stricken *Ajax* was "a female slave [Milly] brought up by Mrs. [Robert] Wickliffe, who possessed a superior education and gifted mind, and was intended for a teacher in Liberia. With her was her son Alfred who was to become a minister." [12] Later it was learned that Milly had died of the scourge, but Alfred "reached the shores of Africa, and became one of Liberia's leading citizens." [13]

Among the liberated blacks from Kentucky who

10. *Ibid.,* pp. 70–71.

11. *New York Commercial Advertiser,* June 23, 1833. Eleven of the freed blacks on board the *Ajax* had belonged to the Rev. Robert J. Breckinridge and six to Senator Robert Wickliffe.

12. *Lexington Observer & Reporter,* June 27, 1833.

13. See Chapter XII for an account of Milly and Alfred, in the Breckinridge-Wickliffe debates and pamphlets.

escaped the ravages of cholera while a fellow passenger on the trip to Africa with Milly and Alfred, in the spring of 1833, was David Richardson, who, after a year's residence in Liberia, sent word to his old friends back in Lexington that he was doing well and was likely to prosper: "I am very well pleased with this county," he said, "and I believe we can make a good living here if we are industrious. We have settled on a ten-acre farm and are carrying on after the manners of the place—raising corn, potatoes, cassada, plantains and bananas which is very good food. I would advise anyone coming to this place to bring everything necessary, such as money, clothing and cheap cloth—knowing that in every new country these things are scarce and very dear. . . ." [14]

During the summer months of 1833 the Asiatic cholera raged in Kentucky, and this epidemic greatly retarded the progress of colonization. "The very general prevalence of the cholera all around us has paralyzed everything," wrote Thornton Mills to James Birney on July 1, 1833. "Multitudes have died throughout this region [central Kentucky]. Lexington and Paris have been severely scourged, and other places have had it less severely. . . ." [15]

But by the fall of 1833 the pestilence had generally subsided, and it was thought that the public mind had become sufficiently settled to make further appeals for funds. In a very optimistic moment, Dr. John M. Blackburn, of Versailles, reported: "I have been very suc-

14. Letter dated March 14, 1834, Monrovia, Liberia, from David Richardson, ex-slave of W. L. Breckinridge, to William Tucker, at Lexington, Kentucky, quoted in the *Lexington Observer & Reporter*, August 13, 1834.

15. Thornton Mills, Frankfort, Kentucky, to James Birney, at Huntsville, Alabama, in Dumond, *Letters of James Gillespie Birney*, I, 80.

cessful in collecting funds. The cause is advancing gloriously in this State. God grant it may soon girt the Union." [16]

Despite the enthusiastic views of Mr. Blackburn and others, the colonization scheme remained sluggish for the next eight or ten years, and in view of the shortage of funds it is not surprising that the number of free Negroes transported from Kentucky to Liberia was in fact very small.[17] However, the efforts of the Kentucky Colonization Society were not relaxed, and in 1844 an agitation was started to establish a separate colony in Africa.

Early in 1845 the Reverend Alexander M. Cowan, state colonization agent, began a vigorous campaign to raise five thousand dollars to be used in purchasing a suitable tract of land on which the free people of color in Kentucky might be settled. Newspapers, churches and other organizations actively espoused the project and, as a result, the required sum was raised before the end of the year.[18] With this money a tract of land forty miles square was purchased in Liberia from the American Colonization Society. This new colony, located on the north bank of the St. Paul River, fifteen miles from Monrovia, was named "Kentucky in Liberia," and its capital called "Clay Ashland," in honor of Henry Clay and his country place in Fayette County, Kentucky.[19]

16. Blackburn to James Birney, Washington, D. C., November 8, 1833, *ibid.*, I, 95.

17. The numbers of liberated slaves transported from Kentucky to Liberia during the following years were: 1834–39, none; 1840, 12; 1841, 20; 1842, 14; 1843, 18; 1844, 21; 1845, 36.—*African Repository,* XXIII, 65.

18. *Frankfort Commonwealth,* September 30, 1845.

19. Alexander M. Cowan, *Liberia as I Found It in 1858,* p. 67. Henry Clay, himself a slaveholder at "Ashland," was a strong supporter of gradual emancipation and firmly believed that African colonization was the logical and practical way to rid Kentucky of free Negroes, and, as he said,

Special inducements were now offered to attract the free Negroes and to make them contented and prosperous after their arrival in this newly-established colony. Those who were unable to pay their transportation expenses were to be provided for with funds raised in Kentucky and were to be supported for six months after their arrival in Africa. Each head of a family or single adult was promised a building lot in the town of Clay Ashland, with five acres adjoining, or, if he settled two miles from town, fifty acres, or if three miles, one hundred acres of land.[20]

Late in November, 1845, the Kentucky society, somewhat elated over its recent success, chartered the barque *Rothschild* to transport about two hundred prospective emigrants to its new settlement, but the boat did not leave New Orleans until the following January, 1846, and then only with thirty-five freed slaves from Kentucky, although there were a large number from other states in the Mississippi Valley. Of the thirty-five colored emigrants who went out from Kentucky, twenty were men, six were women, and nine were children.[21] Only two had previously been free Negroes. Twelve were church members; two were ministers. There were three carpenters, one blacksmith and one shoemaker.

"the only remedy for a chronic disease."—*National Intelligencer*, September 10, 1836.

20. *Presbyterian Herald*, Louisville, January 15, 1846.

21. "Of these emigrants," said a local paper, "15 were from Jessamine County, set free by the late Mrs. Meaux and one free man. Six were from Fayette County; four set free by the late Dr. James Fishback and two by Mrs. Fishback, his widow. Nine from Clark County; eight set free by the late Major Martin; one a free woman the wife of one of Mr. Martin's servants. Two from Daviess County, one from Warren, two from Dayton, Ohio. Two of the manumitted servants from Fayette County and two from Bourbon County preferred to go back, after they had been assembled at Louisville for the trip to New Orleans."—*Western Citizen*, January 23, 1846.

Governor Joseph J. Roberts, of Liberia, personally welcomed this first band of colored immigrants to Kentucky in Liberia, but was no doubt surprised at the way some of them reacted to their new opportunities for freedom. Two turned back at the outset. In the words of the chief executive of the African Republic: "The vessel that took the emigrants from Kentucky arrived in Liberia on 15th of March [1846], having had a passage of 47 days. . . . It must be remembered that in Liberia as in every other country, it requires some exertions for men to place themselves in easy circumstances. Do send us some of your enterprising men from Kentucky. Two of the emigrants, Johnson and Martin, will return in the vessel that brought them out—they were unwilling to land their baggage in Liberia. . . ." [22]

It is from the account of a repatriated black, who made this initial trip to Kentucky in Liberia, that we gain a close insight into actual conditions and the opportunities for the freed slaves which, as Moses Jackson pointed out, were none too good. Writing back to his old friend Eliot West, at Nicholasville, from "Kentucky, Leiberia, Western Africa," under date of March 22, 1846, this former Bluegrass slave reported: "The present state of affairs here is not very flattering, the people here from all that I have seen and heard, take but little interest in the improvement of the country.

"They generally engage in trading with the natives for Corn, Wood and Pam [palm] Oil, which they barter agane for such things as they need, with merchant vessels and neglect almost entirely the cultivation of the ground. The generability of the farms do not exceed 5

22. Letter to Rev. A. M. Cowan, Paris, Kentucky, quoted in *Western Citizen,* May 23, 1846. Governor Roberts was a colored man, as were all landholders or officials of Liberia.

acres and the largest that I have heard of does not exceed 15 acres. Fifteen acres is considered a large farm and so it is for one man to tend it the way they tend it with the hoe. They use neither horses, mules or oxen and they say these animals cannot stand it in performing labours in this climate. There is none of these animals in use here and but two horses in [this] Colony that I can hear of."

Revealing the general dissatisfaction of some of the colonists and the lack of farming tools, he continued: "I want you to send out to me some Grindstones & Chopping Axes by the [next] Expedition and I place the money in Governor Robert's hands to be sent you by the vessel when she returns for they are very scarce here and not a grindstone in reach to sharpen our tools.

"We are settled about 12 miles from Sea Shore on the north bank of the St. Pall [Paul] river in a perfect wilderness and living in bamboo houses. . . . I feel doubtful whether we shall be able to do much good here or not. Six of those who came with us are so discouraged that they are going to return on the same vessel—some of [Rev. James] Fishback's people and some of Mr. [Major Martin, of Clark County] Martin's. . . . Tell Uncle Pleas that we have snakes here from 15 to 20 feet long . . . deer are as common as hogs or sheep in pastures in Kentucky. My respects to all enquiring friends." As an afterthought, he added: "Tell Absolom Woodfork that I cannot as a friend recommend him to come out here until I have seen more of this place." [23]

However, letters written back show that, in spite of the hardships of their new homes in Liberia, some pre-

23. Original letter owned by Judge Samuel M. Wilson, of Lexington, Kentucky.

ferred to be freemen in Africa rather than to live in Kentucky where slavery was a recognized institution. Nelson Sanders, for years a faithful and trusted slave of the Reverend James Fishback, of Lexington, was manumitted by the will of his master, who died in 1845. He was among those first thirty-five freed blacks who went to Kentucky in Liberia with the expedition which left New Orleans in January, 1846. After more than two years' residence in Liberia, Sanders wrote to Mrs. Susan Fishback, widow of his old master, and, addressing her as his "Dear Friend & Benefactor," expressed his sincere gratitude for his blessings and chances in the new country: "As the Liberia packet is about to sail from Africa to America, with the greatest pleasure I embrace the opportunity to write to you [24] . . . as for myself as far as an individual is concerned, I am now in the enjoyment of comfortable health for which I give praise to the Supreme Ruler of the Universe.

"You have perhaps been informed previous to this intelligence concerning the large numbers of Kentuckians besides those of your family of blacks who embarked with me, some of whom have fallen victims of the African fever, but we who survived, are all doing well. I am aware that some persons have falsely [lied] concerning us, and have given woeful accounts of Liberia . . . it is entirely wrong.

"Liberia is unquestionably the happyest territory for the black man that could be selected on the globe, we enjoy liberty and our lives in a degree which is impossible for the negro to enjoy in any other country. Here

24. "Rev. H. W. Ellis, who writes my letter is Pastor of the First Presbyterian Church in Monrovia, and the best friend that I have found in Africa." This colored minister doubtless wrote many other letters for the colored colonists, as few of them could read or write.

is the place whence the man of Color, especially a black color originated, here it should terminate if possible. . . . My shipmates and countrymen, viz, Ware, Jackson, Scott & others are getting on finely & wishes to be remembered to their friends in Kentucky. I now take leave of you for the present, but I hope not forever, for I trust you will condescend to write to me in Africa at least once more, if only to answer this letter; no more at present. I remain your ever grateful servant." [25]

Many liberal-minded and kindhearted slaveholders in Kentucky provided in their wills for their faithful servants, in many cases directing that at the death of their respective owners they be sent to Liberia. The Reverend James Fishback, of Lexington, willed that "if any one or more of my slaves desire to go to Liberia, it is my will that they do so and that fifty dollars be given each one who desires to go, when he or she leaves the shores of the United States, not to return again—at that time I will that they may be emancipated. . . ." [26]

Another Fayette County slave owner, Nancy Markey, bequeathed "unto each of my servants, David, Samuel and Minty, two hundred dollars and to my servant, Lucy, one hundred dollars provided they *goe to Lyberia*. If Minty does not go, $500 to be reserved by my executors for her comfort. . . ." [27]

In Muhlenberg County one benevolent master provided for the "comfort & happiness" of his slaves and wrote in his will that he wished to colonize them,

25. Letter dated "Monrovia, Liberia, Western Africa, January 5, 1848." Original letter owned by Judge Samuel M. Wilson, of Lexington.

26. Fayette County Court, Will Book Q, p. 416, probated December 12, 1845.

27. *Ibid.*, Will Book S, p. 243, dated June 6, 1849.

"should the newly-established Republic of Liberia continue to flourish. I desire," said he, "that my slaves be removed to that country and the money raised from the sale of my property be applied to their outfit and settlement in that country." [28]

Major Richard Bibb, a large slaveholder and planter of Logan County, made a rather unique and remarkable will which, yellowed with age and falling to pieces, is still to be seen at the courthouse in Russellville. By this instrument he liberated all of his slaves, fifty-one in number, valued at $25,000, to take effect "from and after the first day of January next" after his death, and willed "that all of them, who have not wives or husbands in bondage, be sent to Liberia. I give to my slaves hereby emancipated $5,000 to be divided out among them and paid out to them from time to time according to the discretion of my executors. . . ." [29]

Of these fifty-one manumitted slaves, only thirty-two, as heretofore stated, ever left Kentucky for Liberia.[30] Several years later, Abel Long, a Negro preacher of Russellville, went to Liberia as a missionary. When he returned to Logan County he reported that he had been unable to find any of the Bibb Negroes, although he understood a number of them had died of the tropical diseases and was informed that at least two of the women were alive at that time, but that "they had gone into the jungle and lapsed into native barbarity." [31]

Many Kentucky slaves, while enjoying the benevolent features of slavery, were adverse to accepting free-

28. Muhlenberg County Court, Will Book 3, p. 153, dated July 7, 1850.

29. Marmaduke B. Morton, *Kentuckians are Different,* p. 141.

30. These thirty-two liberated slaves were a part of the first shipment from Kentucky to Liberia on the brig *Ajax* in the spring of 1833. See footnote 8, *supra.*

31. Morton, *op. cit.,* p. 141.

dom with the stipulation that they be deported to far-off Liberia, where conditions were primitive and life hard and uncertain. They were content, in many cases, to remain in bondage under their present masters, to live among their friends and loved ones and enjoy the happy surroundings of their birthplace. Then, too, they knew little of self-reliant freedom and cared less for the responsibilities that went with it.

Luther Stephens, a well-to-do slaveholder of Fayette County, recorded in his will a typical case of this kind: "I owned a negro woman named Louisa, and gave her the privilege of being free on condition she should go to Liberia, which offer she refused, preferring to be sold and remain a slave [in Fayette County]; her sale produced three hundred and fifty dollars. It is my will," recited Stephens, "that one-half of this amount be given to the American Tract Society, the other half to the American Bible Society. . . ." [32]

By 1845 the demand for cotton hands in the Far South operated as a decided set-back to the colonization scheme, since in Kentucky and other border slave states, the money value of Negroes was too high to make manumission very popular.[33] Then, again, many manumitted slaves, upon being emancipated, preferred to migrate northward and settle in the little colored settlements already established in the free states of Ohio, Illinois, Indiana and Michigan, where living conditions were much easier than in Kentucky in Liberia, and

32. Fayette County Court, Will Book Q, p. 454, January 20, 1845.

33. Ten years earlier, James Birney, at Danville, saw the futility of the colonization plan when he wrote Lewis Tappan: "Who in Kentucky will furnish all the slaves needed for colonization, between the ages of 17 and 20, the most valuable period of their lives, as articles of commerce, whilst the slave driver is pervading every corner of our state with money in his pockets?"—Dumond, *op. cit.*, I, 178.

where they could still copy the customs and pursue some of the practices of the white man's civilization which they had learned in the two or three generations since their removal from Africa.

Despite the many difficulties that had to be overcome and the constant assaults from the anti-slavery leaders, the colonization advocates kept up their crusade in Kentucky, sending out a few colored emigrants to Africa each year. But results became more and more disheartening, and many persons now believed that colonization probably would die of its own weight, as the cost of transportation was far too much in excess of the good that was to be gained from it. However, early in 1848 there was a slight renewal of interest in the enterprise and twenty-eight emancipated Negroes from Kentucky left on the barque *Nehemiah Rich* for Africa in an "expedition" carrying a total of 129 former slaves.[34]

By 1851 it was plainly evident that the Kentucky Colonization Society was waging a losing fight, for only 297 liberated blacks had been transported from Kentucky to Liberia,[35] and there still remained over ten thousand free Negroes in the state.[36] In an effort to relieve this growing menace to slaveholders and to strengthen the cause of colonization, the Kentucky legislature, by an act passed on March 24, 1851, required all slaves, upon being emancipated, to leave the state and likewise forbade free Negroes of other states from entering Kentucky.[37]

Occasionally however, the dying embers of this

34. *Western Citizen,* March 20, 1848.
35. *34th Annual Report, American Colonization Society,* p. 84.
36. *Negro Population in the United States* (Washington, D. C., 1916), p. 192.
37. *Revised Statutes of Kentucky, 1852,* p. 645.

worthy but impractical social experiment still flickered feebly. Charles Henderson, of Danville, liberated twenty-two of his slaves in May, 1853, and provided them with transportation to Liberia on the schooner *Banshee* with maintenance for six months after they reached the land of their forefathers.[38]

Two years later, through the revived and concerted efforts of the Kentucky Colonization Society, there were assembled at Baltimore fifty-two former Bluegrass slaves, who, on May 8, 1855, embarked for Liberia on the brig *Cora.* "They were all in good spirits," observed an eyewitness, "from the time of leaving Lexington to the time of sailing. They gave no trouble; were not molested on the way, paid no attention to the various opinions expressed to them that they were foolish to go to Liberia." [39] This was the last "expedition" of any consequence to leave the Bluegrass State for Kentucky in Liberia.

The adherents to the plan of colonization—a forlorn hope from the very first—steadily lost faith in the cause.[40] During the whole of the year 1858 only twenty liberated blacks could be found in Kentucky who were willing to go to Liberia, and with that last shipment the Kentucky Colonization Society came virtually to an end.[41] It was now clearly apparent that the amount of money necessary for successful operation was many times larger than that which could have been raised,

38. Roe, *Aunt Leanna, or Early Scenes in Kentucky,* p. 248.

39. *Western Citizen,* June 1, 1855.

40. On March 3, 1856, the Kentucky legislature passed an act appropriating $5,000 annually to the Kentucky Colonization Society, which, at the time, was thought would give a great impetus to the movement. However, from lack of funds and the waning interest in colonization, nothing came of this state appropriation.

41. *42nd Annual Report, American Colonization Society,* pp. 53–56.

even had all slave owners been willing—which they were not—to emancipate their blacks without compensation. At this time it was estimated that sixty-seven dollars was needed to transport each colored emigrant to Liberia and to provide for his upkeep for six months after his arrival on the Dark Continent.[42]

None of the settlements in Liberia flourished. One after another the agents succumbed to disease; some of the dissatisfied colonists returned to the United States; many perished of tropical fevers and numbers lapsed into a state of idleness, want and semi-savagery. Farms and small holdings were deserted; disasters in many forms and consequent despair stalked the colonized Liberians.

Kentucky in Liberia received the small band of colored emigrants that were sent out—never in any appreciable numbers—each year by the state society.[43] Like all the others, this colony, modeled somewhat after "Maryland in Liberia," failed to prosper and furnished a strong argument that under the most favorable conditions emancipated Negroes, when thrown upon their own resources and responsibilities, were wholly incapable of maintaining any economic, social or governmental system of their own. Thus, the scheme of African colonization which Henry Clay earlier in the century had advocated as both "practical and logical" proved, after some thirty years of trials and privations, to be nothing more than a great fantastic dream.

42. *Western Citizen,* June 1, 1858.

43. During the thirty years of its existence, 1829–1859, the Kentucky Colonization Society sent a total of 658 emigrants to Liberia, or a little less than 22 per annum.—*African Repository,* April, 1860, p. 115.

CHAPTER XII

CRUSADERS FOR FREEDOM

When Kentucky was framing her first constitution, the opponents of slavery made a determined effort to prevent the adoption of Article IX, which left slavery virtually undisturbed in the newly-formed state. The Reverend David Rice, father of the Presbyterian Church in the West and one of the most influential men of his time, was the ablest and most active of these early anti-slavery crusaders. In a vigorous speech before the convention at Danville, in April, 1792, he loudly proclaimed the evils of slavery and the probable deterioration of the state if the institution were allowed to persist and, in conclusion, pleaded that the convention "resolve unconditionally to put an end to slavery in Kentucky." This speech, *Slavery Inconsistent with Justice and Good Policy,* appeared in pamphlet form three months before the Constitutional Convention and had the distinction of being the first anti-slavery tract published in Kentucky.[1]

1. Father Rice's pamphlet, under the pseudonym "Philanthropos," was printed by John Bradford, at Lexington, in January, 1792, and later reprinted in Robert H. Bishop's *Outline of the History of the Church in Kentucky* (Lexington, 1824). During the Civil War it was again reprinted under the title: *A Kentucky Protest against Slavery* (New York, 1862).

ROBERT WICKLIFFE

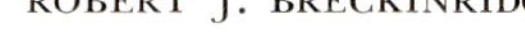

ROBERT J. BRECKINRIDGE

JAMES G. BIRNEY

JOHN G. FEE

Associated with "Father" Rice in these early anti-slavery struggles were six ministers of the Presbyterian, Baptist and Methodist churches and ten lay members of the Constitutional Convention, who firmly believed that, if the spread of slavery was to be prevented, it must never be allowed to obtain the slightest foothold in new territory. However, the efforts of these resolute clergymen and their associates met with little success, for the majority of the framers of Kentucky's first constitution were slaveholders, who adopted provisions which not only recognized, but even protected, slavery.[2]

This first victory for the slaveholding forces, however, did not end the agitation. Between 1792 and the meeting of the second convention in 1799, the slavery opponents kept up a running fight, hoping to secure an anti-slavery clause in the second constitution. For the most part, the opposition of this early period centered in the Baptist and Methodist churches, while the Presbyterians pursued a more conservative course. Young Henry Clay, lately arrived from Virgina, favored gradual emancipation, but the predominating influence of George Nicholas and John Breckinridge was cast on the side of slavery. Provisions favoring Negro bondage were likewise incorporated in the second constitution, and again the anti-slavery forces lost their early fight, a fight that was not to stop here, but was to continue throughout the entire period of slavery.

After the adoption of the state constitutions of 1792

2. Article IX, nevertheless, contained some mitigating provisions, as for example, that the legislature "shall pass laws to permit the owners of slaves to emancipate them," and "to oblige the owners of slaves to treat them with humanity, to provide for their necessary clothing and provision, and to abstain from all injuries to them extending to life or limb." The measure for restricting slavery was defeated by a vote of twenty-six to sixteen.

and 1799, anti-slavery effort continued unabated, especially in the churches. Almost every religious group sponsored some type of anti-slavery program. Most active in this movement were the three leading denominations in Kentucky, the Baptists, Presbyterians and Methodists, while the Catholics, Episcopalians and Disciples or Reformers stood by and figured less prominently in the slavery agitation.

For several years the question of slavery continued to agitate individual churches in Kentucky, although the general associations assumed an attitude of noninterference and took no action in the matter. Emancipating parties were formed in some of the churches, whose adherents proclaimed slavery contrary to God's sacred laws and refused to commune with those who practiced it. Because the Salem Association of Kentucky Baptists refused to pronounce slavery an evil, Mill Creek Church in Jefferson County withdrew in 1794. Under the leadership of Josiah Dodge and Joshua Carmen, the dissatisfied members of Cox's Creek, Lick Creek and Cedar Creek churches formed an independent church in Nelson County, six miles northwest of Bardstown, whose members refused to commune with slaveholders.[3]

Many ministers openly preached emancipation from their pulpits, sometimes even in the presence of slaves. For this conduct they were bitterly assailed, since it was believed that the promulgation of such sentiments would create insubordination and unrest among the slaves.

Many slaveholders were brought before the associations, conferences and church sessions for questioning

3. James H. Spencer, *History of the Kentucky Baptists from 1769–1886*, I, 163, 184, 187.

in regard to their slavery views and activities. Many more were called before the pulpits of their respective churches to be rebuked for their "iniquitous practices." These "martyred" individuals soon left the churches which opposed their holding slaves and established churches of their own, often of the same denomination. Hence there grew up a marked degree of tolerance in the churches as a whole, so that the denominations and ministers became more and more lenient with the "hardened sinners" who persisted in owning slaves.

Early in 1808 the emancipating Baptists formed the Kentucky Abolition Society, the first distinctly anti-slavery organization in the state.[4] While composed largely of the Baptist Licking-Locust Association and the Friends of Humanity,[5] this society embraced a considerable number of anti-slavery advocates from other religious sects throughout the state. In a slaveholding section, such a society, whose chief aim was the liberation of the blacks, naturally incurred severe criticism. Members were openly accused of talking against slavery and slaveholders in the presence of and even "to multitudes of ignorant negroes" who might "pervert the most proper reasonings to improper purposes."

Despite adverse public criticism, the society prospered, and so well pleased were the members with its showing that in 1821 they decided to widen the scope of its activities. As the columns of Kentucky newspapers were closed, as a rule, to all abolition discussion and agitation, this society established an anti-slavery paper,

4. Asa E. Martin, *The Anti-Slavery Movement in Kentucky Prior to 1850*, pp. 42, 43.

5. In Kentucky a society called Friends of Humanity was formed in 1807 with eleven clergymen and thirteen laymen signing the articles of agreement. They were more commonly known as the "Emancipators," and remained in existence until the latter part of 1813.

the *Abolition Intelligencer and Missionary Messenger,* at Shelbyville, in the early part of May, 1822, under the editorship of the Reverend John Finley Crowe, a Presbyterian minister, later identified with Hanover College, in Indiana.

This short-lived monthly magazine, which avowed the extinction of slavery to be its principal object, found existing sentiment too weak to support it and, being unable to buttress its position, ceased publication in April, 1823, after only twelve numbers had been issued. When the next to the last issue of this pioneer anti-slavery periodical came out, the paid subscribers in Kentucky and Tennessee numbered fewer than four hundred,[6] and the society itself counted not more than one hundred and seventy-five members on its rolls. At that time there were only two anti-slavery newspapers published in the United States, the *Abolition Intelligencer* and Benjamin Lundy's *Genius of Universal Emancipation,* published at Greeneville, Tennessee, which in 1824 was removed to Baltimore, where it subsequently ran for several years.

During the middle eighteen-twenties the efforts of the anti-slavery faction to force complete abolition on the people of Kentucky lacked the backing of a wide-spread or crystallized public sentiment. In 1827 the Kentucky Abolition Society died a natural death, whereupon the undismayed opponents of the system of black bondage changed their method of attack. This came about through the formation of those national and state colonization societies advocating gradual emancipation and transportation of freed slaves back to Africa.[7] This

6. *Abolition Intelligencer,* March, 1823. Of the twelve issues printed, nine are in the library of the Wisconsin Historical Society, Madison.

7. The first president of the American Colonization Society was Bush-

new movement of gradual emancipation began to attract much of the public attention and drew into its ranks numerous Kentucky slaveholders who had heretofore manifested little or no interest in the abolition movement, or had generally disapproved it.

It had been clearly demonstrated that slavery in Kentucky, once entrenched, seemed to thrive and prosper on opposition. Robert Wickliffe, the "Old Duke," for many years senator from Fayette County, was now the leader of the radical pro-slavery faction in Lexington, while Robert J. Breckinridge and Cassius M. Clay were spokesmen for those who favored gradual emancipation. Dissension had started in 1828, when a bill was introduced in the legislature to prohibit the importation of slaves into Kentucky, and the emancipation society organized in Lexington the following year further inflamed the public mind.

Several tragic encounters between adherents of the two factions intensified the situation in Lexington, the center of Kentucky's largest slaveholding section. Young Charles Wickliffe on March 9, 1829, shot and killed Thomas R. Benning, editor of the *Gazette,* for publishing a derogatory article concerning the pro-slavery activities of his father, Senator Wickliffe.[8] Several months later this impetuous son of the "Old Duke" challenged George J. Trotter, the new editor of the *Gazette,* and they met under the code duello on October ninth, in a woodland near the Scott County line. Pistols were

rod Washington, nephew of General George Washington. Many distinguished men and philanthropists from both the North and the South were included among its membership, and at various times such men as John Marshall, James Madison, James Monroe and Henry Clay headed the organization. The Kentucky Colonization Society was founded in 1829, seven years before Henry Clay was president of the national body.

8. *Kentucky Reporter,* March 11, July 8, 1829.

named as weapons at the mortal distance of eight feet, and at the first fire young Wickliffe was instantly killed with a bullet squarely through his chest.[9]

During the spring of 1830 a series of caustic, anti-slavery articles, signed "B," appeared in the columns of the *Reporter*. They came from the prolific and pungent pen of Robert J. Breckinridge, son of John Breckinridge, Attorney-General in the cabinet of Thomas Jefferson, and they excited such violent discussion that, two months later, he was forced to withdraw as a candidate for the legislature and to retire from politics at the early age of thirty. His efforts, however, were not altogether in vain, for on September 6, 1831, forty-eight slaveholders "of influence and standing" met in Lexington and formed a society whose members pledged the emancipation of the future offspring of their slaves at the age of twenty-one.[10]

To the alarmed citizens of central Kentucky, the pro-slavery leaders conjured up the spectre of a servile insurrection, should these forty-eight slaveholders succeed in emancipating their slaves; while the emancipationists viewed the excited feelings thus aroused as symptoms of a palpable attempt to suppress public discussion and to inflict more severe discipline on the Negroes. There was much uneasiness among the slaves themselves and, while no Negroes had been executed for fifteen years previous to 1831 in Fayette County for such crimes as murder, rape, arson and burglary, all punishable by death, the jails were now filled with Negroes charged with offenses of this kind. On August 13, 1831, four Negroes were publicly hanged from the

9. *Ibid.*, October 14, 1829.
10. William Birney, *James G. Birney and his Times*, p. 127.

same scaffold in the yard of Megowan's jail, in Lexington, before a crowd estimated to contain between five and ten thousand persons.[11]

On the first day of January of the same year, William Lloyd Garrison, at Boston, began the publication of his paper, *The Liberator,* devoted wholly to the cause of abolition, and two years later, in December, 1833, he and his associates founded the American Anti-Slavery Society, at Philadelphia. This new movement, greatly stimulating the struggling upsurge in Kentucky, called for immediate abolition and violently and indiscriminately denounced Southern slaveholders. Many anti-slavery papers, notably *The Liberator,* the *Anti-Slavery Bugle,* and even a juvenile magazine, the *Slave's Friend,* were often sent free through the mails to persons of known or suspected anti-slavery sentiments in Kentucky. This abolition literature, some of which, by means of cartoons and crude wood cuts, deliberately suggested to the slaves the possibility of gaining their freedom by running off or by revolt, was highly obnoxious to the Bluegrass slaveholders.

Although many Kentuckians favored some sort of gradual emancipation, the impracticability of bringing it to pass was impressing itself upon a larger and larger number. The constant assault from Northern abolitionists by incendiary propaganda and slave stealings was fast exhausting the patience of the people, and, with the increase of anti-slavery sentiment in the North, all of this had the effect of solidifying public opinion in Kentucky concerning slavery. An abolition society, organized and fostered by native Kentuckians, had enjoyed but a brief existence and an emancipation society,

11. *Western Citizen,* Paris, August 20, 1831.

it now seemed, would fail for want of public support.

Slaveholders of Mercer, Lincoln and surrounding counties were greatly aroused by the activities of James G. Birney, a native of Kentucky, who, after some years' residence as a planter in Huntsville, Alabama, returned to his native state in November, 1833, and, after settling on a farm near Danville, freed all his slaves.[12] Although a slaveholder, he had been active in the colonization movement in Alabama until convinced of its futility and, upon his return to Kentucky, he became an out-and-out abolitionist. Shortly after arrival in his home town of Danville, he organized The Kentucky Society for the Relief of the State of Kentucky from Slavery, with nine charter members. For the next two or three years this organization showed some promise of life, increasing to about twenty members and building up a few branches, but it soon thereafter died down. Undiscouraged by the failure of this and another society, known as the Ashmun Association, Birney in March, 1835, organized the Kentucky Anti-Slavery Society, with headquarters in Danville.

Birney had by this time attracted the attention of national abolitionists and secured the co-operation of such well-known anti-slavery leaders as Benjamin Lundy and William Lloyd Garrison. Soon Birney had succeeded in getting Garrison to include the Kentucky society within the scope of his American Anti-Slavery Society, which had been organized two years before. Birney's unpopularity in an already outraged community was further increased when it became known that he planned the establishment at Danville of an

12. Mercer County Court, Deed Book 19, p. 32, June 2, 1834.

abolitionist paper, *The Philanthropist,* which was to appear early in August, 1835.

No sooner were the principles of Birney's proposed paper, *The Philanthropist,* the intended mouthpiece of the Kentucky Anti-Slavery Society, and its connections with Garrison's national society generally known, than opposition to the undertaking was expressed by slaveholders in all parts of the state. Garrison's plan, as sponsored by Birney, called for complete abolition and gave no heed to plans for partial or progressive emancipation, which had been proposed in Kentucky on every occasion when the existence of slavery was questioned. Kentuckians were not yet willing to try so desperate a remedy as immediate emancipation or total abolition, neither were they willing to take unsought advice from outsiders on a question which they considered to be particularly their own concern. Mass meetings were held in many sections and resolutions were adopted to prevent the publication of *The Philanthropist,* "peacefully if we can, forcibly if we must." Threats of violence were openly made against any and all men who might countenance the paper or aid in its circulation.

Public indignation soon reached a high pitch; a committee of thirty-three citizens from neighboring counties waited upon the obstinate Birney: "We admonish you, Sir!" warned the spokesman of the group, "as citizens of the same neighborhood, as members of the same society in which you live and move, and for whose harmony and quiet we feel the most sincere solicitude, to beware how you make an experiment here, which no American slave-holding community has found itself able to bear." [13] But Birney, not to be intimidated, went on with the preparations to publish his anti-slavery paper.

Mr. S. S. Dismukes, the printer, gravely concerned over his own safety, secretly sold out his establishment and left Danville under cover of darkness, while threats were freely spread abroad that any printer undertaking the job would do so at the risk of his life.[14] Remembering the mail sack incident at Charleston, a few weeks before,[15] the postmaster at Danville declared he would receive no abolition papers in his post office, if Birney printed them. Finally convinced that Mercer County was no place for his anti-slavery paper, Birney fled to Cincinnati, with threats of mob violence ringing in his ears.[16] With him went the last vestige of the Kentucky Anti-Slavery Society.

Cassius M. Clay had now come upon the scene as one of the most active and fearless of the anti-slavery crusaders. Son of General Green Clay, a prominent slaveholder of Madison County, young "Cash" went to Yale College in 1831 and there, under the influence of William Lloyd Garrison, became so thoroughly steeped in the doctrines of abolitionism that, to him, slavehold-

13. Birney, *op. cit.*, pp. 181–83.

14. *Autobiography of Dr. J. J. Polk*, pp. 34–35.

15. On July 29, 1835, an angry mob of slaveholders in Charleston, South Carolina, broke open the post office, seized a mail sack of abolitionist literature and publicly burned it on the courthouse square. As a result of this incident, the Postmaster General excused Southern postmasters from delivering abolition literature to persons to whom it was directed.

16. Undaunted by his failure to establish an anti-slavery press in Kentucky, Birney, nevertheless, devoted the remainder of his life to the cause of abolition. His paper, *The Philanthropist*, later established in Cincinnati, was twice attacked and destroyed by a mob during the year 1836. In 1840 and 1844 Birney became the presidential candidate on the National Anti-Slavery or Liberal party ticket, polling over 62,000 votes in the second campaign.

ing was a most flagrant violation of human rights as well as a great moral and religious wrong. After attending one of the great anti-slavery leader's lectures, he wrote: "I felt all the horrors of slavery; but my parents were slaveholders; all my known kindred in Kentucky were slaveholders; and I regarded it, as I did other evils of humanity, as the fixed law of nature or of God. . . . Garrison dragged out the monster . . . and left him stabbed to the vitals, and dying at the feet of every logical and honest mind. . . . I then resolved that, when I had the strength, if ever, I would give slavery a death struggle." [17]

After two years spent at Yale, Cassius Clay returned to Kentucky, where he entered the field of politics, and began the free expression of his views. Clay's views, moulded somewhat by Garrison, only deepened as the slavery cloud darkened in Kentucky, and the "Lion of White Hall" flaunted his abolitionist theories in the faces of the slavocracy as boldly and fearlessly as if the whole world were on his side. He well realized the danger of his course, and no one who knew Cassius Clay ventured to deny that he had the courage of his convictions, or to question the fact that he was a man, if one ever existed, who feared no foe.

In 1841 an act was introduced in the Kentucky legislature for repealing the law of 1833, which prevented the importation of slaves into Kentucky, but it failed to pass. Clay seized this occasion to denounce slavery and its defenders in the savage language which he knew so well how to use. To the threats of slave owners, he replied that neither pistols, knives nor mobs could force him to change his course toward the institution,

17. *Memoirs,* pp. 56–57.

and warned them that, although ready to sacrifice his life, if need be, in the cause, they would not find him "a tame victim of either force or denunciation."

Thus, Clay by his fiery speeches was drawn into open war with the slave power, and on every stump vehemently denounced the institution. Slaveholders of Lexington and surrounding territory frequently held torchlight processions in the city, as a show of strength, and were in turn often imitated by the emancipationists. The "Old Duke's" son, young Robert, was now Clay's rival in the race for the legislature from Fayette County. An altercation between the two men, growing out of the slavery issue, led to a challenge by Clay and its acceptance to combat by his adversary.

In the early morning hours of May 15, 1841, the two duelists met on a "field of honor" near Louisville. Pistols at ten paces were chosen by Wickliffe, and, from the prominence of the men engaged, it was a matter of great public interest, many predicting that it would end in certain tragedy. At the word, both men fired, but neither bullet found its mark. Then, upon the proposal of the seconds, Colonel William R. McKee for Clay, and Albert Sidney Johnston for Wickliffe, it was agreed that the affair be called off. No apology was made on either side and no reconciliation was proposed and, as Clay said, "we left the ground enemies, as we came." [18]

Clay's arch-foes, the Wickliffes, father and son, continued to play an important role in the slavery struggle then fiercely raging in Kentucky, with Lexington as a storm center. Robert Wickliffe, Sr., and the Reverend Robert J. Breckinridge were not only opponents on the slavery question, but bitter personal enemies, and they

18. *Ibid.*, pp. 80–81.

engaged in a series of vitriolic newspaper and pamphlet debates on the Negro Law and slavery in general. The elder Wickliffe was a conscientious objector to duels, and his cloth prevented Breckinridge from appearing on the field of honor, so that for years the battle raged by tongue and pen alone.[19]

Many of their debates were characterized by vituperation and personal abuse and, on one occasion, at the courthouse in Lexington, on November 9, 1840, Dr. Breckinridge publicly declared Robert Wickliffe a man lacking in integrity, a poltroon and a lawbreaker.[20] Several days later the "Old Duke," not to be outdone, caustically responded: "I know many have advised me to silence, and to leave the wretched hypocrite [Breckinridge] to sink under the weight of his own vileness and the castigations his imprudence and falsehoods have brought upon him from other and more able pens than mine. . . . I know, full well, that he that wrestles with a skunk must receive some of its odor. . . . I know that I do myself no good; but in again nailing him to the post as a counterfeit and a hypocrite, not only a disgrace to his church but to his species, I hope to do some good to others upon whom he audaciously pours his venom. . . ."[21]

For months Wickliffe claimed that the Presbyterian minister had been "meanly pouring forth his filth on me through the prostituted columns of the *Lexington*

19. It was truly the day of the pamphleteer. These fiery speeches and accusations were hurriedly printed as pamphlets and constitute today some of the prized exhibits of Kentuckiana collectors. Many of Breckinridge's pamphlets were printed at the expense of Henry Clay, Robert S. Todd and other friends, and were widely distributed from Todd's store in Lexington.

20. *Speech of Robert Wickliffe in reply to Rev. Robert J. Breckinridge* (Lexington, 1841), p. 5. Original in author's collection.

21. *Ibid.*, pp. 5–6.

Intelligencer and the *Louisville Journal*." At length, becoming sorely vexed at this "outpouring of filth," Wickliffe, in the early part of 1843, delivered an address in answer "To the Billingsgate Abuse of Robert *Judas* Breckinridge, otherwise called Robert Jefferson Breckinridge," in which the "Old Duke" resorted to the device of mixing slavery with Dr. Breckinridge's personal affairs, and caustically took him to task about "beautiful Louisa," a comely octoroon slave, whom, as the pamphlet charged, "he kept amongst his slaves that he had not gambled off." [22]

Chagrined and enraged over such an accusation, Breckinridge retaliated against his arch-enemy by charging that he "extorted" twelve hundred dollars from his wife, the former Mrs. James Russell, for the liberation of her grandson Alfred, "a well-behaved, bright and intelligent mulatto lad of fine appearance." [23] After having liberated Alfred at "such tremendous sacrifice," as Breckinridge charged, Mrs. Wickliffe hurriedly sent Alfred and his slave mother, Milly, off to Liberia, where they were last heard from living in poverty "on the barbarous shores of Africa." [24] Such speeches and pamphlets, while not very instructive as to Negro slavery, were masterpieces of vituperation and venom and clearly showed the implacable enmity that long existed between the "Old Duke" and the Reverend Doctor.

In the race for Congress in 1843, young Robert

22. *A Further Reply of Robert Wickliffe, etc.* (Lexington, Kentucky Gazette Print, 1843), pp. 56–57. Original in author's collection.

23. Todd's heirs *vs.* Robert Wickliffe, Fayette Circuit Court, File 1166, January 18, 1850.

24. *The Third Defense of Robert J. Breckinridge against the Calumnies of Robert Wickliffe,* pp. 76–77. Copy of pamphlet in author's collection. For a full account of the story of Milly and Alfred, see Townsend, *Lincoln and His Wife's Home Town,* pp. 205–13.

Wickliffe was a candidate against Garrett Davis, who was being warmly supported by Robert S. Todd, Cassius M. Clay, Henry Clay and other conservative Whigs of Lexington. Handbills were frequently distributed by both parties, some attacking, some defending slavery, as the "Old Duke's" son and Cash Clay stumped the Bluegrass for their respective parties.

Now the pro-slavery faction of the Bluegrass had imported reinforcement from New Orleans in the person of one Samuel M. Brown, a strong slavery advocate and political bully of powerful physique, who came to Lexington with the reputation of having had "forty fights and never lost a battle." Shortly after Brown's arrival, in the summer of 1843, a large political rally was held at Russell Cave Springs, seven miles north of Lexington, in Fayette County. As young Bob Wickliffe addressed the crowd, his arch-enemy, Cassius Clay, challenged one of his statements, whereupon, Clay was promptly felled by a blow from the newcomer Brown, of New Orleans.

Clay, regaining his feet, drew a bowie knife from his shirt bosom and rushed at his assailant, who, brandishing his pistol, shouted: "Clear the way and let me kill the damned rascal!" Brown withheld his fire until Clay was within a few feet of him, and then, taking deliberate aim, fired pointblank at his heart. But before he could fire again, Clay was upon him, and with fierce thrusts of his knife laid his skull open to the brain, dug out an eye and cut off an ear. Then the proud hero of "forty fights" was thrown over the bluff and rolled down into the waters of Russell's Cave.

Clay was rushed to a near-by farmhouse and, upon examination, was found to have escaped unharmed, the bullet from Brown's pistol having struck the silver-lined scabbard of his bowie knife, leaving only a red spot over his heart.[25]

At the next term of the Fayette Circuit Court, Clay was indicted for mayhem,[26] and he engaged his friend and kinsman, the renowned Henry Clay, to defend him. Crowds filled the court room to once more hear the "Gallant Harry," for it had been a long time since he had appeared in a criminal case, but the audience soon knew that he was still the same masterly advocate as of yore.

Public sentiment, strongly pro-slavery, weighed heavily against the defendant, but Clay's keen cross-examination and his dramatic, eloquent plea to the jury won the day, brought in a verdict of acquittal, and kept clear his record of never having lost a criminal case.

This victory for the anti-slavery forces in Lexington continued to widen the gap between the two factions and became the all-absorbing topic of the day. By the small group of emancipationists, who had been long overawed by the aggressive supremacy of the slave-owning class in Kentucky, Cash Clay was now eagerly accepted as their leader. He was known as a fearless combatant, when aroused, and he possessed an iron will that carried him rough-shod over all obstacles.

By 1845 he was fully prepared to renew his fight against slavery in Kentucky. After several of his editorials had appeared in the local newspapers, he was denied further space in the *Observer,* for, as the editor commented, his articles had grown so "militant and

25. Clay, *op. cit.*, pp. 83–85.
26. Commonwealth of Kentucky *vs.* Cassius M. Clay, Fayette Circuit Court, Order Book 29, p. 300, September 30, 1843.

From an oil portrait

CASSIUS M. CLAY AS A STUDENT AT YALE

OFFICE OF CLAY'S TRUE AMERICAN, LEXINGTON

provocative" in tone that he felt compelled to decline them for publication.

But the intrepid Clay, clearly foreseeing such a situation and being a man of means, now undertook to carry out his long-cherished plan to launch a newspaper of his own, through whose columns he could freely attack the slaveholders and at the same time wield the editorial cudgel in behalf of emancipation. However, he well knew the dangers and difficulties that confronted such an undertaking, for he vividly recalled the harrowing experience of James G. Birney ten years before. Clay, nevertheless, despite the warnings of his friends and the mutterings of the slavocracy, calmly and cautiously went about his task.

For his printing establishment Clay selected a three-story red brick building known as "Number 6" North Mill Street, Lexington. Such an undertaking would, of course, expose him to the danger of mob violence, so he accordingly set out to defend himself in case of an attack. He fortified the outside doors and casings of the building with sheet iron and planted two four-pound brass cannon, loaded with Minié balls and nails, at the head of the long narrow steps leading up to the second floor, where the office and presses were located. In addition, the office was equipped with a stand of rifles, several shotguns and a dozen Mexican lances. Clay, as a last extremity, prepared an avenue of escape through a trap door in the roof and means by which he could touch off, from the outside, several kegs of powder secreted in one corner of the room, which would blow up the printing office and its invaders.[27]

On the third day of June, 1845, *The True American,*

27. Clay, *op. cit.,* p. 107.

a weekly newspaper, with the motto "God and Liberty" at its masthead, made its appearance upon the streets of Lexington. On many sides it was severely denounced, but its subscribers, some three hundred scattered over Kentucky and seventeen hundred out of the state, greeted the new champion of freedom with a warm and hearty welcome. In New York City, it was acclaimed by Horace Greeley, editor of the *Tribune*, as "the first paper which ever bearded the monster in his den, and dared him to a most unequal encounter." [28]

Clay's paper not only advocated abolition, but civil and political rights for the slave population, and warned the slaveholders that the abolitionists were becoming quite as reckless as the slaveholders themselves, and might, if provoked too far, display the same bold and aggressive spirit. Throughout the Bluegrass this modest four-page sheet was received with bitter scorn and contempt.

Hints were quietly given out that force was now necessary to suppress *The True American* and, by the time the paper was two weeks old, various and sundry threats had been made against the life of the editor, one of which, scrawled in blood, reflected the temper of the times:

> "C. M. Clay:
>
> You are meaner than the autocrats of hell. You may think you can awe and curse the people of Kentucky to your infamous course. You will find, when it is too late for life, the people are no cowards. Eternal hatred is locked up in the bosoms of braver men, your betters, for you. The hemp is ready for your neck. Your life cannot be spared. Plenty thirst for your blood—are deter-

28. Townsend, *op. cit.*, p. 116.

mined to have it. It is unknown to you and your friends, if you have any, and in a way you little dream of.

Revengers." [29]

But Clay, the vigorous, fearless, anti-slavery leader, continued to put forth bitter and vitriolic attacks against slavery through the columns of *The True American,* despite the grim warnings of the "Revengers" and others who would have liked to have seen him done bodily harm. With each succeeding issue of the paper, the temper of the populace became more and more inflamed. During the summer battle at the polls, the proslavery party suffered a stinging defeat, attributed by many to the activities and influence of Clay's paper. This, and the hatred and the bitter feelings stirred up over the Webster-Fairbank Negro stealing of the year before, together with the proddings of a rabid abolitionist press right in their midst, so angered the defenders of slavery that, on August 14, 1845, a committee of infuriated citizens gathered at the courthouse to discuss plans for checking the publication of this emancipation paper.

Clay, who had lain ill with typhoid fever since July twelfth, upon hearing of the meeting of citizens who favored the suppression of his paper, got out of bed, though weak and feeble, and went straight to the courthouse to personally defend himself. Lying prostrate upon a bench in the circuit court room, he denounced in a voice scarcely audible the "apostate" Whig, Thomas F. Marshall, who was acting as spokesman for the assembly. Then he demanded a hearing, which was denied, and the meeting adjourned.

29. *The True American,* June 17, 1845, *et seq.*

Later, in the afternoon, a committee of three delivered an ultimatum to Clay, as he lay on his sick bed, demanding that he discontinue his paper, which, as the communication stated, "is dangerous to the peace of our community and to the safety of our homes and families." In his usual defiant manner, Clay drafted a caustic reply and challenge: "Your advice with regard to my personal safety," he said, "is worthy of the source whence it emanated, and meets with the same contempt from me which the purpose of your mission excites. Go tell your secret conclave of cowardly assassins that C. M. Clay knows his rights and how to defend them." [30]

This reply further incensed the pro-slavery crowd, and handbills, speedily circulated about the streets of Lexington and adjoining territory, informed the readers that a large mass meeting would be held on Monday, the eighteenth, in the city, to take further steps toward the suppression of the "filthy abolition" paper. Well knowing that Clay had a legal right to defend his office against invasion, which would doubtless result in bloodshed, his adversaries devised a plan to seize his printing plant under process of law.

On the morning of the eighteenth, Judge George R. Trotter, of the police court, quietly issued an injunction against *The True American* and all its appurtenances.[31] With tears in his eyes, Clay, while still confined to his sick bed, delivered the keys to his plant over to the city marshal, when served with the writ of seizure. Several hours later, at eleven o'clock, a crowd of twelve

30. *History and Record of the Proceedings of the People of Lexington & Vicinity, in the Suppression of "The True American" and Appeal of C. M. Clay to Kentucky & the World.* Pamphlet in the collection of Dr. Waller O. Bullock, of Lexington.

31. *Lexington Observer & Reporter,* August 20, 1845.

hundred men assembled in the courthouse yard, unaware of the secret court proceedings which had taken place earlier in the morning. As the meeting came to order, Waller Bullock was chosen chairman, whereupon Thomas F. Marshall, whom Clay had dubbed the "apostate Whig," addressed the crowd at length, and, in conclusion, proposed several resolutions, one of which was that "no abolition press ought to be tolerated in Kentucky, and none shall be in this city or vicinity." [32]

A committee of sixty, headed by James B. Clay, William B. Kinkead, and George W. Johnson, was appointed from the crowd and proceeded promptly, but quietly, to Number 6 North Mill Street, where they found the city marshal on guard. After a "formal protest," he surrendered the keys to Clay's printing office. "The committee" was quiet and orderly in going about its work, and by late afternoon all the presses and equipment of *The True American* had been dismantled, boxed up and sent to the freight depot.[33] Late that night the equipment, thus forcibly removed, was shipped across the Ohio River into free territory, consigned to Messrs. January and Taylor, of Cincinnati.

Of course, the *Observer & Reporter,* strongly proslavery in sentiment, warmly defended the action of the committee of sixty and congratulated the community upon "the rare spectacle of an innumerable body of

32. *Frankfort Commonwealth,* August 26, 1845; *Niles' Weekly Register,* LXVIII (August 30, 1845), 408.

33. "Monday, August 18, 1845. Great excitement about Cassius M. Clay and his office; at 11 o'clock the citizens met at the court-house and were called to order by Waller Bullock, chairman. T. Marshall read an address —sixty men were appointed to pack up the type in Clay's office and send it to the depot . . . everything was done quietly—Clay is sick."—Manuscript diary of a young Transylvania University law student, J. E. Kenton, in possession of L. C. Terrell, of Lexington.

citizens, meeting as a matter of course with highly excited feelings, yet so far subduing and moderating their spirit as to accomplish their purpose without the slightest damage to property or the effusion of a drop of blood." [34]

Many of the Northern newspapers, however, violently denounced the "outbreak of the mob at Lexington" and, as their criticisms grew louder and more rabid, the local press waxed warm and exclaimed: "Howl on, ye wolves! Kentucky is ready to meet and repel your whole bloodthirsty piratical crew!" [35]

As an aftermath of the mob outbreak at Lexington, fully one hundred and fifty men, wearing black masks and calling themselves the "black Indians," marched through the streets of the city on the following evening, maltreating many Negroes and tarring and feathering others on the public square.[36] Before the crowd had finished its work, they "broke the ribs of one man, the hands of another, and so injured the eye of a third that the poor fellow will lose it. . . ." [37]

The ruthless suppression of *The True American* was the inevitable result of the unceasing warfare waged by the pro-slavery element,[38] led by Robert Wickliffe

34. August 20, 1845. Several of the more prominent members of the committee of sixty went through the formality of a trial before Judge Trotter on September 15, 1845, where "after full argument, the jury, without hesitating, gave a verdict of not guilty."—*Ibid.*, October 8, 1845.

35. *Ibid.*, August 30, 1845.

36. "Understand that the 'black Indians' were out again last night, whipping, beating, tarring & feathering numerous colored persons. Considerable excitement among the free blacks. Many citizens are of the opinion that Clay's paper is directly responsible for this outbreak of violence upon the slaves and free negroes."—*Ibid.*, August 20, 1845. See also *Western Citizen*, August 29, 1845.

37. Sangamo, Illinois, *Journal*, September 11, 1845.

38. After his return from the Mexican War, Cassius M. Clay brought suit against the "committee" for damages done to his printing press, and, upon change of venue to Jessamine County, was allowed damages of

during the middle and latter eighteen-forties against what they contemptuously called the "Negro Law," or the Non-Importation Act of 1833. Bills for its repeal had been introduced in each successive legislature since 1833, sometimes passing in the Senate, only to be regularly defeated in the House.

For more than a decade, a social and political storm had been slowly gathering, a storm which, if its full force should be reached, threatened to burst forth in a revolution that would likely upset the aristocratic Bluegrass society, give a larger measure of democracy to the common people, break the chains of human bondage and sweep away a picturesque old order which had ruled Kentucky for generations. This impending upheaval was the outgrowth of the movement for gradual emancipation,[39] championed, from first to last, by Dr. Robert J. Breckinridge, Henry Clay, John J. Crittenden, President John C. Young of Centre College, Senator Joseph R. Underwood, Cassius M. Clay, James Speed, President Howard Malcom of Georgetown College, Bland Ballard, Judge S. S. Nicholas, Dr. Stuart Robinson and many others.[40] Arrayed in the ranks of the pro-slavery cause were the Wickliffes, Ben Hardin, Thomas F. Marshall, James Guthrie, Archibald Dixon, William Preston, John C. Breckinridge, President

---

$2,500.—*Western Citizen,* April 7, 1848. Clay's paper, after its suppression in Lexington, was set up in Cincinnati and ran for several months. Later, on June 19, 1847, it was again set up at Louisville as *The Examiner* and continued in operation until the latter part of 1849.

39. "The measure is certainly gaining friends in Kentucky, and in a convention which is proposed for amending the constitution of the state, this subject [gradual emancipation] will be brought up, and its expediency warmly advocated."—Dr. C. W. Short, of Louisville, January 30, 1848, to his uncle, William Short, at Philadelphia. Letter in Filson Club Library, Louisville.

40. James M. Pendleton, *Reminiscences of a Long Life,* pp. 93–94.

Henry B. Bascom of Transylvania University, James B. Clay and many other able and prominent public men.

To the anti-slavery forces, prospects for gradual emancipation in Kentucky now seemed brighter than ever before, for a reluctant legislature had, early in February, issued the call for a convention to assemble at Frankfort on October 1, 1849, to draft a new state constitution. Friends of emancipation now set about, with all their force and strength, to muster reinforcements to insert a provision in the new constitution for the gradual abolition of slavery in the state. Henry Clay wrote an able letter on the subject, which was widely circulated, and his declaration gave a powerful impetus to the cause of emancipation in Kentucky. He advocated that all slaves born in the state should be freed after they reached a certain age—males at twenty-eight, and females at twenty-one years.

During June and July, as the campaign progressed, public excitement mounted to fever heat and there was scarcely a village, crossroads or voting place where a political speech or joint debate was not held, often resulting in personal encounters. For three days President John C. Young, of Centre College, waged a warm and vigorous debate with Captain George B. Kinkead, a pro-slavery orator, in the First Presbyterian Church at Danville.[41] At a pro-slavery mass meeting in Trimble County, resolutions were adopted calling upon Henry Clay to resign his seat in the United States Senate because of his views on emancipation.[42] During a heated slavery debate at the courthouse in Paducah, Judge

41. *Louisville Weekly Journal,* May 26, 1849.
42. *Ibid.,* June 9, 1849.

James Campbell shot and killed the Honorable Benedict Austin, his opposing candidate for the forthcoming convention.[43]

By 1849 Fayette had become the largest slaveholding county in Kentucky, and "Old Fayette," as the *Louisville Courier* observed, "is the theatre of a more lively discussion on the subject of slavery than any other portion of the state." [44] At the near-by village of Foxtown, on the Lexington-Richmond turnpike, there occurred a tragedy on June fifteenth, which further widened the breach between the contending parties.

On this occasion, Squire Turner, the pro-slavery candidate for the convention from Madison County, while addressing a political gathering, poured forth a scurrilous attack upon Cassius M. Clay and his suppressed paper, *The True American.* When he had finished, Clay mounted the speaker's stand and in his usually defiant manner, launched a vigorous, abusive counter-attack on his rival candidate. He was soon interrupted by Cyrus Turner, eldest son of the Squire, who, wildly waving his hands rushed toward the speaker, shouting: "You're a damned liar!" whereupon Clay jumped off the platform to meet him and was dealt a blow in the face by young Turner.

Clay soon found himself surrounded by the friends of his adversary, and, as he attempted to draw his bowie knife, he was struck on the head with a club and the weapon jerked from his grasp. Then Thomas Turner, brother of Cyrus, leveled a six-barrelled revolver at Clay's head and snapped it three times, but the percussion caps failed to explode. Clay, who had been

43. *Lexington Observer & Reporter,* July 18, 1849.
44. July 4, 1849.

stabbed from behind, defended himself as best he could, and to keep from being stabbed again, seized the open blade of his knife with his naked hand and wrenched it from the hands of his adversary. This nearly severed several of his fingers. Blinded with fury and pain, Clay, with a superhuman effort, shook off those who held him and singling out Cyrus Turner, plunged the knife in his abdomen up to the hilt. Turner died within a few hours and Clay was carried away so seriously wounded that he was not expected to live.[45]

Bitterness between the two parties became more intense as the news of the "fatal rencontre" at Foxtown spread throughout Kentucky, and even to other states. Turner was acclaimed by the pro-slavery party as a martyr who had fallen "in the great cause of white supremacy" before the bowie knife of that "abolitionist madman, C. M. Clay," who had some time before been denounced as "a damned nigger agitator" by his enemies in Lexington.[46]

On the other hand, the emancipation forces disclaimed any blame for the fatal encounter, charging that the affair was nothing more than an attempt on the part of the pro-slavery faction to intimidate and coerce, which had again been thwarted by Cash Clay, the great champion of human liberty.[47]

When the Constitutional Convention finally assem-

45. On the following Wednesday, June 20, 1849, the *Observer & Reporter* said of the Foxtown fight: "Mr. Clay still lives, but his adversary Mr. Turner lingered in great agony until 12 o'clock on Saturday night when he expired." See also the *Louisville Weekly Journal,* June 30, July 14, 1849.

46. Townsend, *op. cit.,* p. 198.

47. "We learn that Capt. C. M. Clay has been removed from Foxtown to his residence, and that he is still doing well, and no doubt is entertained by his physicians of his speedy recovery from the wound he received."—*Richmond Chronicle,* June 21, 1849.

bled at Frankfort in October, 1849, it was found that not a single emancipation candidate had been elected, although they had polled thousands of votes.[48] With the overwhelming defeat of the anti-slavery party, which was attributed by many to too much state agitation and too much interference by the abolitionists in the North, the cause of abolition, it now seemed, was forever lost in Kentucky.[49]

Greatly weakened, though undaunted, by failure to gain their end in the 1849 convention, the emancipationists never lost hope of the ultimate success of their efforts to bring about the liberation of the enslaved blacks. In 1851 their leader, Cassius M. Clay, canvassed the state for the governorship of Kentucky on a platform of gradual emancipation, with George D. Blakey as his lieutenant. Meeting with bitter opposition everywhere he spoke, Clay, with his brace of pistols and bowie knife concealed in his belt, loudly voiced his anti-slavery convictions, but was overwhelmingly defeated in the race by Lazarus W. Powell, the Democratic candidate.[50] Emancipation now appeared even more difficult of achievement than ever, and the institution of slavery, it seemed, was far more strongly entrenched and safeguarded in Kentucky than it had been for many years.

48. *Report of the Debates and Proceedings of the Convention for the Revision of the Constitution of the State of Kentucky, 1849* (Frankfort, 1849). This report is complete in one volume of 1,186 pages.

49. Hambleton Tapp, "Robert J. Breckinridge and the Year 1849," *Filson Club History Quarterly,* XII (July, 1938), 146–50.

50. Clay, *op. cit.,* p. 212. During his candidacy Clay was supported by the small, weekly anti-slavery newspaper, *Progress of the Age,* which referred to him (April 19, 1851) as "the Peoples Candidate." This short-lived and mild-mannered emancipation newssheet, printed in Lexington, ceased publication shortly after the election, in which Clay polled only 3,621 votes.

However the Kentucky slaveholders had little time to enjoy a much-needed respite from the activities of the abolitionists. They were suddenly aroused and thrown into the greatest excitement over the appearance of Mrs. Harriet Beecher Stowe's famous anti-slavery novel, *Uncle Tom's Cabin,* which was first published in book form on March 2, 1852. Having appeared as a serial in the Washington *National Era,* an anti-slavery newspaper, it had attracted little attention, but when published in book form its popularity was immediate and great. Ten thousand copies were sold in ten days and three hundred thousand copies in a single year; eight power presses, running day and night, were not able to supply the demand.

Living across the Ohio River in Cincinnati, where her husband was connected with the Lane Theological Seminary, Mrs. Stowe collected many stories from fugitive slaves fleeing from Kentucky, and by personal visits to the General Thomas Kennedy plantation, in Garrard County, and at the Marshall Key house in the village of Washington, in Mason County, she was brought into intimate contact with Kentucky slavery and saw it at its best.[51] From these Kentucky slaves' own lips and information gleaned elsewhere, Mrs. Stowe painted in the liveliest colors of fiction a lurid and grossly exaggerated picture of the horrors of slavery in the United States, which stirred the reader's passions from their innermost depths and plumbed the abyss of human sentiment. This "monstrous caricature," the greatest propaganda novel ever written, instantly provoked an outbreak of furious indignation, which greatly strengthened the abolitionist cause in Kentucky and in

51. Charles E. Stowe, *The Life of Harriet B. Stowe,* p. 71.

the South, where the book's unpopularity was matched only by its popularity in the North.[52]

Once again, in December, 1855, an attempt was made to establish an abolitionist newspaper in Lexington, with J. Brady, a rabid anti-slavery crusader and New England schoolteacher as the editor. Still fresh in the public mind was the furor and hostility caused by Clay's *True American* some years before, and, as the *Louisville Times* warned: "Those that commence the paper had better get all the hair taken off their heads, so that the Lexington people will only have the trouble of taking off their skin." Brady was attacked by "a ferocious gang of poor whites," all burning, as was said, with a desire "to taste the blood of an abolitionist," and, after "wrecking their vengeance upon him," the angry mob "amid jeers, taunts and low vulgarity" drove the would-be editor out of town.[53]

For several years previous, there had been published at Newport, in Campbell County, an abolition newspaper called the *Newport News,* by William S. Bailey, a machinist of that town. This small anti-slavery news-sheet had at first attracted little attention, "because it

52. Most of the characters of this novel have been identified: Thomas Kennedy, Jr., and his wife were Mr. and Mrs. Shelby of the Kentucky plantation; Little Eva was their daughter Nancy; Samuel and Rachel Halliday were Mr. and Mrs. Levi Coffin, of Cincinnati; John Van Trompe was John Van Zandt, of Cincinnati; Lewis, a slave, was George Harris; Aunt Chloe, Eliza and others were slaves on the old Kennedy plantation. Uncle Tom, the central figure of Mrs. Stowe's novel, has often been erroneously credited to one Josiah Henson, an escaped slave from Daviess County. This famous character was a composite picture of several old and faithful slaves whom Mrs. Stowe knew and interviewed. In a letter written to the editor of the *Indianapolis News,* July 27, 1882, Mrs. Stowe set at rest forever the long-disputed subject as to the real Uncle Tom of her *Uncle Tom's Cabin.* "I will say," she wrote, "that the character of Uncle Tom was not the biography of any one man." Copy of letter in author's collection.

53. Carleton, *The Suppressed Book about Slavery,* pp. 166, 242–43.

was supported by contributions from abolitionists in the North and read by nobody in Kentucky, or other slave states."[54] But after some months of operation the paper became quite obnoxious, paying little heed to the violent opposition it had created among neighboring slaveholders, who, at length, finding their efforts to suppress it ineffectual, set fire to the premises on October 5, 1851, "and burned down the presses, equipment, machine-shop and all."[55]

Assisted by friends and workmen, Bailey managed to set up another press in his home and, securing a fresh supply of type, renamed his paper the *Free South*. Despite repeated warnings, he continued to issue his paper containing violent abolition literature. Bailey, the editor, was now forced to set his own type, assisted by his wife and children, for no printer, under threats of bodily harm, dared to work in his plant. With great difficulty this journal was published, as one observer noted in 1857: "Father, mother and children, and even the little ones, toiling, amid obloquy, reproach, and savage foes, to redeem their state from the dreadful sin and curse of slavery."[56]

Through the editorial columns of his paper, Bailey urged the slaveholding whites of Kentucky to use their votes to exterminate slavery and, on December 31, 1858, issued a stirring call to battle: "Workingmen of Kentucky, think of yourselves! See you not that the system of slavery enslaves all who labor for an honest living.

54. *Western Citizen,* Paris, November 4, 1859. See also the *Free South,* March 9, 1859, in which Bailey himself said that he would have starved had he not received support from the abolitionists in the North.

55. Eliza Wigham, *The Anti-Slavery Cause in America,* p. 47.

56. *Ibid.,* p. 48.

You, white men, are the best slave property of the South, and it is your votes that makes you so." [57]

Following John Brown's raid on Harpers Ferry, the *Free South* became the object of severe criticism and malediction because of its alleged views favorable to Brown's part in the Virginia incident. It was now determined, in the excited state of the public mind, to abate the paper as a nuisance. Accordingly, on the night of October 28, 1859, an infuriated crowd of citizens and slaveholders broke into Bailey's house, wrecked the presses, dragged the forms and type "through the streets of Newport, and flung them into the river." [58]

Next morning the mob began its work of demolishing Bailey's office and home. "Battering down the door, they entered with abusive and malicious language, broke up the furniture and fixtures and carried off everything they wanted, leaving the house a perfect wreck." [59] Again it had been demonstrated that an abolitionist press was not to be tolerated in slaveholding Kentucky, even though it was on the border line just across the Ohio River from free territory.

Several months after the destruction of Bailey's press in Newport, there was considerable excitement and near bloodshed in the little settlement of Berea, in Madison County, on the outer fringe of the Bluegrass. Here, a few years earlier, Cassius M. Clay had established an anti-slavery colony; a church was organized and Berea School founded with the aid of the Reverend John G.

57. *Free South,* Newport, December 31, 1858.

58. *Kentucky Statesman,* Lexington, November 8, 1859.

59. *The Liberator,* Boston, January 27, 1860. Bailey and his family fled from Kentucky, their lives having more than once been threatened by an angry mob.

Fee, an abolitionist preacher, who had been "unfrocked" for his anti-slavery preachings in his churches in Lewis and Bracken counties.[60] He was later joined by the Reverend James S. Davis, John G. Hanson and others who preached the abolition doctrine.

Berea College, the outgrowth of this school, was founded in 1858, and was made possible largely by contributions from people in Northern states. This new institution of learning was intended primarily for the education of Negroes, slave and free, of both sexes. Such an undertaking was highly obnoxious to slaveholding Kentuckians, because the school also received white students, and this "audacious step," coming at such a time, was viewed with alarm as a daring move toward a social equality of the races. Many slave owners, secretly but steadily, planned the suppression of the school and the banishment of its supporters.

This feeling of disfavor and indignation was further aggravated by the John Brown raid in 1859, so much so, indeed, that mass meetings were held in the courthouse at Richmond and in various parts of Madison County, where resolutions were passed that "Rev. John G. Fee and other noisy and incendiary abolitionists in this county should be driven from it." [61] On the twenty-third of December an armed mob of sixty-two men, composed of the "wealthiest and most respectable citizens,"

60. By a presentment, the grand jury of Bracken County charged that "one John G. Fee, a resident of Lewis County and who professes to be a minister of the Gospel frequently intrudes himself into our quiet community and promulgates doctrines upon the subject of negro slavery which we regard as dangerous to the peace and good order of society, which every good citizen ought, in our opinion, to deprecate as fraught with nothing but evil to the country."—Bracken Circuit Court, Order Book H, p. 473, September 17, 1850.

61. *The Daily Commonwealth,* Frankfort, December 28, 1859.

rode up to Fee's home at dusk and, ordering him to come outside, notified him to leave the state with his family in ten days, under penalty of death. Several families of the anti-slavery colony were likewise visited by the mob and ordered to leave along with Fee and his co-workers.

On the following day, December 24, 1859, an appeal was sent by these panic-stricken Bereans to Governor Magoffin for protection, but the chief executive, mindful of the excited state of the public feelings, offered no help and advised the threatened abolitionists to comply with the warnings.[62]

Stripped of their property and with every means of livelihood gone, these families, which numbered about forty persons in all, were thus driven from their homes in Madison County late in December, 1859, and reached Cincinnati several days later. Noting their arrival, the *Cincinnati Commercial* lamented their sad plight, listing among the exiles: "Reverend J. S. Davis, principal of the flourishing school at Berea and his family." [63] Fee later returned to Kentucky and, upon resuming his abolition teachings, was "waylaid, shot at, clubbed, stoned and subjected to constant persecutions of various kinds" in the counties of Lewis, Mason and Rockcastle,[64] and, finally, was ferried across the Ohio River by enraged slaveholders of Bracken County, who threatened to hang him should he return to Kentucky.

Looking back upon those distant days, it is little won-

62. John G. Fee, *Autobiography*, pp. 148–49.

63. December 31, 1859; January 4, 1860.

64. "Reverend John G. Fee, who is somewhat notorious as a Kentucky abolitionist, was recently driven out of Rockcastle County, who, after being warned to desist in his teachings, was tarred and feathered and ducked in a neighboring pond."—*Western Citizen,* August 7, 1860.

der that, to their adherents, the bitter struggle and personal sacrifices of abolitionist crusaders from Father Rice to the Reverend John Fee often seemed worse than futile. Even the milder, more reasonable and practical doctrines of gradual emancipation so staunchly advocated by men like Cassius M. Clay and Robert J. Breckinridge apparently fell on heedless ears.

On the surface, near the end of the eighteen-fifties the "peculiar institution" had lost none of its outstanding characteristics. The strong ties of affection which bound the cabin to the big house could not always prevent cruel masters or callous overseers from rawhiding the backs of helpless slaves. Coarse, hardhearted "nigger tradahs" ruthlessly separated husband and wife, parent and child on the auction block; runaways furtively pushed leaky skiffs into the dark waters of the winding Ohio, following the North Star to freedom, while the breeze of moonlit summer nights bore the twanging rhythm of banjos and guitars and the melody of deep, rich voices. Slavery with all its lights and shadows stood apparently unchanged and, as many believed, unchangeable.

But the unsung efforts of those early anti-slavery martyrs whose tragic idealism lost them home, friends, property and sometimes even life itself had not wholly been in vain. In field, shop and factory, around the family hearthstone at evening, or the big stove in the village store, the plain, quiet people slowly pondered the declarations of a droll, earnest, Kentucky-born, circuit-riding lawyer that the Union could not "endure permanently half slave and half free," and that, conceding slave owners to be "as good as the average of people elsewhere," still, "no man is good enough to govern another man without that other's consent." [65]

And so, finally and inevitably came the fateful twelfth of April, 1861. Housetops, wharves and shoreline along the Battery of South Carolina's historic Charleston were thronged with an anxious multitude tensely waiting through the damp, chilly hours of early morning. Then, as the dim outlines of Fort Sumter became visible through the harbor mists, one of Fort Johnson's mortars belched a spreading column of flames, a thick white ball of smoke, rising high into the air, curved slowly and gracefully toward Fort Sumter's shadowy ramparts.

The dull roar of that Confederate cannon sounded the death knell of slavery, a social order at once kindly yet cruel, benevolent though despotic, in the song-celebrated "land of the free." Kentucky's most romantic and picturesque era had come forever to an end.

65. Lincoln's speech at Peoria, Illinois, October 16, 1854, Nicolay and Hay, *Complete Works of Abraham Lincoln,* II, 228.

SELECTED BIBLIOGRAPHY

References to manuscripts, newspapers and periodicals will be found in the notes.

Adams, Alice D. *The Neglected Period of Anti-Slavery in America, 1808–1831.* Boston, 1908.

Alexander, Archibald. *A History of Colonization on the Western Coast of Africa.* Philadelphia, 1846.

Allen, James Lane. *The Blue-Grass Region of Kentucky.* New York, 1892.

Allen, Thomas N. *Chronicles of Oldfields.* Seattle (Wash.), 1909.

Anderson, John. *The Story of the Life of John Anderson, the Fugitive Slave.* London, 1863.

Andrews, E. A. *Slavery and the Domestic Slave Trade in the United States.* Boston, 1836.

Avey, Elijah. *The Capture and Execution of John Brown.* Elgin (Ill.), 1906.

Bakeless, John. *Daniel Boone, Master of the Wilderness.* New York, 1939.

Ballagh, James C. *A History of Slavery in Virginia.* Baltimore, 1902.

Bancroft, Frederic. *Slave-Trading in the Old South.* Baltimore, 1931.

Barker, Eugene C. *The Life of Stephen F. Austin.* Nashville, 1925.

Bascom, Henry B. *Methodism and Slavery.* Frankfort, 1845.

Bernhard, Karl. *Travels through North America, during the Years 1825 and 1826.* 2 vols. Philadelphia, 1828.

Bibb, Henry. *Narrative of the Life and Adventures of Henry Bibb, an American Slave.* New York, 1849.

Birney, William. *James G. Birney and his Times.* New York, 1890.

Bishop, Robert H. *Outline of the History of the Church in the State of Kentucky.* Lexington, 1824.

Bradford, John. *The General Instructor: or the Office, Duty, and Authority of the Justices of the Peace, Sheriffs, Coroners and Constables in the State of Kentucky.* Lexington, 1800.

Brown, Samuel R. *The Western Gazetteer.* Auburn (N. Y.), 1817.

Brown, Thomas. *Brown's Three Years in the Kentucky Prisons.* Indianapolis, 1858. (Pamphlet.)

Brown, William W. *The Black Man, his Antecedents, his Genius and his Achievements.* Boston, 1865.

——. *Narrative of William W. Brown, a Fugitive Slave.* Boston, 1847.

Browning, Orville H. *The Diary of Orville H. Browning.* 2 vols. Springfield (Ill.), 1925.

Buckingham, James S. *The Eastern and Western States of America.* 3 vols. London, 1842.

Bullitt, Thomas W., ed. *My Life at Oxmoor.* Louisville, 1911.

Carleton, George W. *The Suppressed Book about Slavery.* New York, 1864.

Carroll, Joseph C. *Slave Insurrections in the United States, 1800–1865.* Boston, 1938.

Castleman, John B. *Active Service.* Louisville, 1917.

Catterall, Helen T. *Judicial Cases Concerning American Slavery and the Negro,* Vol 1. Washington, 1926.

Clark, Thomas D. *A History of Kentucky.* New York, 1937.

Clarke, Lewis. *Narrative of the Sufferings of Lewis Clarke.* Boston, 1845.

Clarke, Lewis and Milton. *Narrative of the Sufferings of Lewis and Milton Clarke among the Slaveholders of Kentucky.* Boston, 1846.

Clay, Cassius M. *Cassius Marcellus Clay, Life and Memoirs, Writings and Speeches.* Cincinnati, 1886.

Cockrum, William M. *Pioneer History of Indiana.* Oakland City (Ind.), 1907.

Coffin, Levi. *Reminiscences of Levi Coffin.* Cincinnati, 1876.

Coleman, J. Winston, Jr. *Stage-Coach Days in the Bluegrass.* Louisville, 1935.

Collins, Richard H. *History of Kentucky.* 2 vols. Covington, 1874.

Connelly, Emma M. *The Story of Kentucky.* Boston, 1890.

Cotterill, Robert S. *History of Pioneer Kentucky.* Cincinnati, 1917.

Cowan, Alexander M. *Liberia as I Found It in 1858.* Frankfort, 1858.

Cuming, Fortescue. *Sketches of a Tour to the Western Country.* Pittsburgh, 1810.

Dorris, Jonathan T. *Old Cane Springs.* Louisville, 1936.

Drew, Benjamin. *The Refugee; or Narratives of Fugitive Slaves in Canada.* Boston, 1856.

Duke, Basil W. *Reminiscences of General Basil W. Duke, C.S.A.* New York, 1911.

Dumond, Dwight L., ed. *Letters of James Gillespie Birney, 1831–1857.* 2 vols. New York, 1938.

Eaton, Clement. *Freedom of Thought in the Old South.* Durham (N. C.), 1940.

Elliott, Charles. *Sinfulness of American Slavery.* 2 vols. Cincinnati, 1850.

Evans, Estwick. *A Pedestrious Tour.* Concord (N. H.), 1819.

Fairbank, Calvin. *During Slavery Times.* Chicago, 1890.

Fearon, Henry B. *Sketches of America.* London, 1819.

Featherstonhaugh, George W. *Excursion through the Slave States.* 2 vols. London, 1844.

Fedric, Francis. *Slave Life in Virginia and Kentucky.* London, 1863.

Fee, John G. *Autobiography of John G. Fee.* Chicago, 1891.

Flint, Timothy. *Recollections of the Last Ten Years.* Boston, 1826.

Fordham, Elias P. *Personal Narrative.* Cleveland, 1906.

Fox, Early L. *The American Colonization Society, 1817–1840.* Baltimore, 1919.

Galbreath, Charles B. *History of Ohio.* 5 vols. New York, 1925.

Goddell, William. *The American Slave Code, in Theory and Practice.* New York, 1853.

Gray, Thomas R. *The Confession, Trial and Execution of Nat Turner.* Baltimore, 1831. (Pamphlet.)

Green, Elisha W. *Life of the Rev. Elisha W. Green.* Maysville (Ky.), 1888.

Griffith, Mattie. *Autobiography of a Female Slave.* New York, 1857.

Harlan, Mary B. *Ellen; or the Chained Mother and Pictures of Kentucky Slavery.* Cincinnati, 1853.

Hart, Albert B. *Slavery and Abolition, 1831–1841.* New York, 1906.

Haviland, Laura S. *A Woman's Life Work: Labors and Experiences of Laura S. Haviland.* Cincinnati, 1882.

Helm, Katherine. *Mary, Wife of Lincoln.* New York, 1928.

Helper, Hinton R. *The Impending Crisis of the South: How to Meet It.* New York, 1857.

Henson, Josiah. *Father Henson's Story of His Own Life.* Boston, 1858.

Hundley, D. R. *Social Relations in Our Southern States.* New York, 1860.

Imlay, Gilbert. *A Topographical Description of the Western Territory*. London, 1797.

Ingraham, Joseph H. *The Southwest: by a Yankee*. 2 vols. New York, 1835.

Jackson, Andrew. *Narrative and Writings of Andrew Jackson, of Kentucky*. Syracuse (N. Y.), 1847. (Pamphlet.)

Jay, William. *Miscellaneous Writings on Slavery*. Boston, 1853.

Jenkins, William S. *Pro-Slavery Thought in the Old South*. Chapel Hill, 1935.

Johnson, Oliver. *William Lloyd Garrison and his Times*. Boston, 1880.

Johnston, Elizabeth B. *Christmas in Kentucky, 1862*. Washington, 1892. (Pamphlet.)

Johnston, J. Stoddard. *Memorial History of Louisville*. 2 vols. Chicago, 1896.

Littell, William. *The Statute Law of Kentucky*. 5 vols. Frankfort, 1809–1819.

Little, Lucius P. *Ben Hardin: His Times and Contemporaries*. Louisville, 1887.

Lloyd, Arthur Y. *The Slavery Controversy, 1831–1860*. Chapel Hill, 1939.

Lugenbeel, James W. *Sketches of Liberia*. Washington, 1853.

McDougall, Marion G. *Fugitive Slaves, 1619–1865*. Boston, 1891.

McDougle, Ivan E. *Slavery in Kentucky, 1792–1865*. Lancaster (Pa.), 1918.

Mahan, John B. *The Trial of Rev. John B. Mahan for Felony in the Mason Circuit Court of Kentucky, 1838*. Cincinnati, 1838. (Pamphlet.)

Martin, Asa E. *The Anti-Slavery Movement in Kentucky Prior to 1850*. Louisville, 1918.

Mather, Otis M. *Six Generations of LaRues and Allied Families*. Hodgenville (Ky.), 1921.

Melish, John. *Travels through the United States, 1806–1811*. 2 vols. Philadelphia, 1815.

Michaux, François A. *Travels to the West of the Alleghany Mountains*. London, 1805.

Mitchell, William W. *The Under-Ground Railroad*. London, 1860.

Monette, John W. *History of the Discovery and Settlement of the Valley of the Mississippi*. 2 vols. New York, 1846.

Morton, Marmaduke B. *Kentuckians are Different*. Louisville, 1938.

Nicolay, John G., and Hay, J. *Complete Works of Abraham Lincoln*. 12 vols. New York, 1905.

Olmsted, Frederick L. *The Cotton Kingdom.* 2 vols. New York, 1862.

Parsons, C. G. *Inside View of Slavery, or a Tour among the Planters.* Boston, 1855.

Paxton, James D. *Letters on Slavery.* Lexington, 1833.

Pendleton, James M. *Reminiscences of a Long Life.* Louisville, 1891.

Perrin, W. H., and Battle, J. H. *Counties of Todd and Christian, Kentucky.* Chicago, 1884.

Phillips, Ulrich B. *Life and Labor in the Old South.* Boston, 1929.

Polk, J. J. *Autobiography of Dr. J. J. Polk.* Louisville, 1867.

Ridenour, George L. *Early Times in Meade County, Kentucky.* Louisville, 1929.

Roe, Elizabeth A. *Aunt Leanna, or Early Scenes in Kentucky.* Chicago, 1855.

Russell, Ward. *Church Life in the Bluegrass.* Lexington, 1933.

Shaler, Nathaniel S. *The Autobiography of Nathaniel S. Shaler.* Boston, 1909.

Shewmaker, William O. *Pisgah and Her People.* Lexington, 1935.

Siebert, Wilbur H. *The Underground Railroad from Slavery to Freedom.* New York and London, 1898.

——. *The Underground Railroad in Massachusetts.* Worcester (Mass.), 1936.

Smith, Harry. *Fifty Years of Slavery in the United States of America.* Grand Rapids (Mich.), 1891.

Smith, Zachariah F. *The History of Kentucky.* Louisville, 1886.

Sneed, William C. *History and Mode of Management of the Kentucky Penitentiary.* Frankfort, 1860.

Speed, James. *James Speed, A Personality.* Louisville, 1914.

Speed, Thomas. *The Wilderness Road.* Louisville, 1886.

——. *Records and Memorials of the Speed Family.* Louisville, 1892.

Spencer, James H. *A History of the Kentucky Baptists from 1769–1886.* 2 vols. n.p., 1886.

Staples, Charles R. *The History of Pioneer Lexington.* Lexington, 1939.

Starling, Edmund L. *History of Henderson County, Kentucky.* Henderson, 1887.

State of Ohio vs. Forbes & Armitage, Tried before the Franklin Circuit Court of Kentucky, April 10, 1846. n.p., 1846. (Pamphlet.)

Stowe, Charles E. *The Life of Harriet B. Stowe.* Boston and New York, 1889.

Stowe, Harriet B. *Key to Uncle Tom's Cabin.* Boston, 1853.

——. *Uncle Tom's Cabin, or Life among the Lowly.* Boston, 1879.

Sturge, Joseph. *A Visit to the United States in 1841.* London, 1842.

Sydnor, Charles S. *Slavery in Mississippi.* New York, 1933.

Tower, Philo. *Slavery Unmasked.* Rochester (N. Y.), 1856.

Townsend, William H. *Lincoln and his Wife's Home Town.* Indianapolis, 1929.

Trotter, H. *First Impressions of the New World.* London, 1859.

Van Deusen, Glyndon. *The Life of Henry Clay.* Boston, 1937.

Van Meter, Benjamin F. *A Dead Issue and the Live One.* Louisville, 1913.

Warren, Louis A. *The Slavery Atmosphere of Lincoln's Youth.* Fort Wayne (Ind.), 1933. (Pamphlet.)

Watts, William C. *Chronicles of a Kentucky Settlement.* New York, 1897.

Webster, Delia A. *A History of the Trial of Miss Delia A. Webster at Lexington, Kentucky, December 17–21, 1844, before the Hon. Richard Buckner, on a Charge of Aiding Slaves to escape from that Commonwealth.* Vergennes (Vt.), 1845.

Webster Kentucky Farm Association, Its Origin and Object. Boston, 1858. (Pamphlet.)

Weld, Theodore D. *American Slavery As It Is: Testimony of a Thousand Witnesses.* New York, 1839.

Weston, George W. *The Progress of Slavery.* Washington, 1857.

Wigham, Eliza. *The Anti-Slavery Cause in America and its Martyrs.* London, 1863.

Williams, C. S. *Lexington Directory, City Guide and Business Mirror, 1859–1860.* Lexington, 1859.

Wilmot, Franklin A. *Disclosures and Confessions of Franklin A. Wilmot, the Slave Thief and Negro Runner.* Philadelphia, 1860.

Wilson, Samuel M., and Bodley, T. *History of Kentucky.* 4 vols. Chicago, 1928.

Wood, Norman B. *The White Side of a Black Subject.* Chicago, 1894.

INDEX